Peachpit Learning Series

OS X Mountain Lion

Lynn Beighley

 Peachpit Press

OS X Mountain Lion: Peachpit Learning Series
LYNN BEIGHLEY

Copyright ©2013 Robin Williams, John Tollett, and Lynn Beighley
Peachpit Press
1249 Eighth Street
Berkeley, CA 94710
510.524.2178   voice
510.524.2221   fax

Find us on the web at www.peachpit.com
To report errors, please send a note to errata@peachpit.com
Peachpit Press is a division of Pearson Education

Project Editor: Valerie Witte
Production Editor: David Van Ness
Copyeditor: Liz Welch
Composition: Lynn Beighley
Indexer: Valerie Haynes Perry
Cover design: Charlene Charles-Will
Interior design: Kim Scott
Prepress: David Van Ness

ISBN 13:   978-0-321-85851-1
ISBN 10:   0-321-85851-4

10 9 8 7 6 5 4 3 2 1
Printed and bound in the United States of America

Explore, play, and share.

ynn

Contents

MAKE IT YOUR OWN MAC

TECH STUFF

OS X Basics for New Mac Users

1

GOALS

Become familiar and comfortable with the Desktop, Finder, and Home

Get to know the Finder windows and how to use them

Create your own folders

Understand the Dock

Use the Trash basket

Know how and when to use keyboard shortcuts

Learn to watch for tool tips and other visual clues

Know where to go for more information

Introduction to the OS X Desktop

If you have a Mac running Mountain Lion (OS X version 10.8), you're ready to jump right in! In this lesson you'll become familiar with using the basic features of your Mac and its Desktop/Finder.

This book assumes you are familiar with how to operate a computer—how to use a mouse or trackpad, select items from menus, distinguish one icon from another, move files and folders and windows around, how and why to save the documents you create, etc.

Get to Know Your Desktop and Finder

When you turn on your Mac, you first see your **Desktop,** shown below. This is also called the **Finder** (although technically the Finder is the application that runs the Desktop). Whenever you see a direction that tells you to go to the Desktop or to the Finder, this is where you need to go.

Application menu.
This menu names the application that is "active" at the moment.

Apple menu.

Menu bar.

Spotlight. See Lesson 21. **Notifications.** See Lesson 18.

Desktop.
This entire background area is the Desktop.

Finder window.
See pages 5–7.

Finder icon.
See the next two pages.

Dock.
See pages 22–23.

Documents and **Downloads** folders.
See pages 24–25.

Trash.
See pages 26–27.

> **TIP** —— You might *see* the Desktop but not actually *be* in the Finder. Get in the habit of checking the application menu (shown top-left and on the opposite page). When you are really in the Finder or at the Desktop, the application menu will say "Finder."

> **TIP** —— For an uncluttered Desktop appearance, the "Hard Disk" icon (usually shown in the top-right corner) is not visible by default in Mountain Lion. If you're accustomed to seeing it there and want to bring it back, see Lesson 16.

Make sure you can get to the Desktop or Finder whenever necessary

Think of the Finder as your home base. As you work on your Mac, you will be using a number of applications, but you'll often want to get back to the Finder. The name of the *active* application, the one that's currently open and available to use (including the Finder), will always be displayed in the application menu. Keep an eye on that menu.

To go to the Finder at any time, do one of these things:

- Single-click on any blank area of the Desktop.

- Single-click on any Finder window (shown below) that you see.

- Single-click the Finder icon in the Dock (shown on the opposite page).

Make sure the **application menu** says "Finder," as shown circled below.

The Finder is the active application.

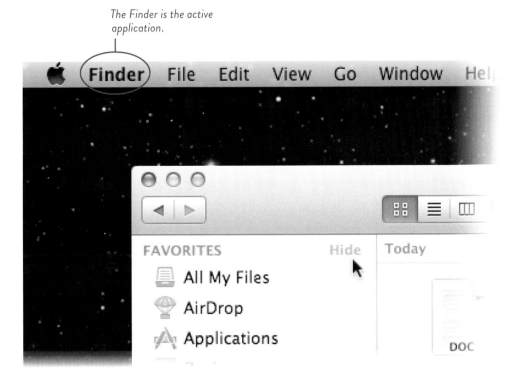

Get to Know Your Finder Window

Below, you see a typical **Finder window.** This is called a *Finder* window to distinguish it from similar (but different) windows you use in your applications. You access just about everything on your Mac through a Finder window, and you store everything you create in a Finder window. A window can open into a number of different views, so take a few minutes to read the following pages about the views you might see, and read Lesson 16 about customizing the windows.

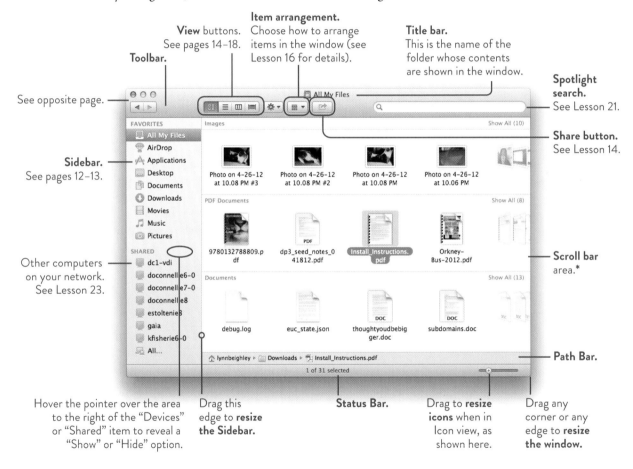

Item arrangement.
Choose how to arrange items in the window (see Lesson 16 for details).

View buttons. See pages 14–18.

Toolbar.

Title bar. This is the name of the folder whose contents are shown in the window.

Spotlight search. See Lesson 21.

See opposite page.

Sidebar. See pages 12–13.

Share button. See Lesson 14.

Other computers on your network. See Lesson 23.

Scroll bar area.*

Path Bar.

Hover the pointer over the area to the right of the "Devices" or "Shared" item to reveal a "Show" or "Hide" option.

Drag this edge to **resize the Sidebar.**

Status Bar.

Drag to **resize icons** when in Icon view, as shown here.

Drag any corner or any edge to **resize the window.**

To move a window, *press* on the title bar or status bar and drag it.

*Important: Scroll bars are hidden until you start to scroll by dragging a mouse, swiping a trackpad with two fingers, or swiping a Magic Mouse with one finger.

If you use an older mouse or you want the scroll bars to be visible, go to System Preferences, choose "Appearance," then set "Show scroll bars" to "Always."

Become comfortable with "swiping"

Mountain Lion has many features that are more useful and easier to work with if you use one of the Multi-Touch devices such as a Magic Mouse, a Magic Trackpad, or a built-in trackpad on your laptop with *gestures* enabled. For instance, in the window shown on the opposite page, swipe left or right to display the files. See page 19.

Use the buttons in the Finder Window

There are several buttons in the Toolbar of every Finder window.

Red, yellow, and green buttons ● ● ●

- Single-click the **red button to close** the window.
- Single-click the **yellow button to minimize** the window, which adds a tiny icon down in the Dock, on the right side. To open the window again, single-click its icon in the Dock. Try it.
- Single-click the **green button to toggle** between the previous window size and the current window size.

Previous and Next buttons ◀ ▶

These buttons go back and forward through the contents of windows you have viewed (just like the *Previous* and *Next* buttons on web pages). Every time you open a new window, these buttons start over.

Hide/Show the Toolbar, Sidebar, Path Bar, and Status Bar

To hide the Toolbar, Sidebar, Path Bar, or Status Bar, go to the View menu, then choose "Hide Toolbar" (or "Hide Sidebar" etc.). If an item is already hidden, the menu says "Show Toolbar," etc.

Toolbar. —

Sidebar. —

The same window with the Toolbar, Sidebar, Path Bar, and Status Bar hidden.

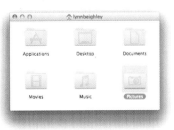

Status Bar.   The **Path Bar** shows a location path to the *selected* item.

Get to Know Your Sidebar and Its Home Folders

When you open a Finder window in Mountain Lion, the default is to show you the contents of the folder named **All My Files,** which displays every file you've ever created or copied to your computer, arranged in rows of categories (see page 13 for more details about All My Files). The other items in the Sidebar are folders that are actually stored in what's called your Home folder, where everything you create is saved; putting the Home folders in the Sidebar saves you one step in that you don't have to first open your Home folder to access them. (Also see Lesson 2.)

If you're an experienced Mac user, you might notice that Apple seems to want us to transition away from using the traditional OS X Home folder to using the Sidebar to access the folders. You can put your Home folder in the Sidebar, as described below.

- **To open a Finder window,** single-click on the Finder icon (shown to the left) in the Dock (the Dock is that row of icons usually found across the bottom of your screen). A Finder window provides access to everything on your Mac.

- **To put your Home folder in the Sidebar** (skip this if you don't miss your Home folder or don't even know what it is): From the "Finder" menu at the top of your screen, choose "Preferences..." (shown below, right). Click the "Sidebar" icon in the toolbar. Put a check next to your Home folder name and icon. Click the little red close button in the corner to put it away.

I put a Home folder in the Sidebar above so you could see the folders that are stored in it.

In the preferences (shown to the right), you can uncheck any items you don't need to see in the Sidebar.

The Public folder is used for sharing files; see Lesson 23.

What each folder in your Sidebar is for

All My Files All your document and image files (not folders) are displayed in this window. You cannot put anything in this folder yourself. See page 13.

AirDrop Don't worry if you don't see this item. This is a window for sharing files; see Lesson 23.

Applications This folder holds all your applications that came with your Mac, and when you install new ones, they will go in this folder. See Lesson 3.

Desktop This folder holds any files that might be sitting directly on the Desktop (see page 4). Putting files on the Desktop is like keeping them on your office desk instead of putting them in a filing cabinet. Having this folder to hold the same files means you can get to them when you're not actually at the Desktop, as when you want to open a file from within an application.

Documents At first, your Mac makes sure every document you create is safely tucked into this Documents folder. Later, you can create your own folders (see pages 10–11) and store your documents in them.

Downloads This folder holds most of the files that you download through Bonjour, iChat, or the Internet. Files that come to you through email will also end up here if you click the "Save" button in an email message. The Downloads folder in the Dock holds exactly the same files. See pages 24–25.

Movies The iMovie application uses this folder to automatically store the files necessary for creating the movies you make. You can also store movies here that you've acquired from any source other than iMovie, such as from the Internet or email.

Music The iTunes application uses this folder to automatically keep track of all the music files you buy and all of your playlists.

Pictures The iPhoto application uses this folder to automatically keep track of all your photos and albums. Use it to store any photos, or folders of photos, even if they haven't been imported into iPhoto.

Do not change the names of the folders in the Home folder or throw them away unless you are very clear on what you're doing and why you're making that choice. You can, however, **Command-drag any folder out of the Sidebar;** if you ever want to replace that folder, open your Home folder and drag it back in.

Create Your Own Folders

You can create your own **folders** where you can **store** your documents and **organize** your files. For instance, you might want a folder in which to store all your financial documents, another folder for all your newsletter files, and yet another for the screenplays you're writing. All of these documents *could* go inside the Documents folder, but that's like putting every document in your office in one big manila folder.

Think of the folders on your Mac as manila folders in a metal filing cabinet. When you save a file, save it directly into your custom folders.

- **To make a new folder,** go to the File menu and choose "New Folder." It is ready to name—go ahead and type the new name, then hit Return. Click anywhere to deselect the folder.

  The new folder appears *inside the window whose name is in the title bar* (shown circled, below). That is, if you want to put the new folder into the Documents folder, first open the Documents folder before you make the new one.

In my Documents folder, I made a new folder called "My Writing." Inside that folder, I made these six new folders.

■ **To rename a folder:**

1 Single-click the folder to select it.

2 Hit the Return key to highlight the name (you'll see a blue outline around the name). *Or* single-click on the name.

3 Type to replace the existing name. (You don't need to delete the original name first.)

4 Hit Return or Enter to set the name.

■ **To open a folder,** double-click it.

■ **To go back** to the contents of the previous folder, single-click the left-pointing triangle, called the Previous button (shown to the left).

■ **To move a folder,** just drag it to another window or another folder.

■ **To put something inside a folder,** drag the item and drop it on top of the folder icon or into its column. *Or* save a file directly into that folder (see Lesson 2 for details).

In Column View (shown and explained on page 16), notice that I have folders inside of folders. Picture it like a filing cabinet in which you store file folders, and the understanding of organizing your information will come easily.

Take Advantage of the Sidebar

The **Sidebar** of every Finder window is customizable—you can add or remove any folder or document as often as you like. Items in the Sidebar are always *aliases,* or icons that merely *represent* the real file. This means you can delete an icon from the Sidebar and it does not delete the actual file that it represents.

Each of the icons in the Sidebar represents a file or folder somewhere else on your hard disk.

Because a folder or document in the Sidebar is a *picture* (alias) of the real thing, you can drop files into the icon in the Sidebar (drag and drop them) *or* into the original folder and they go to the same place.

Try it: Drop a file into the Documents folder in the Sidebar, then open the Documents folder in the Home window and you'll see the new document.

Add a folder or document to the Sidebar. This makes it easier to find a folder and put other files in it, and it makes a document easier to find and open (just single-click it). It's also easier when you are working in an application and want to save a file, because the folder shows up in the sidebar of Open and Save As dialogs.

- **To add a folder or document to the Sidebar,** drag the icon from any window or from the Desktop and drop it into the Sidebar.

- Use the Finder preferences to add hard disk icons and more (as explained on the opposite page).

Remove folder or document icons from the Sidebar that you don't use. Don't worry—removing the picture of a folder from the Sidebar does not throw away the original folder nor anything in it.

- **To remove an item from the Sidebar,** hold down the Command key, click on the name with the mouse, and drag it out of the Sidebar. Let go when the mouse pointer is on the Desktop. As you can see, the icon disappears in a puff of smoke. Notice that although I removed the Movies folder from the Sidebar, the original Movies folder is still safe and sound in the Home window (as shown on the opposite page).

Customize the Sidebar to contain just the items you want to see: Click on the Desktop to make the Finder the current active application, then from the Finder menu (next to the Apple icon), choose "Preferences…." Click the "Sidebar" icon in the toolbar (circled, above-right). Check the items you want to show in the Sidebar, and uncheck items that you don't want. If you uncheck all items in a category, such as "Devices," the entire category, including the header, disappears from the Finder window sidebar.

All My Files

This item in your Sidebar displays every file and photo you ever create or store on your Mac. This is not a useful feature when you've got lots and lots of files in one window, although if you set the arrangement by date, the latest things you've worked on will show up first. *You* can't add files to this window—it is done automatically; you might think you are dropping a file in this window, but the Mac stores the file in an appropriate folder and just shows you the icon. You *can* delete files or rename them, and you are actually deleting or renaming the original file. Keep the Path Bar visible (see page 7) so you know where the files are located.

The default for the All My Files view is that it is *arranged by* Kind, which is what puts all the files in rows, each row being a category; within these rows, the first items you see are the newest. This makes it handy to find something you were recently working on—open All My Files and your most recent documents are right there.

See Lesson 16 to learn to control the arrangement in this window and others.

Change the View of the Finder Window

You can change the visual display of the files inside any window—show them as icons, as a list of items, in columns of information, or slideshow-like. You might prefer one view for certain files and a different view for others. Experiment with the **four different views** and decide for yourself how you like to work.

- ■ **To change views,** single-click one of the four little View buttons.

 From left to right, the View buttons display Icon View, List View, Column View, and Cover Flow view.

The Icon View

Icon View displays every file as an **icon,** or small picture. Double-click an icon to open it. To view the icons in categorized rows like you see in the "All My Files" window on page 6, see Lesson 16.

Show View Options.

Icon View button.

Sidebar.

Drag this slider to resize icons.

Drag this slider to resize icons.

Enhanced Icon View: Enlarge the icons with the size slider for easy viewing. You can preview multipage documents and movies right in the icon: In the View Options (as shown above-right), check "Show icon preview" (if it isn't already selected).

 Hover the pointer over the icon of a multipage document. To browse through the pages, click the left and right arrows that appear at the bottom of the icon.

 Hover the pointer over the icon of a movie, then click the Play button that appears.

14

The List View

In the **List View,** you can organize the list of files alphabetically by names, by the dates the files were last modified, by what kind of items they are, and other options. You can also see the contents of more than one folder at once.

List View button.

The **blue column heading** is a *visual clue* that the contents are organized, or "sorted," by that heading. You can see, above, that the files in this window are sorted by "Name." To organize the contents by the dates they were modified, size, or kind, single-click that column heading (you might have to open the window wider or scroll to the right to see the other columns and headings). **If you cannot make any changes to the columns, it probably has an "arrangement" applied; see Lesson 16.**

The **tiny triangle** in the column heading (circled above, right) is a *visual clue* that tells you whether the information is sorted from first to last or last to first.

Try it: Single-click the triangle to reverse the sort order.

In the List View, single-click vs. double-click:

Folder icon: Single-click the **disclosure triangle** to the left of a folder to display its contents as a sublist, as shown circled above, left. You can view the contents of more than one folder at once.

Double-click the **folder icon** to display its contents in the window, which will *replace* the contents you currently see in the window.

Document icon: Double-click a document to open not only that document, but also the application it was created in.

Application icon: Double-click an application icon to open the application.

The Column View

Viewing a Finder window in **columns** allows you to see the contents of a selected folder or hard disk and easily keep track of where each file is located. You can also view the contents of another folder without losing sight of the first one. This view helps you understand where everything is kept in your computer.

If you have photographs, graphic images, movies, or PDFs in your folders, the last column displays **previews** of the items. You can even play a small movie in this preview column, if a movie file is selected. Some documents can display previews as well.

Column View button.

To resize an individual column, drag one of the vertical divider lines. **To expand the column** to reveal the longest file name, double-click the divider line.

To resize all columns, Option-drag a vertical line (hold down the Option key while you drag a line). You might see small "thumb" marks at the bottom of the column divider; if so, you must drag that thumb mark to move the column.

The **Path Bar** shows another view of the path to the selected file. Double-click any folder shown in the Path Bar (or in the Column View) to open it.

You won't see additional columns to the right until you **single-click** a folder or a file—then a new column to the right appears to display the contents of that folder or a preview of the file. A triangle indicates that file is a folder that can contain other files.

In the example above, you can see that the "top-level" folder is the Home folder, "lynnbeighley." In "lynnbeighley," I selected the folder "Pictures" (I clicked once on it) and in that folder I selected "travel," and in that folder I selected "rome" and then selected an image. The last column displays a preview of the selected file and information about it.

In the Column View, single-click files to display columns:

Documents

Folder icon: Single-click a folder to display its contents in the column to the right. If there is no column to the right, one will appear.

subdomains.doc

Document icon: Single-click a document to see a preview in the column to the right. Not all documents can provide content previews, but the preview will at least give you information about that file.

Double-click a document to open not only that document, but also the application it was created in.

TextEdit

Application icon: Single-click an application icon to preview information about it, such as its version and date of modification.

Double-click an application icon to open that application.

TIP —— You can customize many features about the Finder windows, such as the font size, the icon size, even the color inside the window. You can organize the List View by different columns of information, choose to turn off the preview in Column View, and more. See Lesson 16.

TIP —— No matter which view you are in, you can always open a folder into a **new, separate window:** Hold down the Command key and double-click any folder in any view (the original window stays open).

Hold down the Option key and double-click a folder to open the folder in a new window **and** close the original window.

The Cover Flow View

The Cover Flow View displays your files graphically in a slideshow-like format at the top of the window. To flip through them, click on the icons on either side of the center image, drag the slider bar, or click the items in the list below the Cover Flow pane. You can also use the arrow keys on your keyboard to move through the Cover Flow View.

For the columns below the Cover Flow pane, organize and use them just as you would in List View, as described on the previous pages. If you find you can't move the columns, it means there is an "arrangement" applied; go to the *Arrange* menu (see callout, below) and choose "None."

Cover Flow View button.   Arrange menu.   Double-click a Cover Flow image to open that document or application.

Single-click any item in the Sidebar to display it or its contents in the window.

Single-click an icon here to display it in the Cover Flow View window above.

Double-click an icon here to open that document or application.

Drag this "thumb grip" to enlarge the Cover Flow area of the window.

Drag the slider bar to navigate through the Cover Flow files.*

*Important: The slider bar is hidden by default. To make it visible, go to System Preferences, choose "Appearance," then set "Show scroll bars" to "Always."

Use Gestures to Navigate Your Mac

Mountain Lion can take advantage of something called *gestures*—movements of your fingers on a special Multi-Touch input device. These devices include the Apple Magic Mouse, the Apple Magic Trackpad that you can use with your desktop computer, and trackpads that are built into newer Apple laptops. Below are some of the basic Multi-Touch gestures that you can use with these special devices (if you don't have one, ignore this page). Note: A *tap* is a *gentle* tap, not a click.

Some of these gestures might be different for you because you can customize them in the Mouse or Trackpad system preferences (see Lesson 16). This preferences pane also shows you little movies of how things work. Gestures might be confusing at first, but it's surprising how quickly you get accustomed to your favorite ones.

On a Magic Mouse

To go forward or back through web pages, swipe left or right with *one finger.*

To show all open windows of an application, hover over the application's icon in the Dock, then swipe *up* with *two fingers.*

To flip between Launchpad screens (see Lesson 3), swipe left or right on the Multi-Touch surface with *three fingers.*

To switch between Spaces (see Lesson 17), swipe left or right with *two fingers.*

To open Mission Control (see Lesson 17), double-tap with *two fingers* on the Multi-Touch surface. To return to the Desktop, double-tap with two fingers again, *or* click one of the items in Mission Control (a file, app, or Space).

On a Magic Trackpad or built-in MultiTouch trackpad

To go forward or back through web pages, swipe left or right with *two fingers.*

To show all open windows of an application, hover over the app's icon in the Dock, then swipe *up* with *two fingers.*

To flip between Launchpad screens (Lesson 3), swipe left or right with *two fingers.*

To show the Desktop and hide all open windows in the screen edges, *spread four fingers* on the Multi-Touch surface. To return, *pinch* four fingers.

To switch between screens and Spaces, swipe left or right with *three fingers.*

To open Mission Control, swipe *up* with *three fingers.* To return to the Desktop, swipe *down* with *three fingers, or* click one of the items shown in Mission Control (a file, app, or Space).

Quick Look

Quick Look lets you quickly preview almost any kind of file without actually opening it. Select a file, then press the Spacebar to preview it in Quick Look.

To put a Quick Look button in the toolbar of Finder windows: Right-click on a window toolbar; choose "Customize Toolbar...." From the sheet that drops down, drag the Quick Look button and drop it on the window's toolbar. Click "Done."

When you preview a text file, you can scroll through the document. When you preview a Keynote presentation, you'll see your slides and notes. When you preview a PDF with many pages, you can scroll through the pages.

To open a Quick Look preview, select one or more files, then do any of the following:

- Tap the Spacebar.
- Click the Quick Look button described above, *or* press Command Y.
- Go to the File menu and choose "Quick Look *filename*."
- Right-click and choose "Quick Look *filename*."

Once a Quick Look preview is open, you can single-click other files in the Finder or use the arrow keys to cycle through files, and they will appear in that preview.

If more than one file is open in Quick Look, you can use the *Previous* and *Next* arrow buttons (shown below) to cycle through the files.

Click to enlarge the preview. Click again to return to original preview size.

Open with an application appropriate for the file type.

Close Quick Look.

Show selected files as an Index Sheet (see the next page).

Share with others through email, Messages, Twitter, and more (see Lesson 14).

Drag any corner or edge to enlarge.

To view multiple files as an index sheet, click the "Index Sheet" button (shown to the left and on the previous page).

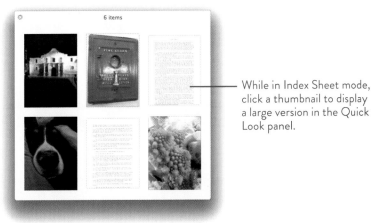

While in Index Sheet mode, click a thumbnail to display a large version in the Quick Look panel.

A selection of various file types, shown in Quick Look's Index Sheet.

Quick Look also works in email and Messages. When you see a web address (a URL) in email or Messages, hover the cursor over the URL to reveal a Data Detector icon to its right (circled, below, left). Click that icon to display the web page in Quick Look.

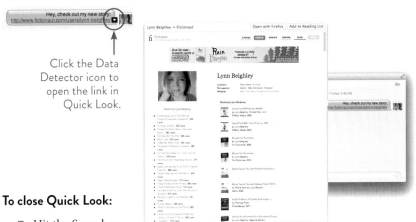

Click the Data Detector icon to open the link in Quick Look.

To close Quick Look:

- Hit the Spacebar.
- Press Command Y.
- Click the **X** in the upper-left corner of the Quick Look window.
- Go to the File menu and choose "Close Quick Look."

Use the Dock

The **Dock** is that strip of icons across the bottom of the screen (see "Is the Dock Missing?"). The specific icons that appear in the Dock will change as you open and close applications, view photos, or customize what's in the Dock. "Hover" your mouse over an icon (position the pointer and hold it there, but don't click) to see a label appear that tells you the name of the application or file.

- **To open an application or document** from the Dock, single-click its icon.

Keep an eye on the application menu in the top-left corner of the screen (as explained on pages 4–5) to verify which application is the currently "active" application. You can also enable a visual clue that tells you which applications in the Dock are open. Right-click the *dividing line* in the Dock, choose "Dock Preferences," then select "Show indicator lights for open applications." A **tiny blue light** appears under the icon of open applications (as shown below, under three applications).

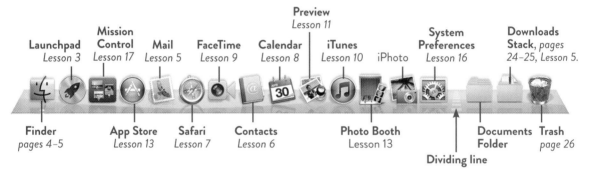

You can **rearrange** any of the icons. You can **add** or **remove** applications from the *left* side of the dividing line (see callouts, above), and you can **add** or **remove** folders, documents, and web page locations from the *right* side of the dividing line:

- **To rearrange an icon,** press the mouse on it and drag it left or right. The other icons will move over to make room.

- **To add an application icon,** first open the Applications folder (click the Applications icon in the Sidebar of any Finder window) *or* open Launchpad (see page 49). Drag an application icon down to the Dock, to the *left* side of the dividing line. The existing icons will move over to make room.

- Whenever you open an application, its icon is automatically and temporarily put in the Dock. **To keep an application icon in the Dock,** press on the icon while it's in the Dock, choose "Options," then choose "Keep in Dock."

- **To add an often-used folder or a document,** drag it to the *right* side of the dividing line. Then you can easily open it with a single click.

- **To remove any icon from the Dock,** press on it with the mouse and drag it upward, off the Dock. Let go of the mouse and the icon will disappear in a poof of smoke. This doesn't delete anything but the icon from the Dock! *Never* will you delete any original item by removing its icon from the Dock. You can also Control-click (or right-click) a Dock item, choose "Options," then choose "Remove from Dock."

- **To add a web page,** open your browser application, Safari (see Lesson 7 about Safari). Go to the web page that you want to have easy access to in your Dock. Drag the tiny icon that you see on the left of the web page address in the location field (circled below) and drop it in the Dock—on the *right* side of the dividing line.

    The advantage of putting a web page icon in your Dock is that while you're working in any application, you can click that web icon and your browser opens to that page—you don't have to go find your browser first and then find the bookmark.

Both the Documents folder and the Downloads stack, shown on the previous page, can be changed to regular folder icons, as shown above. See the following page.

Is the Dock missing?

The Dock can be customized in many ways. It might be on either side of the screen instead of at the bottom, or it might even be hidden. If you don't see the Dock anywhere, push your mouse to the far left, the far right, or the deep bottom of the screen and the hidden Dock will appear from one of those edges. See Lesson 16 for details on how to customize the Dock to fit your needs.

Documents and Downloads folders in the Dock

The right side of the Dock holds copies of the Documents and Downloads folders
that are stored in your Home folder. The icons in the Dock provide convenient
access to the files you've created or downloaded to your Mac through Bonjour,
Messages, or the Internet. Files attached to email will also end up in the Downloads
folder when you click the "Save" button in an email message.

Documents folder.   Downloads folder, shown as a *stack* of icons.

You can choose to display these folders in the Dock as a **Folder** icon (as the
Documents folder shown above) or as a **Stack** icon (also shown above):

1 Control-click one of the folders to get the pop-up menu shown below.

2 In the "Display as" section of the pop-up menu, choose "Folder" or "Stack."

   If you choose "Stack," the icon on top of the Stack is the most recent file added
   to the folder. Dazzling, but not very useful. I prefer the Folder display.

You can also choose to **remove** these icons from your Dock—just drag the icons
out of the Dock and drop them on the Desktop. The original folders in your Home
folder are still there, safe and sound.

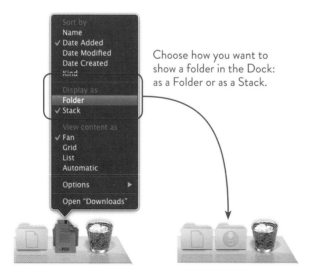

Choose how you want to
show a folder in the Dock:
as a Folder or as a Stack.

To view its contents, single-click the folder or stack icon.

You can **choose how to display the contents:** Control-click (or right-click) the Folder or Stack to open the pop-up menu shown on the previous page. From the "View content as" section, choose "Fan," "Grid," or "List." If you choose to view content as "Automatic," the Stack opens in Fan view when 11 or fewer items are present; more than 11 items opens in Grid view. Single-click a file or folder to open it. Each view includes an "Open in Finder" command.

Click this icon to show the folder contents in a normal Finder window.

View contents as a Fan.   View contents as a Grid.

The Grid view of contents makes navigation of folders easy: Click a folder in Grid view (below, left) to see its contents (below, right). To return to the previous folder, click the return path button (to the previous folder) in the top-left corner.

When there are too many items to display, a dark gray scroll bar appears on the right side of the window.

To previous folder.

Current folder.

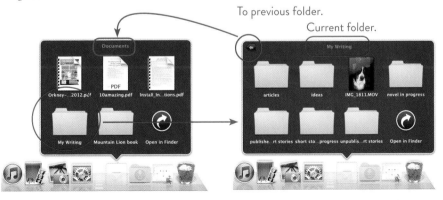

25

Use the Trash

The **Trash basket** in the Dock is where you throw away any files you don't want.

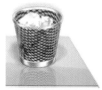

- **To put a file in the Trash,** press on any file in the Finder and drag it to the Trash basket. When the ***tip*** *of the pointer* touches the basket, the basket changes color—this means you're in the right place. Let go of the mouse button and that file is in the Trash. Remember, it's the ***tip*** *of the pointer,* not the icon image, that selects the Trash basket.

  You can also use a contextual menu to trash things; see Lesson 2.

- **To empty the Trash,** press *(don't click)* on the Trash icon and a little menu pops up with an option that says, "Empty Trash." Choose that option, *or* go to the Finder menu and choose "Empty Trash."

When you empty the Trash, you'll get a **warning** asking if that's what you really want to do. Some people like to have this reminder; others hate it. You can tell your Mac to stop reminding you about emptying the Trash (next page).

■ **To turn the Trash warning off (or on):**

  1 From the Finder menu, choose "Preferences…."

  2 Click the "Advanced" icon in the toolbar at the top.

  3 Uncheck (or check) the box "Show warning before emptying the Trash."

  4 Click the red button in the upper left of the pane to put it away.

■ **To see what's in the Trash,** single-click the Trash icon in the Dock. This opens the Trash window, as shown below.

■ **To take an item out of the Trash,** single-click the Trash icon to open its window. If there is an item you don't want to throw away, drag it out of the window and put it back where you want it.

  Or select one or more items in the Trash window, go to the File menu, and choose "Put Back" (or use the keyboard shortcut, Command Delete).

  Or see Lesson 2 about contextual menus. One of the options for a trashed item is "Put Back."

Take Advantage of Keyboard Shortcuts

Most actions that you can do with the mouse and menus can also be done with
keyboard shortcuts. Often this is not only faster, but more convenient because you
don't have to take your hands off the keyboard to pick up and maneuver the mouse.
You will see lots of keyboard shortcuts in the menus across the top of the screen,
such as the ones shown below in the Edit menu. **Use a keyboard shortcut** *instead*
of going to the menu.

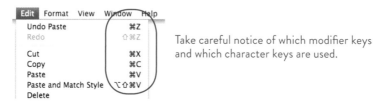

Take careful notice of which modifier keys
and which character keys are used.

Recognize the common modifier keys

Keyboard shortcuts work with **modifier keys,** which are those keys that don't do
anything by themselves. For instance, the Shift key doesn't do anything when you
press it down by itself, *but it modifies the behavior of other keys.*

Each key has a **symbol** by which it is known. These are the key symbols you will see
in menus and charts:

⇧	**Shift**	↻	**Escape (esc)**
⌘	**Command**	⇕ ⇕	**PageUp or PageDown**
⌥	**Option**	⌫	**Delete**
^	**Control**	↑↓←→	**Arrow keys**
↵	**Return**	⌅	**Enter**
F2, F10	**Fkeys**	`	**Grave accent** (tilde key)

Fkeys are those keys across the top of the keyboard that are labeled with the letter
F and a number, such as F2 or F13.

The **fn** key (function key) enables individual keys to do more than one function.

Keyboard shortcuts typically use one or more modifier key(s), plus one number,
character, or Fkey, as you can see in the example of the Edit menu above: The
keyboard shortcut to copy *selected* text is ⌘C, or Command C.

Use a keyboard shortcut

The trick to using a keyboard shortcut is this: *Hold down* the modifier keys all together and keep them held down, then *tap* the associated letter, number, or Fkey *just once* for each time you want to perform an action.

For instance, the keyboard shortcut to close a window is Command W, so hold the Command key down and tap the letter W just once. If there are three windows open on your Desktop, you can hold the Command key down and tap the letter W three times and it will close three windows.

Notice gray versus black commands

When commands in a menu are gray instead of black, the Mac is giving you an important *visual clue.* Here's a short exercise to demonstrate.

1 Click an empty spot on the Desktop.

2 Now take a look through the Finder menus and notice the shortcuts for different actions or commands. Notice how many commands are gray.

   If a command is **gray,** that means you cannot use that command at the moment. Often this is because you have not *selected* an item first, an item to which the command should apply. For instance, you can't use the command to close a window unless an open window is *selected.*

3 Now open a Finder window (if there isn't one already) and *select* a **folder icon** (click *once* on it).

4 Look at the File menu again, and notice how many more commands are available (they're in **black,** not gray).

5 In the File menu, find the keyboard shortcut to "Open," but don't choose the command from the menu—just notice and remember the shortcut (Command O). Click somewhere off the menu to make the menu go away.

6 Make sure a folder is selected. Now use the keyboard shortcut, Command O, to open it.

Learn More about OS X

There are a number of ways to learn more about your Mac and how to use it, all available right from your Desktop. Keep these tips in mind as you spend time on your Mac—you will learn a lot from them.

Tool tips

Most applications and dialog boxes provide **tool tips** that pop up when you hover your pointer over an item. They tell you what the items do. Just hold the pointer still over a button or icon for about three seconds; if there is a tool tip, it will appear, as shown in the examples below.

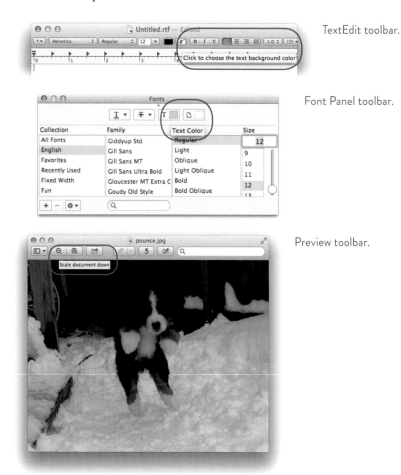

TextEdit toolbar.

Font Panel toolbar.

Preview toolbar.

Hover tips

As mentioned on the opposite page, tool tips appear when you *hover* the pointer.
For instance, you've probably already noticed that when you hover over an item in the
Dock, the name of that item appears. Actually, all kinds of things appear when you
hover—try it on everything! Below are some examples. Remember, "hover" means to
hold your mouse still while pointing to an item—don't click or press the button.

In Mail, hover over a name in an email to see
which address it came from.

In Messages, hover over a
name to see that person's
information.

In Safari (your web browser), hover over a link name to see exactly
where it goes—the destination appears in the Status Bar at the
bottom of the window. (If you don't see this Status Bar, go to the
View menu in Safari and choose "Show Status Bar.")

Help files

No matter where you are on the Mac or which application you are working in, you'll always find **Help** just a click away. At the Finder, go to the Help menu to look up tips and techniques on just about anything.

Every application has a Help menu, and it's always at the far right end of the menu choices, as shown below. Choose the Help option for that particular application, then type in a word or two that you want to look up. You see two different kinds of options available, "Menu Items" and "Help Topics."

Menu Items   This tells you where the item you're looking for can be found in the menus. It doesn't explain anything about that item. When you select an option in the "Menu Items" list, a menu drops down and a big moving arrow points to the item you're looking for.

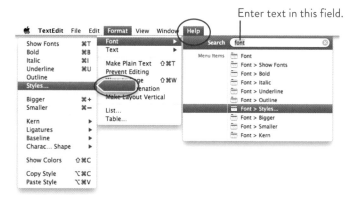

Help Topics   If the software vendor has written information in the Help file, you will see a list of the possible topics. Choose one and the Help file opens to that piece of information.

Support pages

The **Apple web site** has a huge number of support pages. Here you can find manuals that you can view on screen or download (copy) to your computer.

You'll also find discussion pages where other users talk about different products and software packages on the Mac, ask questions, and answer questions.

You can sign up for training at a local Apple store, read the product question-and-answer pages for hardware and software, and more. Go to <u>www.Apple.com/support</u>.

Mac video tutorials

Apple provides lots of video tutorials about Mac basics and Mac applications (such as iPhoto, iMovie, iWeb, GarageBand, iWork, and MobileMe) on its web site. Visit <u>www.Apple.com/findouthow/mac</u> and look for **Video Tutorials.** Or just use Safari to do a Google search for "Mac video tutorials."

iCloud tutorials

If you have multiple Apple devices, or work on more than one Mac, visit the **iCloud page** where you'll learn more about how to take advantage of your data being stored in the cloud and accessible on every newer Apple device you own. Visit <u>www.Apple.com/iCloud</u>.

The basic iCloud service is free for OS X Mountain Lion and can make your Mac experience many times more empowering, enjoyable, and useful.

Apple Support Communities

Join *Apple Support Communities* to find an online community focused on a product or topic you're interested in. Sign in using your Apple ID to find answers to existing questions, ask your own questions, or join a discussion. After you join, you can customize your homepage to show topics you're interested in, read existing discussions to check on the latest issues and tips, post responses, and more. Visit Apple Support Communities at <u>https://discussions.Apple.com</u>.

2

GOALS

Become familiar with the
sections of the Sidebar

Understand
the Library folders

Learn how to select
multiple items in the
different window views

Take advantage of
contextual menus

Save documents into
specific folders

A Bit Beyond the Basics

Feeling comfortable with the techniques and features described in the previous lesson? Carry on into this lesson where you'll learn a few more advanced (but still everyday and useful) features. If anything overwhelms you in this advanced lesson (or any lesson), skip it and come back later.

Understand the Sections of the Sidebar

The Sidebar is divided into sections, each with a purpose.

Favorites

The **Favorites** section displays folders and files on your own computer. To make any file or folder easily accessible, drag it from the right side of the Finder window to this section of the Sidebar. When you no longer need easy access to the item, Command-drag it out of the Sidebar. It disappears in a poof of digital smoke but does not delete the actual file or folder. If you decide to put that item back in the Sidebar, drag it into the Sidebar again.

You can choose which items are displayed in the Sidebar; see Lesson 16.

Shared

The **Shared** section (if you see it in your Sidebar) displays any other computers or disks that you can connect to through your *local* network. A local network is one in which computers in a small area, such as a home or office, are all connected via wires or a wireless connection.

To hide a section in the Sidebar, hover the cursor over the area just to the right of the "Favorites", "Shared", or "Devices" title until the word "Hide" appears. Click "Hide" to *hide* the items.

To show a section, hover the cursor over the same area as above, until the word "Show" appears. Click "Show" to make the items appear in the Sidebar again.

Devices

In the **"Devices" portion of the Sidebar,** you see icons that represent hard disks, other computers on the network, a CD or DVD, an iPod, or any other type of removable media.

Display the contents of each media item the same way you do any of the items in the Sidebar: Single-click the name or the icon.

The **Hard Disk** is your computer, the disk that holds the operating system and all your files. You can rename your hard disk at any time, just as you rename a folder (as explained on page 11).

The **round disk icon** in the Sidebar is a music **CD** inserted in the CD drive. The **square disk icon** called **External Disk** is a removable drive connected to this computer. Removable media always have Eject symbols to the right of the names.

 When you see the **Eject symbol** to the right of an icon (the triangle with a bar under it), that means it is a removable disk of some sort. It might be a CD, a DVD, an iPod, or another computer you are connected to over the network. Click on the symbol to eject or disconnect the item.

TIP —— Choose which devices, if any, appear on your Desktop. See Lesson 16.

View your Home folder from the "Hard Disk"

Below you see another way of looking at your Home folder, using the Column View (as explained in Lesson 1). As you open folders, the contents appear in a new column to the right, creating a visual path.

You can see by the highlight in the Sidebar that I first clicked on the drive icon labeled "Macintosh HD"; the Hard Disk (HD) is where all your files are stored (although you or someone else might have renamed your hard disk). This click displays the folders stored on that Hard Disk; you can see them in the column to the right.

Then I clicked on "Users," which displays my Home folder in the *next* column. If you create any other users, as explained in Lesson 20, you will see all of those users listed in this folder/column.

Then I clicked on "lynnbeighley," which displays my own Home folders in the *next* column.

See the Applications folder in the screenshot below? Notice that it's in the *top level* (first column) of the *Macintosh HD.* Your Applications icon in the Sidebar makes it easy to access this folder so you don't have to dig into the Hard Disk to find it.

Experiment with different ways of getting to your Home folders until you feel comfortable about where things are stored on your Mac.

The name of the currently selected item appears in the title bar.

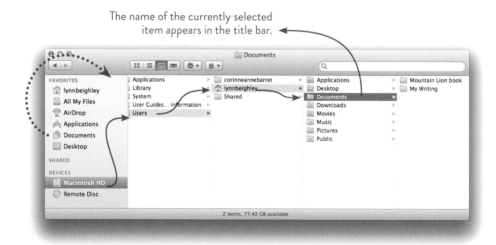

Understand the Various Library Folders

As you work with your Mac, you'll run across a number of folders with the same name: **Library.** Do you see the two Library folders in the illustration below? And there are others.

Library folders contain information that the operating system and certain applications need to function. Unless you have a really good reason and know exactly what you're doing, **leave the Library folders alone—don't put anything in them and don't take anything out.**

The Library folder you see above, in the first column, is at the *top level* of your Hard Disk. It contains files that are critical to running your entire computer, and the files it contains pertain to all users who use this Mac. For instance, the Library folder in the first column has a folder inside called "Fonts," and all fonts that are installed into this top-level folder are available to all users. (For details about multiple user accounts and how to create them, please see Lesson 20.)

The Library folder in the second column, above, is in the *System folder*, a folder that contains files critical to the operation of the computer. Don't change anything in the System folder unless you're expert at working with systems.

A third Library exists in the User's Home folder, but it's hidden. If you know what you're doing and really need to see this hidden Library folder, in the Finder open the Go menu and hold down the Option key. While the Option key is down, select the "Library" item from the menu. This is where your user account stores your application preferences, web page bookmarks, Address Book contact information, email, and other personal information.

That's all you really need to know about your Library folders—and leave them alone for now!

Select Multiple Items in the Finder

To select an individual item in a Finder window, single-click it, as you probably know. But sometimes you might need to select more than one item at a time. **To select multiple items,** there are two ways to do it, as explained below. Once items are a selected together, you can move, trash, open, or change their labels (see Lesson 16 about labels), and more.

In the Icon View

To select multiple items in the Icon View, hold down the **Command key** *or* the **Shift key** and single-click the items you want to group together. You can only select items from one window while in the Icon View.

Or *press* a blank spot in the window and *drag* the cursor around the items you want to select. Any icon that is at least partially enclosed by the rectangle you draw with the cursor will be selected.

Icon View.

The rectangle I dragged partially overlaps six files. After I release the cursor, all six files will be selected.

In the List View, Column View, or Cover Flow View

In these views, using the Shift key is different from using the Command key.

Hold down the **Command key** and single-click multiple items.

In the *List View* and the *Cover Flow View,* you can select items from several different folders *in the same window,* as long as their contents are showing in the list. See the examples on the opposite page.

In the *Column View,* you can select multiple items from *one column at a time.*

List View.

Command-click to select or deselect noncontiguous items.

The **Shift key** lets you select a group of items that are *contiguous,* or next to each other in the list. Single-click on the *first* item you want to select in a list. Then hold down the Shift key and click the *last* item you want in the list. *Everything between the two clicks will be selected.* See the example below.

Cover Flow View.

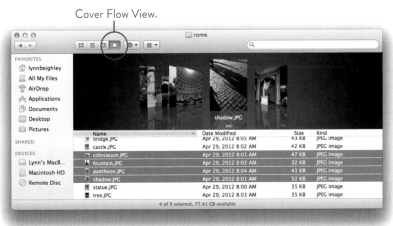

Shift-click to select contiguous items.

To deselect an item from any group in any view: Command-click it.

To deselect all items from any group in any view: Single-click any blank area in the window.

Look for Contextual Menus

These are great. You can Control-click just about anywhere (hold down the Control key—not the *Command key*—and click), and a menu pops up right where you click. This is a **contextual menu** that is specific to the item you Control-click on, meaning what you see in the pop-up menu is dependent on what you click (as opposed to menus in the menu bar or in dialog boxes that always contain the same items).

To display a contextual menu, hold down the Control key and click on an icon, a blank spot on the Desktop, inside a Finder window, on a title bar, toolbar, or just about anywhere. A little menu pops up, as you can see by the examples.

If you have a **two-button mouse,** you don't need the Control key—just use the right-hand button (the secondary mouse button) to display a contextual menu. If your right button isn't working, go to the preferences for Mouse (see Lesson 16) and make sure you have assigned the secondary button.

There is *no visual clue* for a contextual menu—just keep checking. You'll find them in applications, on web pages, in toolbars, in the Sidebar, and everywhere.

A contextual menu on a blank spot on the Desktop.

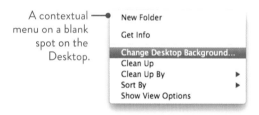

This is great. Select a number of files, and the contextual menu gives you an option to put them all into a new folder. The new folder appears ready for you to type its new name.

A contextual menu on a Toolbar.

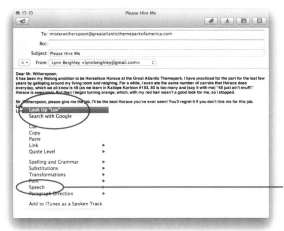

This is an example of a contextual menu in an application:

Control-click (or right-click) a misspelled word in a new email message to get a contextual menu with possible spellings.

Select the correct word, let go of the cursor, and the misspelled word is instantly replaced with the correct one.

Try the "Speech" option—selected text will be read aloud to you.

TIP —— In Finder windows, the **Action menu** does many of the same things as the contextual menu, and more.

Try it: Single-click to select a folder or file, then click the Action button to see what the contextual menu options are.

Open and Save As Dialog Boxes

When you're working in an application and need to open a file you created earlier, most of the time you'll go to the File menu and choose "**Open…**" to get the dialog box shown below. Keep in mind that you can change the view of the Open dialog in the same way you change a Finder window view. Also in the same way, you can select items in the Sidebar to navigate to the folder in which you have stored the file you want to open.

Starting from the Sidebar (or the menu), choose the folders in which you have stored files to find the one you want to open.

It's good to get in the habit of **saving your file directly into its appropriate folder** so you can keep your thousands of files organized. As usual, save your new file right away (Command S). In the dialog that opens, find your folder (or make a new one), and select it so your new file goes straight into it.

The disk or folder name shown here is the one that your new file (or new folder) will be saved into.

If the disk or folder in which you want to save a file is not listed here, click the disclosure triangle to open the fuller window, shown to the right.

Find the specific folder you want to save into. If you haven't created a specific folder, you can do so now: Click the "New Folder" button. That new folder will be stored inside the folder that is currently selected in this window.

OS X Applications in Mountain Lion

3

GOALS

Know your
Applications folder

Understand the
common features
of Apple applications

Access applications
from Launchpad

Use applications in
full-screen mode

Search and shop
the App Store

Realize what CANNOT
be covered in this book

Introduction to OS X Applications

One of the greatest things about Mac applications is that they are consistent, which makes them easy to learn and easy to use—what you learn in one application also applies to just about any other application.

In this short introductory lesson, we present a brief overview of the major applications, or apps, that come with your Mac. All of the Apple applications are integrated with other apps, and they all share certain features and tools. In the following lessons, we'll go into more detail about individual programs, and in Lesson 14 you'll learn how to use the tools that all Apple applications share.

Know Your Applications Folder

In the Sidebar of any Finder window is an icon labeled **Applications.** Single-click this icon to display the contents of the Applications window. These are the programs you will use to create your work on your Mac.

At any time, you can put the application you use most often **in the Dock** so you'll have easy access to it: Just drag the application icon from this window and drop it on the Dock (the other items will move over to make room). If you accidentally lose something from the Dock, you can always go back to the Applications window to drag the item back in.

When you open an application that's not already in the Dock, its icon automatically appears in the Dock. When you quit the application, the icon disappears from the Dock. **To keep the application icon in the Dock,** *press* on it (while it's in the Dock) to show a pop-up menu, choose "Options," then choose "Keep in Dock" (shown below, right).

Some applications that you buy will display their *folders* here in the Applications window instead of the *application icons*.

If you see that an application is stored in a folder, open that folder and find the actual *application* icon to drag to the Dock.

Use the Launchpad

To display a full-screen view of all your application icons, single-click the Launchpad icon in the Dock. Then single-click an application icon to open that app.

If you have more apps than will fit on a screen, the others are shown on additional screens: Swipe left with two fingers on a trackpad; use one or two fingers on a Magic Mouse. Swipe the other direction to return to previous screens. If you have an older mouse, press-and-drag the mouse left or right to switch screens.

Single-click an icon to open that application.

Click a blank space to exit Launchpad.

Launchpad.

These dots tell you how many Launchpad screens are present, and which one is visible. Click a dot to go to that page of apps.

This type of icon indicates a folder (a group) of applications. Single-click it to see all the apps inside.

To add applications to Launchpad: Drag an application icon and drop it on top of the Launchpad icon in the Dock.

To create a new folder (a group) of applications: Drag an icon and drop it on top of another icon that you want to group it with. A folder (it doesn't look like a real folder) is automatically created with both apps inside. Drag and drop any other apps on the same "folder" to add them to the group.

To exit Launchpad: Click on a blank space of the screen, or tap the Esc key.

To open an app *location* in the Finder and exit Launchpad: Control-Command-click the icon. Launchpad closes and a Finder window opens with the app selected.

To delete an app from Launchpad (WARNING: this will delete the app from your entire computer!): Hold down the Option key until all icons start to shake and an **X** appears in the top-left corner of each one. While the Option key is down, click the **X** to remove the app from Launchpad.

Know the Common Features of Mac Apps

Most Mac applications have these features in common.

Windows and window controls

When you open an application, you'll actually be working in a **window.** If you worked through Lesson 1, you already know all about windows, even ones you haven't seen before. You see the same red, yellow, and green buttons to close, minimize, and resize the window. The document name and a tiny icon appear in the title bar. You can drag the title bar or the Status Bar (at the bottom of the window, if it's showing) to move the window.

Application menu

The application menu (directly to the right of the Apple menu) always tells you the name of the currently **active application,** the one you're working in (even if there is no document window open on the screen). You'll always find the Quit command at the bottom of the application menu.

File and Edit menus

File and Edit menus are always the first two menus to the right of the application menu.

Although each application includes specific features in its menus, in the **File menu** you'll always find the commands to **open** an existing document or create a **new** one, **save** the document or **save as** with another name, **close** the active window, and **print** the active document.

From the **Edit menu,** as shown on the right, you can always **undo** or **redo, cut, copy, paste, delete, select all,** check the **spelling and grammar,** and access the **Special Characters.**

Preferences   Every application has its own preferences where you can **customize** the application to suit yourself. Open the preferences from the application menu (shown on the previous page). **To open the preferences for an app,** open the application, then from the application menu, choose "Preferences…." Typically, you'll see a toolbar across the top of the preferences pane; single-click an icon in that toolbar to set the preferences for that particular feature.

Safari preferences with the Tabs pane selected.

Toolbars   Most applications have a Toolbar across the top of the window. Usually, you can **customize** this Toolbar: Check the **View menu** for a command called "Customize Toolbar…," or use the contextual menu (Control-click or right-click on the window's toolbar).

This is a typical sheet that drops down from a toolbar so you can customize it.

Drag icons from this sheet to the toolbar, then click "Done."

Sidebars

Many applications have a Sidebar, or a pane on the side of the window. Single-click an icon in a Sidebar to display its particular contents in the window.

Here the iTunes Store is selected in the iTunes Sidebar.

Special collections

Several applications use collection metaphors such as *Albums* in iPhoto, *Playlists* in iTunes, *Bookmark Collections* in Safari, *Mailboxes* in Mail, *Groups* in Contacts. Use these to store and organize your stuff.

Open and Save As dialog boxes

Whenever you open an existing document or save a new one, the dialog boxes you see to open a new document or save a document always look familiar.

Help files Every application has a Help menu with Help files specific to that application. Use the Help menu you see on your screen; some apps have a keyboard shortcut such as **Command ?** to bring up the Help files. You'll find a search field where you can type in keywords, then hit Return to display the answers. See page 32 for more details.

Action button and menu

 In many application windows, you'll see the Action button (shown to the left) that displays the Action menu. Every application has different options—always click on it to see what is available.

Search

Just about every application has a search feature. It's usually in the upper-right corner of the window, as you can see in the iTunes window on the opposite page. Just exactly what the search feature searches depends on the application. In Contacts, shown below, for example, it lets you search for names. See the individual overviews in the lessons for each application.

Search field. ———

Smart Folders

Many applications have some version of *Smart Folders* that automatically update themselves according to your specified criteria. See Lesson 21 on Spotlight to learn how to take advantage of this great feature.

Other applications have similar types of smart folders: Contacts has *Smart Groups* that will add appropriate contacts to themselves; iTunes has *Smart Playlists* that will add music to themselves; Mail has *Smart Mailboxes* that gather up messages. See the individual lessons for each application.

Preview before you print

At the bottom of most Print dialog boxes (especially in Apple apps) is a button called "PDF." Click this to display a menu where you can choose "Open PDF in Preview." This creates a quick PDF of your document and opens it in the Preview application where you can see what it will look like when printed. If you like the way it looks, continue to print from Preview, or close the preview window and go back to your document to continue printing.

Full-Screen Apps

Many of the applications that come with a Mac can be used in full-screen mode, such as Mail, Safari, Calendar, Preview, iTunes, and iPhoto. Full-screen mode hides Desktop clutter while you work. When you put an app in full-screen mode, it occupies a *Space,* all by itself (see Lesson 17 about Mission Control and Spaces). You can open that Space by choosing it while in Mission Control, or click its icon in the Dock to bring forward the Space that contains that full-screen application.

If you like working in the full-screen mode, you can leave the applications open in their own Spaces, then switch Spaces when you're ready to use a certain one.

To enter full-screen mode, click the *Full-Screen* button, the double-arrow button that appears in the top-right corner of some application windows (shown below).

To exit full-screen mode, move your pointer all the way to the top edge of the screen to reveal the top menu bar, then click the blue *Exit Full-Screen* button.

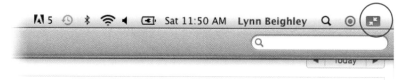

To switch between full-screen apps, do one of the following:

- Click an application icon in the Dock. If the Dock is hidden because you're already working in another full-screen app, move your pointer to the bottom edge of the screen to reveal the Dock.

- Enter Mission Control, then click the Space thumbnail that contains the full-screen app you want to work with.

- Swipe left or right with *two fingers* on the surface of a Magic Mouse to move between *all* Spaces. Or swipe left or right with *three fingers* on the surface of a Multi-Touch trackpad to move between *all* Spaces.

Application Integration

All of the Apple applications share certain tools such as the Spell Checker and Grammar Checker, the Fonts palette, the Colors palette, the Special Character palette, and more. Common tool elements are explained in detail in Lesson 14.

Also keep in mind that all of these applications work together in amazing ways. You can drag text and graphics from one app to another, save files into different formats, save notes or events from Mail directly into Calendar, create a PDF in TextEdit that you can read and annotate in Preview, and more. See the individual application lessons and Lesson 15 for details.

What This Book Can't Cover!

I introduce iTunes in Lesson 10, but I don't cover iPhoto, GarageBand, iWeb, iMovie, or iDVD because they belong to a specialized suite of apps called iLife and are not part of the Mac operating system. Other authors cover those, however, in a variety of books published by Peachpit Press, **www.PeachpitPress.com.** Some iLife books are more than 500 pages, so you can see why I don't cover all of that in this book. At Peachpit you'll also find much more information than I can provide in this introductory book about such programs as Mail, Calendar, and Messages.

Nor do I cover Pages, Numbers, or Keynote in this book because they each deserve their own book. If you have any of those programs, know that Peachpit publishes books about them (including Robin Williams' *Non-Designer's Presentation Book* which is mostly about Keynote), and don't forget that the applications have good Help files built right in.

I suggest you poke around in the preferences for each application, explore the menus, click on things. You'll be surprised at the little treasures you'll constantly encounter.

4

GOALS

TextEdit for Word Processing

TextEdit is a small yet surprisingly powerful word processor. Use it to write memos, letters, diaries, novels, grocery lists, memoirs, or any other text document. You can create simple tables and automatically numbered or bulleted lists, add shadows to type, insert images, search and replace text, and more. But it's not a full-blown word processor such as Apple's Pages (check the App Store in your Dock). Although TextEdit can't do all the fancy things a big word processor can, it's excellent for many projects.

If you've never used a word processor before and you don't know how to open an application and save files, enter text, select text for formatting, cut/copy and paste, etc., please read *The Little Mac Book* first! This lesson assumes you know the basics of working in a word processor.

Create and Save a TextEdit Document

Open TextEdit (it's in your Applications folder and in Launchpad). Then from its File menu, choose "New." A blank window opens for you to start typing.

Choose how you want to see the document: From the Format menu, choose "Wrap to Window" (below, left) or "Wrap to Page" (below, right).

"Wrap to Window" fills the page with no visible margins.

"Wrap to Page" displays the text as it will look when printed on paper.

Save your document as usual (from the File menu, choose "Save…," give it a name, and store it in a folder where you'll find it again). As you continue to work on your TextEdit document, the word "Edited" appears to the right of the document's name in the window. This is a *visual clue* that the document has been changed and you might want to save the changes (press Command S).

An unsaved file has no options next to the document's title.

A saved file displays a disclosure triangle when you mouse over its title.

Once you edit a file, TextEdit lets you know when there are unsaved changes.

Click "Edited" or the triangle to choose from several options related to saving or reverting your file:

Lock prevents further changes. If you try to type, you get an option to *Unlock* it. This is not a secure lock—anyone can click the *Unlock* button.

Revert to Last Saved Version gives you the option to revert to the last time it was saved (either by you or by TextEdit), *or* you can revert to an older version, as explained on the opposite page.

Browse All Versions—see the opposite page.

AutoSave and versions

TextEdit automatically saves your document every hour as you work on it, as well as when you close it (it doesn't ask—it just saves). In addition, you can (and should) save more often (press Command S).

As soon as you save and name a document, TextEdit keeps track of all *previous versions* of that document; that is, every time you save or TextEdit saves, a new version is stored. You can return to any of these versions, as explained below.

To manually save the current version, go to the File menu and choose "Save a Version," or press Command S.

To save a document with another name or in another file format, go to the File menu and choose "Duplicate." Save this new file with a new name.

Restore a previous version

To turn to a previous version of the document, click the top-right corner to get the menu shown below. Choose "Browse All Versions…." All previous versions of your document appear, as shown at the bottom of this page.

Click on the title bars to go back in time to previous versions, *or* click in the vertical timeline to view various versions. When you find the one you want, click the "Restore" button at the bottom of the screen.

The current document version.   Previous document versions.   Timeline.

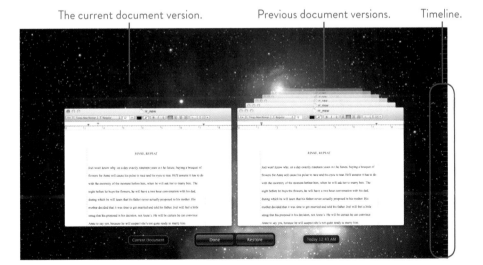

Rename a document

New documents in TextEdit are named "Untitled" by default. When you save a document in TextEdit (choose "Save…" from the File menu), you are prompted with the Save dialog box and given the chance to give your document a name other than "Untitled."

When you save a document, change the name from Untitled to something more descriptive.

You can always change the name of a document, even one you've saved, at any time. If you forgot to give your document a name the first time you saved it, or if the current name ought to be changed to more accurately reflect the contents of the file, click the triangle that appears when you mouse over the document's title and choose the "Rename…" option.

To rename a document, click the arrow and choose "Rename…."

The title of the document becomes editable. Type the new name of the document and press Return.

When you choose "Rename…," the title of the document highlights and becomes editable. Start typing the new title you want to give your document. Press Return when you're finished.

Keep in mind that when you change the name of your document, it changes it for all previous document versions as well.

Move a document

If you want to save the current document in a different location, you can use the Finder to drag it from one place to another. But TextEdit offers you a shortcut.

With the document you wish to move open in TextEdit, click the triangle that appears when you mouse over the document's title and choose the "Move To..." option.

To move a document, click the arrow and choose "Move To...."

Click the "Where" select box to locate the folder where you want to move your file.

With the document you wish to move open in TextEdit, click the triangle that appears when you mouse over the document's title and choose the "Move To..." option. Click the "Where" select box and choose the folder where you want to move the file. If you've activated your iCloud account (learn all about iCloud in Lesson 20), you can store your document remotely and access it with other Apple devices.

Duplicate a document

When you save or move a document, you still have a single copy of the original document. If you need an additional copy of the document, use the "Duplicate" option. As with "Rename..." and "Move To...," the "Duplicate" option is available under the arrow menu next to your document title. Click and choose "Duplicate." A copy of your original document opens in another TextEdit window. The new document is untitled, but displays the original document's title with the word "copy" after it, as shown below. Save the copy by choosing the Save option as discussed at the begining of this lesson.

When you duplicate a document, a copy of the original document opens in a new TextEdit window. The title bar indicates that it's a copy of the original document.

Find and Replace Words or Phrases

Did you write your entire novel using a name that you no longer think suits your main character, such as Smith? And now you've come up with a better name, and need to **replace** the character's last name with Scrooge? No problem:

1 From the Edit menu, choose "Find…," *or* press Command F. A search field appears below the ruler bar.

2 Click the "Replace" checkbox to open a *Replace* text field below the search field.

3 In the *Find* field, type the word you want to find, such as *Smith.*

4 In the *Replace* field, type the word or phrase that will replace the found word, such as *Scrooge.*

5 Find and replace:

    Replace: Replaces the currently selected occurrence of the word or phrase, then automatically finds the next occurrence.

    All: Replace *all* occurrences of the found text. Press (don't click) on the "All" button to see more options.

    To manually find other occurrences of the text, click the *Previous* and *Next* buttons.

    For more search options, click the small double-arrows next to the magnifying glass icon on the left side of the window.

6 Click "Done" to put the Find and Replace fields away.

Previous and Next buttons.

Click for more search options.

Press to show more *replace* and *select* options.

"Insert Pattern" opens a menu of search criteria that includes searches for email, web addresses, or phone numbers.

Paste Text to Match the Existing Text

This is one of my favorite features. Let's say you're writing a term paper and you copy a quote from a web page to add to your paper (properly cited, of course). Typically the copied text pastes in with the typeface, style, size, and color that were originally applied to it. But to add this quotation to your term paper, you want it to look like the rest of your page. Use this great feature instead of the regular paste:

> From the Edit menu, choose **Paste and Match Style,**
> *or* use the keyboard shortcut, Option Shift Command V.

The pasted text will pick up all the formatting *from the character to the left of the flashing insertion point.* This technique works in Mail as well.

Use Your Favorite Text Styles Easily

TextEdit doesn't have the powerful style sheets of a full-blown word processor, but it does make your writing life much easier by letting you create **favorite styles** of basic type features so you can apply them quickly. A "style" contains all of the formatting information, such as typeface, size, color, indents, etc., so you can apply everything to selected text with one click of a button.

These styles are saved with TextEdit, not with an individual document, so you can use the same styles in different documents.

To create your own favorite style:

1   Type some text, any text, and set up the typeface, size, color, linespace, and the ruler the way you want it.

2   Click anywhere in that formatted text.

3   Click the *Paragraph Styles* button, then choose "Show Styles…."

4   In the sheet that slides down (right), click the button, "Add To Favorites."

5   Name the style and choose your options. Click "Add."

To apply a style, select a range of characters, then choose the style name from the *Paragraph Styles* pop-up menu in the toolbar. All of the formatting that you saved with that style will be automatically applied to the selected text.

Tabs and Indents

The tab and indent markers in TextEdit function as in any word processor.

To set a right-aligned tab, single-click in the ruler.

To set any other tab, Control-click (or right-click) in the ruler and choose a tab marker (shown below), *or* double-click a marker to change it.

To remove a tab, drag the marker off the ruler.

To indent just the first line of text *or* both the left and right edges, drag the indent markers shown below.

First lines of paragraphs start at this **First Line Indent** marker.

These are your tab options.

All lines but the first one in a paragraph start at this **Left Indent** marker.

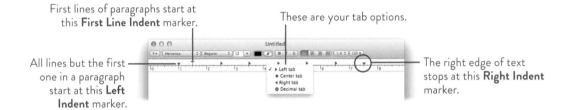

The right edge of text stops at this **Right Indent** marker.

Examples of tab and indent settings

The following are some examples of how to set up your tabs and indents to create certain effects. Remember, after you've set a tab, hit the Tab key *before* you type the text. Once you've got tabs set up, you can select the text, then move the tab and the *selected* text will follow.

The tab applies only to the selected paragraphs—you only need to click inside a paragraph to select the entire paragraph. To select more than one paragraph, press and drag to highlight a range of text in each paragraph. Follow the directions as explained in each window and its caption.

To create an indent, drag the First Line Indent marker to the right. The rest of the text will automatically align at the Left Indent marker.

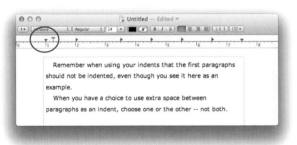

To creat an outdent, where the first line is outdented farther than the other lines: Move the Left Indent marker (the triangle) to the *right* of the First Line Indent marker.

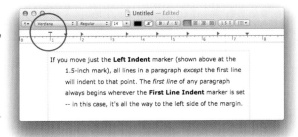

If you move just the **Left Indent** marker (shown above at the 1.5-inch mark), all lines in a paragraph *except* the first line will indent to that point. The *first line* of any paragraph always begins wherever the **First Line Indent** marker is set -- in this case, it's all the way to the left side of the margin.

To indent an individual paragraph on both sides: *Select* the paragraph, then move both the Left Indent and the Right Indent markers inward.

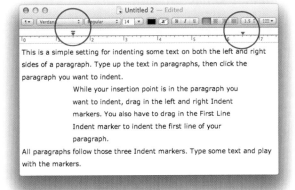

This is a simple setting for indenting some text on both the left and right sides of a paragraph. Type up the text in paragraphs, then click the paragraph you want to indent.

While your insertion point is in the paragraph you want to indent, drag in the left and right Indent markers. You also have to drag in the First Line Indent marker to indent the first line of your paragraph.

All paragraphs follow those three Indent markers. Type some text and play with the markers.

To create columns: Remove all tabs except the few you need, and reposition those about where you want the columns to align. Now hit ONE tab to move the insertion point to the first column, and type. Hit ONE more tab to get to the second column, etc. At the end of the line, hit a Return and start over.

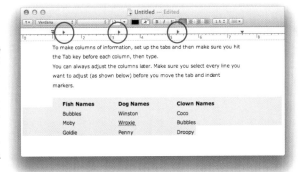

To make columns of information, set up the tabs and then make sure you hit the Tab key before each column, then type.

You can always adjust the columns later. Make sure you select every line you want to adjust (as shown below) before you move the tab and indent markers.

Fish Names	Dog Names	Clown Names
Bubbles	Winston	Coco
Moby	Wroxie	Bubbles
Goldie	Penny	Droopy

This is a common setup. It might seem a little tricky at first, but once you get it, you'll love knowing how to do it. Set the markers as shown and follow the directions.

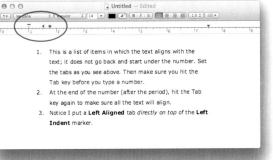

1. This is a list of items in which the text aligns with the text; it does not go back and start under the number. Set the tabs as you see above. Then make sure you hit the Tab key before you type a number.
2. At the end of the number (after the period), hit the Tab key again to make sure all the text will align.
3. Notice I put a **Left Aligned** tab *directly on top of* the **Left Indent** marker.

Create Lists That Number Themselves

If you have a list of items, TextEdit can number them for you with numbers, capital or lowercase letters, or other options. When you add or delete items from the list, TextEdit automatically updates the numbering.

List bullets and numbering button.

List options.

When you click the List button (circled above) and choose a numbering option, the numbers apply to **either** of the following:

> If you **select text** on the page *before* you go to the Lists menu, your choice of list numbering will apply only to the *selected* text.

> If there is no selected text, the flashing **insertion point** is "filled" with the list specifications, and everything you type from that point on will be in the list format. This is a good way to start a new list: Just make sure your insertion point is flashing where you want the list to begin, *then* go to the List menu and choose your numbering system, *then* start typing. Each time you hit a Return, TextEdit considers that line to be the next item in the list.

To end the sequencing of numbers in a list, hit the Return key twice at the end of the last item.

To delete the list numbers, single-click anywhere in the list. Open the Lists menu and choose "None.'"

To easily access the advanced List options after you've started a list, click anywhere within a list, then Control-click (or right-click) in the list to show a contextual menu and choose "List...."

Create Tables

If you like working with tables, you can create simple ones in TextEdit. This table feature also helps ensure that tables created in a Word document will open in some form in TextEdit.

To create a table in TextEdit:

1 Position your insertion point where you want the table to begin.

2 Go to the Format menu and slide down to "Table...."

3 The Table palette appears, as shown below. Choose how many rows and columns you want in the table. You can determine how the text is aligned vertically as well as horizontally in each cell (use the "Alignment" icons), and more. Spend a few minutes to familiarize yourself with the tools.

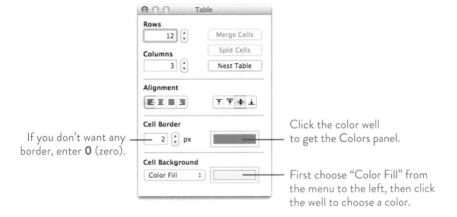

If you don't want any border, enter **0** (zero).

Click the color well to get the Colors panel.

First choose "Color Fill" from the menu to the left, then click the well to choose a color.

As you **type in a cell,** the cell expands downward to fit the text.

Change the formatting of the text as you do on a regular TextEdit page: Select the text first, then choose the settings from the menus or toolbar.

4 **To resize rows and columns,** position your pointer over the edge of a cell. The pointer turns into a two-headed arrow. With that two-headed arrow, press-and-drag on a cell edge to resize it.

Print Automatic Page Numbers

You can add page numbers to a *printed* document (the numbers won't appear on the screen). This feature also automatically adds the name of the document in the upper-left corner of the page (including the extension, probably .rtf), the date and time in the upper-right corner, and the words "Page ___ of ___" in the bottom-right corner. That is, in TextEdit you can't choose one or the other of these—they all appear on the page, or none.

To print the page numbers (and everything else), press Command P (or go to the File menu and choose "Print…"). In the Print dialog box, shown below-left, click "Show Details." In the expanded Print dialog (below, right), check the box to "Print header and footer." Click "Print" to print the document.

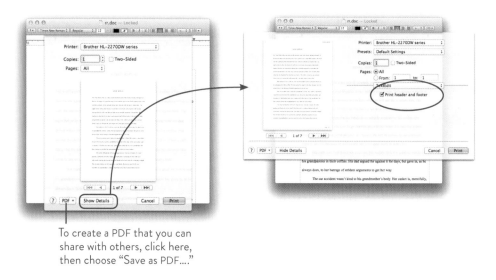

To create a PDF that you can share with others, click here, then choose "Save as PDF…."

Automatic Spelling Correction

TextEdit can automatically correct many spelling errors as you type. To enable this feature, open the TextEdit Preferences (from the TextEdit menu). Make sure the "New Document" tab is chosen. Toward the bottom of the window, check the "Correct spelling automatically" box. Close the Preferences pane.

If TextEdit can't figure out how to spell it or if automatic correction is turned on, you'll probably see a red dotted line under misspelled words. See Lesson 14 to learn to use the spell checker.

Select Noncontiguous Text

This is really quite wonderful. "Contiguous" means "sharing a common border." Very few applications allow you to select individual sections of text that are not physically next to each other (text that is *noncontiguous*). This technique lets you apply formatting or copy, cut, or delete separate sections of text all at once.

To select noncontiguous text:

1 Press-and-drag to select a section of text.

2 Hold down the Command key. Press-and-drag to select some other text that is not contiguous.

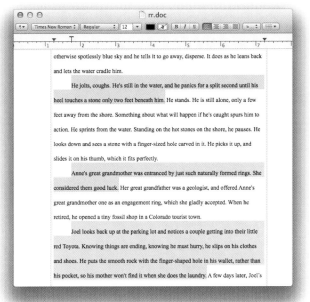

A selection of noncontiguous text.

Show Substitutions

TextEdit "Substitutions" (from the Edit menu or contextual menu) makes automatic substitutions for you as you type. For instance, "Text Replacement" corrects obvious spelling mistakes (it substitutes *the* for *teh,* etc.) and turns a typed fraction, such as 7/8, into a *real* fraction, ⅞. Below are several of the other substitution options.

Use typographer's quotes

TextEdit provides typographer's quotes, or **Smart Quotes.** Smart quotes (and apostrophes) are the curly quotes, not the straight, typewriter quotes. Nothing will make your work look as amateurish as typewriter quotes.

typewriter quotes

smart quotes

It's "QueenB" to you.   It's "QueenB" to you.

The Substitutions panel provides extra options for **Smart Quotes** so you can activate automatic quotation styles for other languages. Turn Smart Quotes *off* when you want to type feet and inch marks. For instance, I am 5' 7" tall, not 5'7" tall. To get this panel, go to the Edit menu, choose "Substitutions," and then choose "Show Substitutions."

Create live web links and email links

It's easy to create web links and email links on a TextEdit page. If you send someone the TextEdit file, that person can click on a web link; her browser will open and go to the page you specify. An email link in the document opens her email program, pre-addressed to whomever you specified.

If you make a PDF of your document (see page 75), the links will work in the PDF.

Create links as you type web addresses:

1 Go to the Edit menu, slide down to "Substitutions," then choose "Smart Links." If there is a checkmark next to "Smart Links," it's already on.

Or Control-click in the document, slide down to "Substitutions," then choose "Smart Links."

2   On your TextEdit page, just type the web address. You don't need the *www* part of the web address, or the *http://* part. If the address ends with .com, .edu, or .org, the link appears automatically. You'll know if it's working because the text will turn into a blue, underlined link.

If the domain (the .com part) is more unusual, such as .info, you'll have to manually add the link, as explained below.

Sometimes the text on the page is not an actual address, but you want the *link* to go to an email or web address. For instance, perhaps you wrote, "Please visit our Mary Sidney web site," and you want the link attached to "Mary Sidney" to go to MarySidney.com, or you want to say Email me! as a link to your actual email address. In either case, use the manual process described below to add a link.

To manually create a web link or an email link on a TextEdit page:

1   Type the text that you want to turn into a link. *This text can be anything— it doesn't have to be the email or web address itself!*

2   Select the text that you just typed in.

3   From the Edit menu, choose "Add Link…."

4   **Web address:** type the address. Make sure you include this code at the beginning of the web address: **http://**

    Email: Type into the field: **mailto:**
    Immediately after the colon, type the entire email address just as you would address it: mailto:**name@domain.com**

5   Click ᴏᴋ.

To remove a link from the text on a TextEdit page:

1   Click in the text *a few characters away from the link* to set the flashing insertion point. Use the left or right arrow keys to move the insertion point into the linked text.

2   From the Edit menu, choose "Add Link…."

3   Click "Remove Link," then click ᴏᴋ.

Use Data Detectors

Data Detectors is one of several **Substitutions** available in TextEdit that enhance your text. The Data Detectors feature, like Smart Links, makes your text interactive. When you hover the cursor over a street address or phone number in a TextEdit document, the cursor draws a marquee around the address and/or phone number. Click the triangle button (circled, below) that appears to show a contextual menu of options. You will see different options depending on what is selected.

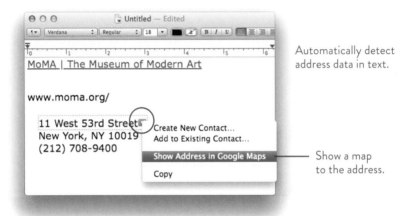

Automatically detect address data in text.

Show a map to the address.

Data detection is probably turned on already. If it isn't: **To turn on data detection,** go to the Edit menu, choose "Substitutions," then select the "Data Detectors" option.

You can also Control-click (or right-click) on any empty spot in the document to open a contextual menu. Slide down to "Substitutions," then choose "Data Detectors." A checkmark next to a Substitution item means it is enabled; select it again **to disable it.**

Change case (as in upper- and lowercase)

The Edit menu also contains a command called **Transformations** to change the *case* of selected letters quickly and easily. That is, you can change a word that starts with a lowercase letter to one that starts with a capital letter, or if someone wrote you something in all caps you can change it to lowercase with the click of a button.

Select some text and Control-click (or right-click) on that selection, *or* simply Control-click (or right-click) directly on an unselected word. From the Edit menu, go to the Transformations submenu and choose "Make Upper Case," "Make Lower Case," or "Capitalize" (which capitalizes just the first letters of each selected word).

Extra Tips and Notes

Ruler: If the ruler isn't showing, press Command R. Without the ruler showing, you can't set tabs, indents, or margins.

Formatting: If text won't let you apply formatting, go to the Format menu and choose "Make Rich Text."

Wrap to Page: If text stretches the entire width of the window, you might want to switch to "Wrap to Page." Go to the Format menu and choose "Wrap to Page."

If your text prints really tiny, go to the Format menu and change "Wrap to Window" to "Wrap to Page."

Complete: To automatically complete a word that you start typing (a word that you're not sure how to spell, or a word that's so long you don't want to type it all), go to the Edit menu and choose "Complete," or use the keyboard shortcut Option Escape. A pop-up menu that contains a list of possible matches opens. Select the word you want from the list, then hit Return (*or* click the word in the list).

Speech: Let your Mac read selected text to you aloud. Go to the Edit menu, choose "Speech," then choose "Start Speaking." To stop the speech, choose "Stop Speaking." To read aloud just a certain portion of text, select that range of text, then choose the "Start Speaking" command.

Look up words in the Dictionary: To look up a word (such as "hegemony") in the Dictionary, select the entire word or phrase, and then right-click on it to open a contextual menu and choose *Look Up "hegemony."* If your trackpad supports multi-touch gestures, double-tap the word with three fingers to look up the selected word, as shown below.

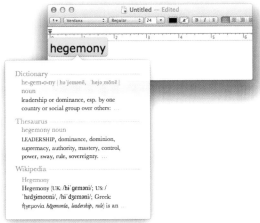

Read Microsoft Word Files

Do you need to send or read **Microsoft Word files,** but you prefer to keep a Microsoft-free environment on your own computer? TextEdit can open Word files and save as Word files. Some of the advanced features will be missing, but this works great for basic text documents, including those with simple tables or numbered/bulleted lists.

If you don't have Microsoft Word installed on your Mac, file names ending with .doc or .docx (which are usually Word files) **automatically open** in TextEdit when you double-click them.

To force a Word document to open in TextEdit (if it doesn't automatically), drag the file and drop it on the TextEdit icon.

If TextEdit is not in your Dock, it's in the Applications folder and in Launchpad: Click the Launchpad icon in the Dock. Find the TextEdit icon, then drag and **drop it in the Dock** so it's always easily accessible.

Change the default application to open Word files

If you own Microsoft Word and want your **.doc files to open in TextEdit,** not Word, you can **change the default application:**

1 Control-click (or right-click) the Word document icon to get its pop-up menu.

2 While the menu is visible, also hold down the Option key. This changes the "Open With" command to "Always Open With."

3 Choose "Always Open With." You'll see TextEdit listed in the pop-out menu. *Or* select "Other...," then choose the application you want to always open the selected file.

Save TextEdit files as Word docs

You can save any TextEdit file as a Microsoft Word document to send to people who want it in that format.

To save a TextEdit file as a Word document:

1 Go to the File menu (or the arrow to the right of the title, see page 61) and choose "Duplicate."

2 Press Command S to save this duplicate.

3 In the "File Format" menu at the bottom of the dialog box, choose "Word 2007 Format (docx)." This automatically adds the Word extension, .docx, to the end of your file name.

   If you don't see an extension at the end of a file name—and you want to— click the disclosure button to the right of the "Save As" field (circled below). Uncheck the box to "Hide Extension." To *show* the extension, of course, check the box.

If you have set your Finder preferences to show all file name extensions (Lesson 16), you won't see this checkbox.

To see the options shown here, single-click this button.

The "File Format" menu lets you save your files in several other formats. Keep this in mind.

Save TextEdit files as PDFs

From the File menu, choose "Print…," then click the "PDF" button (in the bottom-left corner of the Print dialog). Choose "Save as PDF…."

5

GOALS

Mail for Email and Notes

Mail is Apple's application for sending and receiving email. If you have more than one email account on more than one server, Mail can check them all at the same time, and you can send email from any of your accounts right through Mail.

With Mail's stationery, create fancy HTML email messages with special fonts, images, and design—all with the click of a button. And take advantage of the Notes that coordinate instantly with your Calendar information and sync to your iPhone.

For those who use Windows systems at work, Mountain Lion has built-in support for Microsoft Exchange Server. You can use your Mac apps (Mail, Calendar, Contacts) to access Exchange services, such as email, calendar invitations, and Global Address Lists.

Set Up a New Email Account

It's easy to add your email account to Mail if you didn't do it when you first installed Mountain Lion or turned on your new Mac, and it's easy to add a new account. **If your account is already set up, skip to page 83.**

To set up a Mail account (or a Messages account, Calendar settings, iCloud account, and/or to transfer your Contacts):

Mail, Contacts & Calendars

1 Open the "Mail, Contacts & Calendars" preferences: From the Apple menu, choose "System Preferences…," then click the icon shown to the left. You'll see the pane shown below-left.

2 Click the type of existing account you have. You'll be asked for your email address and its password and a couple of other questions. If all goes well, your Mac sets up your account and that's it!

3 At any time you can click the account name on the left, then choose to turn on or off the various services.

To set up a POP account (which is just about any other email account besides the services listed above), click "Other." Enter your email address and password, and if the Mac can set it up, it will.

But it might tell you that it's not able to do it and pass you off to the manual setup, which is shown on the following pages; start with Step 2.

Whether the process on the opposite page makes you set up an account yourself or you just prefer to do it yourself, it's not difficult.

1 Open the Mail app from your toolbar (or from the Application menu in the sidebar of your Finder). The "Welcome to Email" pane appears (shown below). If it doesn't, go to the File menu and choose "Add Account…."

2 Enter the information required, then click "Continue."

3 The next pane asks technical details about your account. If you don't know what kind of account it is, call your Internet service provider and ask. *Generally speaking,* this is how to **choose the type of account:**

This is the name that will be visible to the people to whom you send email.

Choose POP (Post Office Protocol, this is the most common) if you have an email account with your ISP, or if you have a domain name that you paid for and you opted for an email account with it.

Choose IMAP (Internet Mail Access Protocol) if you can access your account on different computers and always see your mail (besides webmail). This is usually with a paid service or a large company intranet (although most POPs can be set up as IMAP if you ask your provider).

Choose Exchange if your company uses the Microsoft Exchange server and the administrator has configured it for IMAP access. See your system administrator for details.

—continued

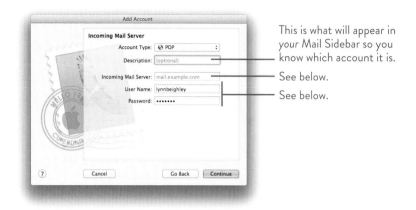

This is what will appear in
your Mail Sidebar so you
know which account it is.

See below.

See below.

Each account type has slightly different information to enter.

For instance, if you choose a POP account, Mail wants to know the **Incoming Mail Server.** It's usually something like *pop.domain.com* or *mail.domain.com.* The "domain," of course, is to be replaced with the domain name of your email. For instance, I use *mail.lynnbeighley.com* for my email that comes from that web site. If you're not sure, check your email host's web site or call and ask for the "incoming mail server."

The **User Name** for a POP account is *usually* your entire email address; occasionally it might be something different altogether. If your email address doesn't work as the user name, ask your provider.

Enter your password as provided by your provider or set up by you when you opted for the email account.

Click "Continue."

4   The **Outgoing Mail Server,** or **SMTP** (Simple Mail Transfer Protocol, shown on the following page) has a couple of options. For instance, your Google mail account will be automatically set up with a Gmail SMTP.

However, I've found that the most reliable SMTP is the one provided by your Internet service provider. For instance, if you use Comcast, your best SMTP is "smtp.comcast.net." That is, *your most reliable outgoing mail server is the company that you pay to connect you to the Internet.* So if Mail is not going out, try changing the SMTP to the one provided by your ISP.

Some ISPs may have a low-end broadband option that does not allow you to have an outgoing mail server, requiring you to use web mail to check and send your mail (and thus read their advertising). If that's your situation and you don't like it, call your provider and upgrade your service so you can get an SMTP address (or change providers).

The **Description** field lets you name this SMTP so you can choose it from certain menus. Enter something that will make it clear to you.

User Authentication: Unless your provider insists (for security reasons), you usually don't have to enter a user name and password for authentication, so for now you can leave those blank. If it doesn't work with those options blank, you'll need to call your provider because the user name and password it wants are typically *not* your email account and password! It wants the user name and password for your provider account, not your email account.

5 In the Account Summary pane that opens, check the "Take account online" box, then click "Create." The new account is now available in Mail.

Edit, delete, add, or put on hold an account

At any time you can add another account, or delete or edit an existing one by using the Mail preferences.

1 Go to the Mail menu and choose "Preferences...."

2 Click the "Accounts" icon in the toolbar.

3 **To edit an existing account,** single-click the account name in the pane, then use the pane on the right to edit.

   To add a new account, single-click the **+** sign at the bottom-left of the Accounts pane. You will see the same information panes as explained on the previous three pages.

   To delete an account, single-click the account name in the pane on the left. Single-click the **−** sign at the bottom of the Accounts pane.

   To put an account on hold, single-click the account name in the pane on the left. Uncheck the box labeled "Enable this account".

4 When finished, close the preferences or click on another icon in the Toolbar. A message will appear asking if you want to save these changes.

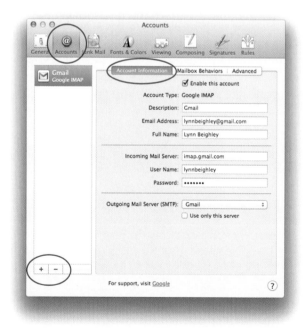

Read Your Email

The default in Mail is to automatically check your mail every five minutes (if you use a dial-up connection, go to the Mail preferences, the "General" tab, and change the "Check for new messages" option to "Manually"). If you have used Mail in the past and hate this redesigned version, you can **revert to the classic version:** Go to the Mail preferences, select the "Viewing" tab, and click "Use classic layout."

To read mail that has arrived:

1   Open Mail: Single-click the Dock icon.

   If you see "Mail" in your menu but no window, go to the File menu and choose "New Viewer Window." You'll see something that looks like the sample below.

2   On the left is a column that displays your messages, each one showing the subject and the first couple of lines of the message. Unread messages have a **blue orb** next to them.

3   **To read a message,** single-click it and the message is displayed on the right side. *Or* double-click a message and it opens into a new, separate window.

To see text labels under the icons, Command-click (or right-click) and choose "Icon and Text."

Click "New Message" to compose and send a message.

Single-click a message to display it on the right.
Double-click a message to open it in its own window.

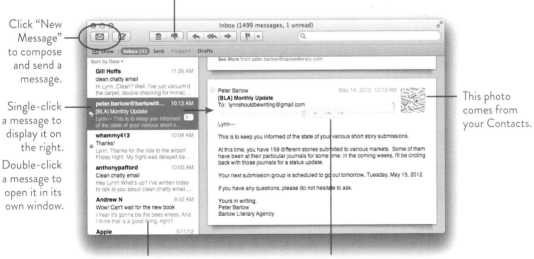

This photo comes from your Contacts.

To determine the number of lines that show in the Message List, go to the Mail menu, choose "Preferences...," click the "Viewing" tab, and choose from the "List Preview" menu.

These symbols are invisible until you hover your cursor in this spot. The symbols mean **delete, reply, reply to all,** or **forward** the message.

—continued

Features of your email window

To resize the window, drag any corner or any edge.

To resize the panes, drag any vertical dividing bar.

To open in full-screen, click these corner arrows.

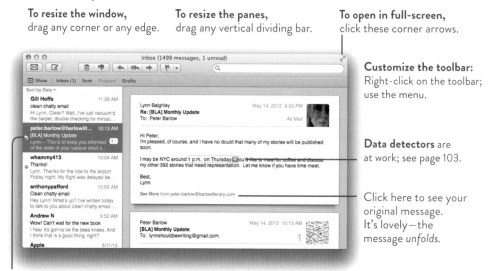

Customize the toolbar: Right-click on the toolbar; use the menu.

Data detectors are at work; see page 103.

Click here to see your original message. It's lovely—the message *unfolds*.

This view shows you an expanded **Conversation,** as indicated here in the **Message List** with a stack of messages; see pages 86–87.

To include the photos from your Address Book, go to the Mail menu, choose "Preferences...," click the "Viewing" tab, and check the box to "Show contact photos."

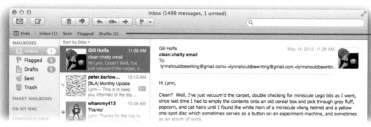

The Favorites Bar. A downward-pointing triangle indicates a menu. Numbers in parentheses indicate unread messages in that mailbox.

The **Favorites Bar** makes it easy to access your most-used options. If it's not showing, go to the View menu and choose "Show Favorites Bar." Drag items from the Sidebar into the Favorites Bar. Drag the items left or right to rearrange. Drag items to the Desktop to remove from the Bar.

Choose how you want to **organize your Message List** from the teeny, tiny, pale gray menu just above the list.

To organize by Date, choose one of the Date options, and then go back to the menu and choose or unchoose "Ascending Order" to view messages by oldest or newest first.

Mail has a seemingly endless variety of ways to present information to you. On this and the following pages we present a few of the many ways to customize Mail to suit your needs. Poke around and experiment with Mail; some of its features are invisible or only appear when necessary.

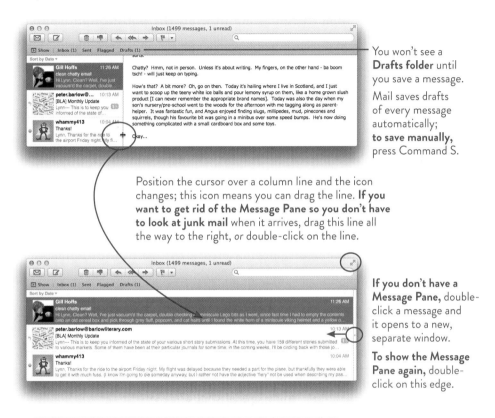

You won't see a **Drafts folder** until you save a message.

Mail saves drafts of every message automatically; **to save manually,** press Command S.

Position the cursor over a column line and the icon changes; this icon means you can drag the line. **If you want to get rid of the Message Pane so you don't have to look at junk mail** when it arrives, drag this line all the way to the right, *or double-click on the line.*

If you don't have a **Message Pane,** double-click a message and it opens to a new, separate window.

To show the Message Pane again, double-click on this edge.

Hide or show the Sidebar.

This view shows the Sidebar, the Message List, and the Message Pane. To resize all the panes or make them disappear or appear, drag the dividing lines, as shown above.

The blue orb tells me this is an unread message.

The green orb tells me this person is online and available in Messages.

—continued

Conversations in your email window

Conversations include everyone who sent a message regarding this subject, numbered in order of being received; if a message in another mailbox *pertains* to this subject, it also appears in the Conversation, but without a number. The examples below show a message *not* included in a Conversation, and then how it appears when it *is* included in a Conversation.

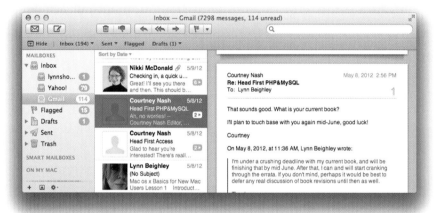

This is a typical Mail layout, with the **Sidebar** showing your Inboxes, the **Message List** showing your mail, and the **Message Pane** showing the email text.

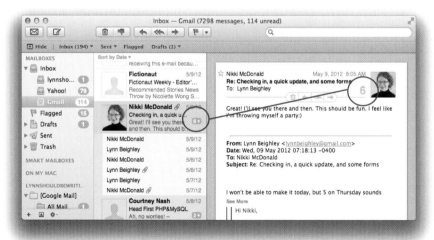

From the View menu, choose "Organize by Conversation." The Message List condenses the related messages and puts the most recent sender at the top with a number in the Message List indicating how many messages are in the Conversation.

All the related messages are in the Message Pane; scroll down to read them. The number in the Message Pane indicates which number message this is in that particular Conversation (also called a *thread*).

Although this looks like *seven* messages, the top part is actually the first message in the list beneath.

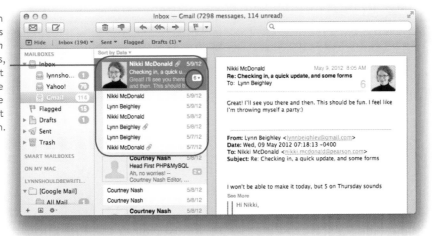

Once your email is in Conversation view, go to the View menu and choose "**Expand All Conversations.**" The newest email in the thread displays rows of previous messages beneath it, as shown above. Once you select a message, you can use your arrow keys to select other messages in that Conversation.

Notice the triangle (circled, above) next to the number in the first message now points downward, indicating the Conversation is expanded. Click that number and it will "collapse" the Conversation (or from the View menu, choose "Collapse All Conversations").

Important note: If you delete the top (most recent) message in a Conversation, *every email in that Conversation goes to the Trash!* To save an individual message from the Conversation, you can move an email from a Conversation and drop it into another mailbox; it remains part of the thread, but it won't get deleted along with the others.

Also be sure to check out the **preferences for Conversations:** From the Mail menu, choose "Preferences...." Click the "Viewing" tab. The bottom portion of the pane provides options for you to consider regarding Conversations. For instance, if you prefer not to view messages by Conversations, you could have related messages highlighted with a color instead.

Compose and Send a Message

To compose and send an email message:

1 **New message:** Click the "New Message" button in the toolbar, *or* press Command N.

Reply, Reply All, Forward: Mouse over the dividing line between return address and the message to show the reply buttons.

Click the A to show or hide the formatting pane.

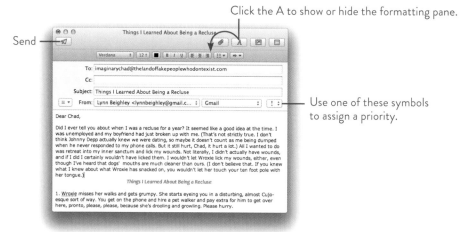

Send

Use one of these symbols to assign a priority.

2 **In the "To" field,** enter an email address.

If this person is in your Address Book or if you've sent a message to him before, as soon as you start typing, the rest of the email address appears. If there is more than one person with those beginning letters, you'll get a list of possibilities. Use the arrow keys to go up or down the list and select the address you want; hit Return to put that address in the field. (Manage addresses you've sent to in the **Previous Recipients** list from the Window menu.)

Or from the Window menu, choose "Address Panel" to bring up a limited version of your Contacts. Double-click on anyone's name to add it to the "To" field. To add someone's email address to the Cc or Bcc fields, select a name in the list, then click the "Cc:" or "Bcc:" button.

3 **In the "Subject" field,** enter a subject that does not sound like junk mail.

4 **In the Message Pane,** type your message. Mail automatically checks your spelling and displays suspect words with a red dotted underline. You can change the font, color, size, alignment, and more, using the Format menu in the toolbar. You can also use the Font panel, Colors panel, Spelling Checker, and all the other os x features—see Lesson 14 for details.

5 **To send an attachment** of some sort, just drag it into the message window and drop it (see pages 105–107 for more details).

6 **Hit the "Send" button** (it looks like a paper airplane). *Or* press Command S to **save it for later;** to open that letter later, go to the Drafts folder in the Sidebar.

Customize the message window

You can **customize** the mail message for every message you open in the future, or just the one you're writing now. To make some settings your defaults, use the "Composing" pane in the Mail preferences (from the Mail menu).

■ Click the *Customize* button to add or delete fields, or to add or delete a return address menu, an SMTP server menu (see pages 80–81), signature options (see pages 98–99), or the priority button (see the opposite page).

Cc: Sends a copy of this message; the main addressee can see Cc addresses.

Bcc: Sends a private copy; no one in the To or Cc field knows this person also received a copy.

Reply to: If you want a return email to go to a different address than the one you are sending it from, put that address here.

As usual, you can Command-click to get the option to Customize the toolbar.

Get photos; see page 91.

Stationery; see the following pages.

Customize the options in this row.

If you have more than one email address set up in Mail, you can choose from which address to send your message.

If you have more than one SMTP available, you can choose it here.

All signatures you have created appear in this menu.

> **TIP** —— **If you can't format the text in a message,** such as change the color or make words bold, go to the Format menu and choose "Make Rich Text." If it says "Make Plain Text" in that menu instead of "Rich Text," that means you're already working in rich text. If you still can't make bold or italic text, then the font you chose does not have bold or italic versions. Check the Fonts panel (press Command T) to see if the font you're using includes bold and italic versions. See Lesson 14 for details.

Use Stationery to Send Fancy Email

It's actually called "HTML" mail, not "fancy" mail. HTML means it has HTML code written into the message for you that creates the layout, the space for photos, the fonts, etc. *You* don't have to write one single piece of code. All you do is choose the stationery template, type your message, and drag photos to replace the existing ones.

To create an email with stationery:

1 Open a new email message (Command N *or* click the "New Message" icon).

2 Single-click the button on the far-right side of the message toolbar; if your text labels are showing, it's called "Show Stationery." (If you don't see that button, open the window wider, or click on the arrow you see where the button should be—that will pop out a menu with "Show Stationery" on it.)

3 A row of stationery templates appears, as shown below. Single-click a category on the left, then choose a template on the right.

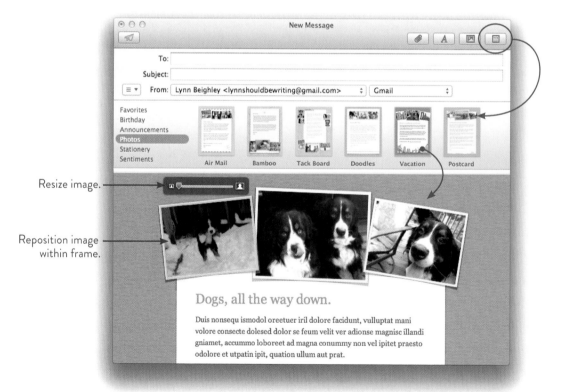

Resize image.

Reposition image within frame.

4 **To replace the text,** click it and Mail automatically selects all the text in that section. Whatever you type replaces that text, but retains the font.

5 **To add photos,** you can do several things.

- Click the "Photo Browser" button in the toolbar (shown below). The Photo Browser displays all the photos in iPhoto, Aperture, and Photo Booth. Just drag an image from the Photo Browser and drop it directly on top of the image you want to replace.

- Drag an image from anywhere on your Mac and drop it on an existing image.

- Open iPhoto and drag an image directly from iPhoto onto an existing image.

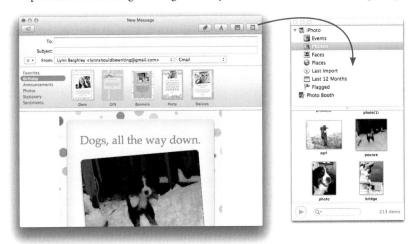

6 **To resize photos,** click an image and a little slider bar appears, as shown on the opposite page. Drag the slider right or left to enlarge or reduce the image.

7 **To reposition the image within the frame,** click the image. Then press-and-drag on the image to reposition it within its frame (you can't reposition the frame itself).

To get back to a blank white page, choose the "Stationery" option, then click the "Original" template.

You can **change templates at any point**—if there are fewer photos in the new template, some of them will disappear. Your text will reappear in the new template.

Click the "Hide Stationery" button so you have more room in which to write.

Save as Stationery

To save your own designs as stationery, set up a message, then go to the File menu and choose "Save as Stationery." A new category appears in the list, called "Custom." Click on it to see your own stationery. **To delete stationery you made,** position your mouse over it, then click the little **X** that appears in the upper-left corner.

Create Mailboxes to Organize Your Mail

Organize your mail with mailboxes in the same way that you make folders in a Finder window to organize all the files on your Mac, or the same way you use folders for papers in your office filing system. Everything in your Sidebar is considered a mailbox, even though most of the "mailboxes" look just like folders.

Once you've got your mailboxes set up, drag messages to your mailbox folders to organize your email. Better yet, use filters (called Rules; see the opposite page) to automatically send incoming mail to the different folders/mailboxes. Also check out pages 96–97 about Smart Mailboxes.

To make new mailboxes, do one of the following:

- From the Mailbox menu, choose "New Mailbox…." You get a dialog that lets you choose where to place that mailbox and what to name it. You can assign a mailbox to a specific Inbox account, or nest it inside an existing mailbox.

- *Or* Control-click (or right-click) directly on the icon in the Sidebar in which you want to put the new mailbox. If you put it in an Inbox account, the mailbox will appear in the lower portion of the Sidebar, under the name of that account.

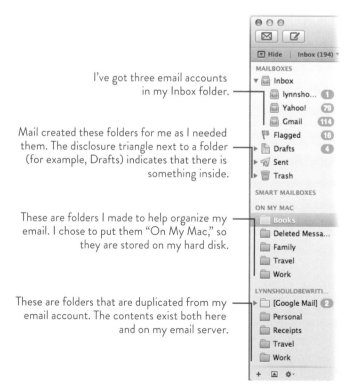

I've got three email accounts in my Inbox folder.

Mail created these folders for me as I needed them. The disclosure triangle next to a folder (for example, Drafts) indicates that there is something inside.

These are folders I made to help organize my email. I chose to put them "On My Mac," so they are stored on my hard disk.

These are folders that are duplicated from my email account. The contents exist both here and on my email server.

Filter Your Incoming Mail with Rules

Create rules, or filters, to do things like **sort incoming mail** into an appropriate mailbox, highlight certain messages in a particular color, automatically forward to a different address, delete a message before it even appears in your box, send an auto-reply, and more. All filters apply to all email accounts unless you specifically choose an account in the Rule itself. If you plan to sort mail into different mailboxes, first create the mailboxes you want so you can organize with them (see opposite page).

To create and apply a rule:

1 From the Mail menu, choose "Preferences...."

2 Single-click the "Rules" icon. Single-click "Add Rule."

3 Choose your parameters for the type of mail coming in and what to do with it. (If you forgot to make a special mailbox for something, you can actually do it while the Rules pane is open on your screen: go to the Mailbox menu and choose "New Mailbox...." The new mailbox immediately appears in the pop-up menu, shown below.)

> In the example below, I first made a new mailbox called "My Fiction."
>
> Then I created a new rule to find any incoming mail "From" my fiction agent, Peter Barlow, by entering the beginning of his email address.
>
> When found, I want that message to move straight into the "My Fiction" folder and play a little sound so I know it arrived.

The choices here, *any* or *all,* are useful to limit your results.

Click the pop-up menu button (under here) to choose the mailbox into which this Rule will move messages.

Click **+** to add more options.

Poke around in here at all the options in all the menus. Add more *conditions* (the first section) and choose more *actions* (the second section).

VIP Email Addresses

Most of us get tons of email, some important, some not so much. You may get email from specific people that you always want to read as soon as possible, whereas other email you can put off reading until you have more time. If you want to pay special attention to emails you get from certain people, you can designate them as VIPs with their email addresses. It makes them stand out, and you can even tell Notifications (see Lesson 18) to notify you only when you get a VIP email.

When you designate an email as a VIP, a copy of all email arriving from that address shows up in a section on the Mail sidebar. Each VIP gets his own subfolder under the VIPs folder.

An easy way to see all your VIP mailboxes is to use this VIPs drop-down menu.

Mail created these folders for me when I designated these email addresses as VIPs. Click on a name to view all email from that person. If you've got a lot of VIPs, you might want to hide these subfolders. Click the disclosure triangle to hide or show this list.

Emails from your VIPs show up both in their folders and in your Inbox. When it's from a VIP, this star appears next to it.

Creating and Removing VIP Email Addresses

Adding and removing VIPs is easy.

To add a VIP:

1   Open a message from the address you want to designate as a VIP.

2   Mouse over the email address and click the arrow on the right to open a menu (shown below).

3   Choose "Add to VIPs." That's it!

You'll now have a new folder under VIPs containing email from this address. Deleting is even easier. Just Control-click on the VIP folder you want to remove and choose "Remove from VIPs." This doesn't delete email from this address, it just removes the VIP folder and no longer designates these emails as VIP emails.

Clicking "Add to VIPs" will create a new VIP mailbox for this address and all email, both old and new, will show up in it.

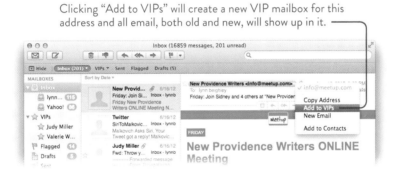

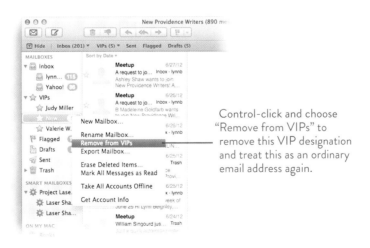

Control-click and choose "Remove from VIPs" to remove this VIP designation and treat this as an ordinary email address again.

Smart Mailboxes

You can create **Smart Mailboxes** that will hold all the email messages that meet certain search criteria. If you are familiar with Rules (filters), as explained on the previous page, you'll notice there are a couple of differences between Rules and Smart Mailboxes.

- A Rule is an *action* that is applied to incoming messages, such as filtering certain email into a certain folder. The *original* email is *moved* into the folder.

- A Smart Mailbox applies your search criteria to mail that is already in your box, not just to future incoming mail.

- A Smart Mailbox contains messages that match search criteria. No action is taken on the messages.

- A Smart Mailbox does not contain the *original* message, thus the same message can be "stored" in a number of Smart Mailboxes.

- A Smart Mailbox automatically updates itself as messages come in or are deleted.

You might be involved in leading a project that involves several people who are each working on an individual part of it. Thus you might use *Rules* to filter their messages into subfolders in a main project folder, and you might use a *Smart Folder* to collect all the email pertaining to this project in one place.

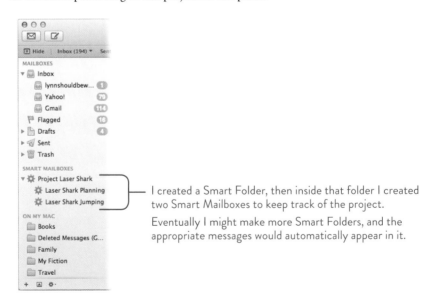

I created a Smart Folder, then inside that folder I created two Smart Mailboxes to keep track of the project.

Eventually I might make more Smart Folders, and the appropriate messages would automatically appear in it.

Create Smart Mailboxes

There are several ways to **create a Smart Mailbox.** You can use the Mailbox menu (below) or the **+** sign at the bottom of the Message List, or use the parameters you've designated in a saved search, explained on page 101.

To create a Smart Mailbox:

1 If you go to the Mailbox menu, you'll see there are two similar options, "New Smart Mailbox Folder..." and "New Smart Mailbox...."

> The **Smart Mailbox Folder** creates a folder with no search parameters; it is simply for organizing other **Smart Mailboxes** inside (as shown on the opposite page). You will only be asked to name the folder and click OK.
>
> If you want your Smart Mailbox to be *inside* of an existing Smart Folder, first select that folder in the Mailboxes Sidebar; if not, make sure a Smart Folder is *not* selected.
>
> *Or* click the **+** sign at the bottom-left and choose "New Smart Mailbox...."

2 You'll see the dialog sheet below. Name your Smart Mailbox, choose your parameters, and click OK.

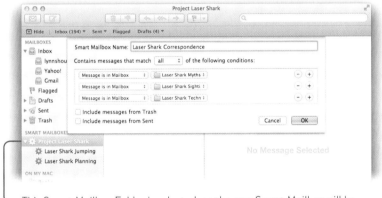

This Smart Mailbox Folder is selected, so the new Smart Mailbox will be placed inside.

Before I created this particular Smart Mailbox, I created the three folders and applied Rules to filter specific messages into each one.

3 If you need to edit the parameters of your new Smart Mailbox, select it, then either Control-click, right-click, or go to the Mailbox menu and choose "Edit Smart Mailbox...."

Add Signatures to Your Messages

An **email signature** is the little blurb you can automatically add to the bottom of your messages. A signature might include your contact information, promotion for your upcoming art show or book publication, your favorite quote, or even a small graphic. You can make more than one signature, then choose which one you want for an individual email message, as a default signature that automatically appears, or you can let Mail randomly choose one for you.

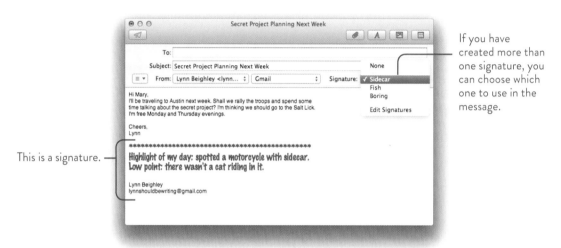

This is a signature.

If you have created more than one signature, you can choose which one to use in the message.

To create a signature:

1 From the Mail menu, choose "Preferences...."

2 Single-click the "Signatures" icon. You'll see the window shown on the opposite page.

3 At the top of the left-hand pane, single-click "All Signatures."

4 In the middle pane, single-click the plus sign (**+**). The new one is called "Signature #1." Name it something more relevant.

5 In the right-hand pane, type your signature. From the Format menu at the top of your screen, choose "Show Fonts," then choose a font, size, style, alignment, and color. You can use Returns and Tab keys in your signature.

   Don't choose a font that you have bought or acquired along the way because most of your recipients probably won't have that same font installed. Use one of the fonts that came with your Mac.

6 If you want an **image** to appear in this signature, drag the image from the Finder and drop it into the right-hand pane. Keep in mind that this should be a very small image, both in file size and in visual size!

If you like, drag an image from the Finder and drop it in this pane.

7 **To assign signatures to email accounts:** Drag a signature from the middle column and drop it on the account name in the left column. You can have lots of signatures, yet choose only certain ones for different email accounts.

8 Each email account can have its own **default signature** that automatically appears in each email message you write: First select an account in the left-hand pane, then use the "Choose Signature" menu circled above (you can always choose a different one from the menu, even if one is assigned as a default).

To use a signature, put the "Signature" menu in your message window:

1 Open a new message as if you're going to write a letter.

2 Single-click the Action button on the left, as shown below, then choose "Customize...."

3 Put a checkmark in the box next to "Signature."

4 Click OK. Now you will see the Signature menu in every new mail message, as shown below. Choose the one you want to use for each individual message.

Action button.

You won't see an option to add signatures if you haven't made any yet!

Search Your Mail

In Mail, the Search feature makes it easy to find just about anything.

1   The default is to search all folders and mailboxes in Mail. To limit the search to a particular inbox or mailbox, select it in the Sidebar; to select more than one, Command-click each one. If you have messages or Notes flagged with various colors, you can choose to limit the color of flag to be included in the search.

2   Enter a word or phrase in the search field (you can use Boolean search terms such as OR, AND, or NOT, as explained in Lesson 21). **NOTE:** The Mail search only finds words that *begin* with the letters you enter. That is, if you search for *quest* you will find *question,* but not *request.*

As you start typing in the Search field, the Favorites Bar turns into a Search Bar and a menu of suggestions in several categories appears.

3   As you type more characters, the results narrow and become more specific. If you see what you think you're looking for, click on that item; the Message List on the left displays only items that match that suggestion.

The Search Bar appears. At any point you can click any item in the Bar to limit your search to that item.

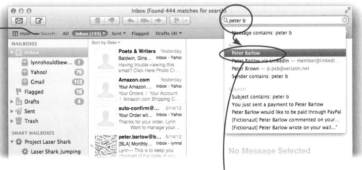

Results are categorized by Dates, People, and Subjects (which has nothing do to with the Subject line in a message).

4   As soon as you select one of the items in the list of suggestions, the Search field gives you yet another option to narrow the search, as shown below. What this option displays depends on the category your choice was in.

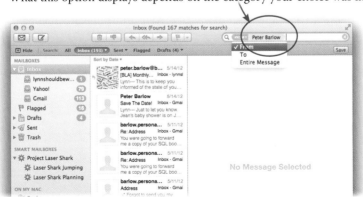

I made a choice in the "People" category, and Mail immediately provides more options to narrow it down, as you can see here.

In this example, I made a choice in the "Subjects" category, so now Mail lets me limit the search phrase to the Subject line of the message or to the entire message.

5 Your results, be they messages or Notes, appear in the Messages List.

6 **To display all your messages again,** click the gray **X** in the search field.
As long as there is even one character in the search field, you will see the search results instead of your mail.

To search within an individual message, open the message and press Command F.

Create a Smart Mailbox from a saved search

You can create a Smart Mailbox (as explained on pages 92–93) by saving a search. Anything that satisfies the search criteria will leave a copy in this mailbox.

1 Do a search as usual, as explained above.

2 If the search gives you what you need and you think you'll want to use the same search again, click the "Save" button (it's just below the Search field).

3 The saved search is automatically named with the search phrase you just used. You can refine your search in the edit box, if you like. When ready, click OK.

4 If you need to edit the parameters of your new Smart Mailbox, select it, then either Control-click, right-click, or go to the Mailbox menu and choose "Edit Smart Mailbox...."

Check Your Dock Icon

When email comes in, your Mail icon in the **Dock** displays a little red badge that tells you how many messages are unread. There is more to that Dock icon than meets the eye:

Single-click this Mail icon to bring the Mail window to the front. (You don't have to quit Mail when you're finished working in it.)

Right-click (or Control-click) the Mail icon to open a pop-up menu of commands and options (below left), such as "Compose New Message." These commands are also available in the File menu and the Application menu.

Press (hold down the mouse button) the Mail icon to pop up a menu with other options (below), such as "Quit," "Hide," and "Keep in Dock."

The appearance and content of this contextual menu changes, depending on if the application is already open or not.

Choose "Show All Windows" to display all your open messages, as shown below.

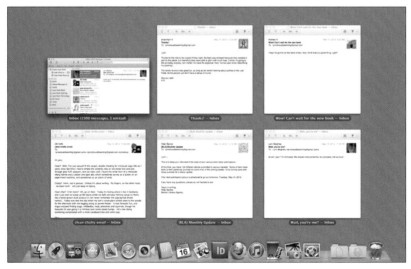

Automatic Data Detection in Messages

This is amazing. As you might have seen in TextEdit, your pointer becomes a data detector, capable of recognizing dates and location information. When you hover the cursor over a day, date, or address in an email message (or a note), the information highlights with a gray dotted outline and adds a data detector button (a triangle symbol, shown below).

If you click the data detector button on a date, you can create an Calendar Event for that date. Click it on an address, and you can show a map of the address or create a new contact in Contacts, using the address information.

Create a Calendar Event from date and time info

1   Hover the pointer over a date in a message. A gray dotted line appears around the date (or month, day of the week, or even a word like "tomorrow").

2   Click the data detector button (the triangle) to show a pop-up calendar with the date inserted (shown at the top of the next page).

   To add the information to Calendar as an Event, click "Add to Calendar" in the top-right corner of the pop-up.

   To expand the pop-up and add more information, or to **edit** the existing information, click the "Edit" button. In the expanded calendar dialog, you can select a calendar to put the Event in, change the time, create alerts, etc.

3   After editing, click "Create."

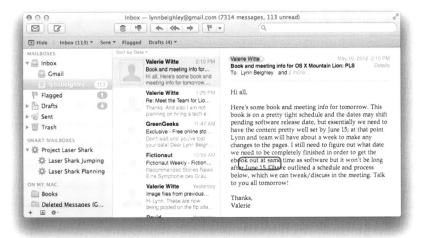

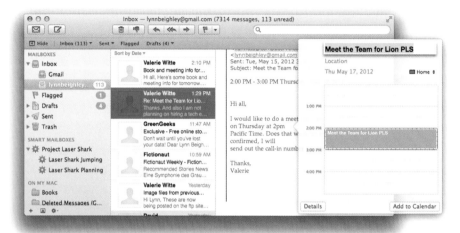

When you click a date or time that's highlighted by the data detector in your pointer, the information is automatically added to a minimal calendar form (above, right).

Create a contact, add to an existing contact, or show a map

1   Hover the pointer over an address in a message. The pointer's data detectors sense location information and border the address with a dotted line and a data detector button (a gray triangle).

2   Click the data detector button to show a pop-up menu of options: "Create New Contact…" (in Contacts), "Add to Existing Contact…," "Show Address in Google Maps," and "Copy".

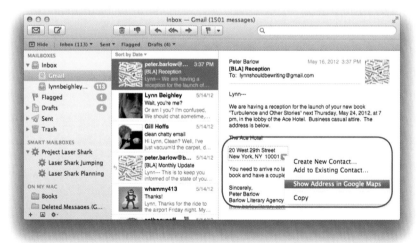

Mail Attachments

One of the greatest things about email is the ability to send files and photos back and forth. Mail has some great features for attachments, making it easier than ever.

To send an attachment:

1   Open a new message window and address and type your message.

2   Click the *Attach* button in the toolbar (the paperclip).

    A sheet drops down from the message window toolbar. Find your file, select it, and click "Choose File." **To select multiple files to attach,** hold down the Command key and single-click each file.

    Or drag a file or photo from anywhere on your Mac and drop it directly into the message window. *Or* click the Photo Browser button in the top-right corner of the message window, then navigate to the photo you want to attach.

3   The file appears in your message window. If it's a one-page PDF or a photo, the actual image appears, as shown below. If the attachment is a multi-page PDF, a text file, or any number of other file types, it appears as a file icon, not an image.

4   Send the email (click the paper airplane button).

Send. ——

Open the Photo Browser
and find photos to attach.

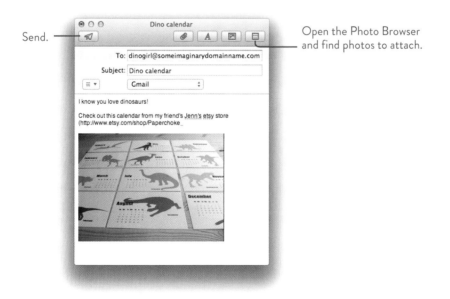

To receive and download an attachment:

1 An attachment appears in a Mail message as an actual image or as a file icon, shown below, left.

2 If it's **a file or photograph,** you can do any of several things:

> Drag the file to the Desktop or directly into any window or folder on your Mac, or into a folder in a Finder window Sidebar.

> *Or* Control-click (or right-click) the file name. Choose an option from the pop-up menu that opens (shown below).

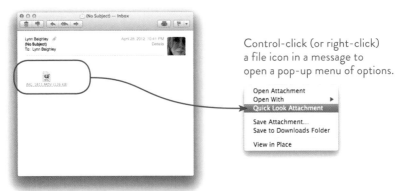

Control-click (or right-click) a file icon in a message to open a pop-up menu of options.

> *Or* if the attachment is an image, save it directly into **iPhoto:** Control-click (or right-click) the photo (or select *all* the photos), then from the pop-up menu, choose "Export to iPhoto."

View lots of photo attachments as a contact sheet

This happens often: Someone sends you **multiple photographs** in an email message. Instead of scrolling through them, you can view them as a contact sheet or as a slideshow, using Quick Look.

From the File menu, choose "Quick Look Attachments." In the Quick Look window:

> Use the arrow buttons in the toolbar to cycle through the photos like a slideshow.

> *Or* click the "Contact Sheet" button to show all photos at once.

> *Or* click the "Open with Preview" button to open all the photos in the Preview app.

> *Or* press (don't click) on the button to open a pop-up menu of other options, such as "Add to iPhoto."

Slideshow buttons.

View as a Contact Sheet.

Click a thumbnail in the Contact Sheet (below) to display the image full-frame, as shown to the left.

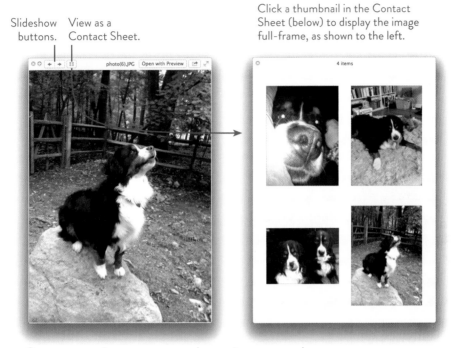

Save attachments to a location you choose

To save one or more file attachments, go to the File menu and choose "Save Attachments…," then choose a location in which to save them. By default the **Downloads folder** is selected (although you can choose any location you want). Open the Downloads folder (in the Dock or in your Finder window Sidebar) to get to the saved files.

A copy of the Downloads folder is in the Dock; you can view the contents as a "Stack" (a stack of icons) or as a "Folder". **To determine how the *folder* is displayed in the Dock,** Control-click (or right-click) the Downloads folder in the Dock to show a pop-up menu, then select "Folder" or "Stack". Next, **to determine how the content of the folder is displayed** when you select the folder in the Dock, choose "Fan," "Grid," or "List".

6

GOALS

Make and edit
contact cards

Add photos
to your contacts

Designate your own card
for automatic fill-in
on web pages

Create mailing lists (Groups)
and Smart Groups

Search your contacts

Print envelopes, a list
of contacts, and more

An introduction to iCloud

Contacts for Keeping Track of People

The Contacts app, as its name suggests, keeps your contact info for you. Enjoy the drag-and-drop ease of creating groups and sending the group a message. Create Smart Groups so that new contacts that meet certain criteria are automatically added to the group. Show a Google map of an address with a single click, and more.

Contacts is integrated with Mail and Calendar so you can easily and quickly send messages and invitations to your contacts. Contacts supports directories hosted on network servers, such as Microsoft Exchange, Lightweight Directory Access Protocol (LDAP) servers, and Internet accounts such as Yahoo!.

Contacts syncs automatically with iCloud (Apple's free automatic storage and syncing solution) to keep all of your devices synced and updated.

How You'll Use Your Contacts

Let's start with a brief description of how you can use this great application.

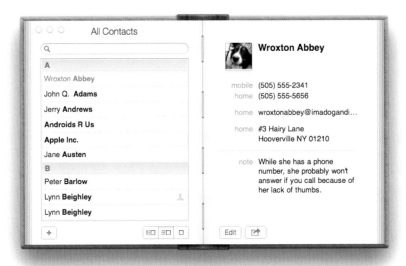

Select a contact on the left to show the contact information on the right.

You can customize individual cards and/or add new *fields* to all of them. For instance, you can add a birthday field or a nickname field. You can change the labels, add a photo or image, and customize the address for another country.

You can create Groups of addresses to make a mailing list so you can mail everyone in the Group with one click.

In Mail, all the contacts you put in your Contacts will be available via the Address *Pane* (you can't add, edit, delete, or group addresses in that pane—you can just access them for emailing; see Lesson 5).

While in Mail (not Contacts) **you can automatically add an address from an email you receive:** Open the email, Control-click (or right-click) the email address in the "From" field to get a contextual menu, then choose "Add to Contacts." If that contact information is already in your Contacts, the pop-up menu item says "Show Contact Card."

Your iPhone or iPad will synchronize with all the addresses or with certain Groups that you specify (when using iCloud to sync your mobile devices). As you add contacts to your iPhone or iPad, they will automatically be added to your Contacts on your Mac the next time you connect and sync your mobile device.

Create and Edit New Cards

To make a new card (sometimes called a **vCard,** or virtual card), click the **+** sign in the bottom-right corner of the "All Contacts" page. The new, blank contact card is displayed on the right page, ready for you to add information.

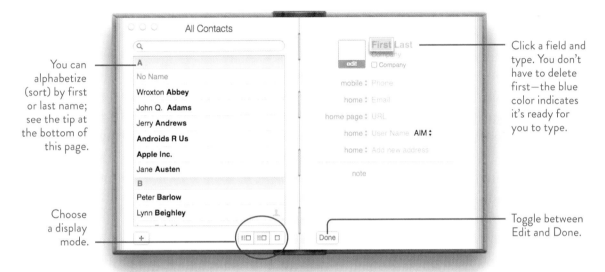

You can alphabetize (sort) by first or last name; see the tip at the bottom of this page.

Choose a display mode.

Click a field and type. You don't have to delete first—the blue color indicates it's ready for you to type.

Toggle between Edit and Done.

To edit an existing card, select the card name on the "All Contacts" page on the left, then click the "Edit" button on the card on the right. When finished, click "Done."

After you fill in a field, hit the Tab key **to highlight the next field,** ready for you to type in it. To skip that field, hit the Tab key again.

To delete a field, click the red button to the left of it (although if a field is empty, it will disappear when you finish editing).

To change an existing field label name, click a *label* (a field name). A menu pops up with a list of other label options. If none of them fits, click the "Custom…" item and create your own label.

To open a card in its own floating window, double-click a contact name.

TIP ——— Only fields that contain information are visible after you leave Edit mode. Check out the preferences for Contacts (from the Contacts application menu): Use the "Phone" pane to automatically format phone numbers so you don't have to type hyphens and parentheses. Use the "General" pane to choose a sort option for names. Use the "Accounts" pane to synchronize your contacts with your Google, Yahoo!, or Exchange accounts.

Add a photo to a card

You can add a photo to any contact card. That photo will appear in email that you receive from that person; it will be transferred to your iPhone so you can see his handsome face when he calls; and you can print it with his contact info.

To add a photo to a contact card:

1 Go to that card in your Contacts.

2 Double-click the empty photo space to the left of the name. A sheet appears:

Capture a picture.   Resize.   Apply an effect.

3 Drag any type of image into the pane, *or* click "Defaults" to use a stand-in photo, choose "Recents" to find a photo you've recently saved to your hard disk, *or* click the camera icon to take a picture of yourself or someone near you.

4 **To resize the image,** drag the slider to the right or left.

   To reposition the image, click and drag it around inside the cropped space.

   To apply an effect, click the *Effects* button to the right of the slider.

5 Click "Done" when you like it.

Add photos via your iPhone

Next time you add someone's contact info to your iPhone, take a photo of that person. When you sync your iPhone to your Mac, this photo will automatically appear in your Contacts; when you get email from this person, his photo will appear in the message.

Designate Your Own Card

In your Contacts, you can designate the card with your contact information on it as "My Card." Other applications, Safari and iChat in particular, will use that information in various ways, such as filling in forms online, accessing your email address, and displaying your photo.

A tiny human silhouette to the right of your name in Contacts marks it as "My Card."

Enter a **card** for yourself in the Contacts. Then go to the Card menu and choose "Make This My Card."

To keep some of the information private so it won't show up if you send your vCard (virtual card) to someone else:

1   Go to the Contacts preferences (under the "Contacts" menu).

2   Click the "vCard" icon in the toolbar.

3   Check the box to "Enable private me card" (if it isn't already). Close the preferences.

4   Go to your own card and click the "Edit" button. You'll see a blue checkbox for each item on your card; the checkmark means it is public information. **Uncheck** the boxes that you want to be private.

Add Fields to One Card or All Cards

The fields for data only appear on the card if there is data in them; otherwise the fields disappear, which is kind of nice. Select a card and click the "Edit" button to see what fields you might have on a card that are not filled in.

You can add a number of other fields to an individual card or to all cards.

To add a field to ONE card:

1   Select that card.

2   From the Card menu in the menu bar across the top of your screen, slide down to "Add Field," and make a choice from the pop-out menu (such as "Birthday").

To add a field to EVERY card:

1   From the Card menu, choose "Add Field," then choose "Edit Template...."

   Or go to the Contacts menu and choose "Preferences...," then from that toolbar, click the "Template" button.

2   Click the "Add Field" button to display its menu. Field names in the list that are gray and checkmarked are already on the card template. Choose any field name that is black and it will be added to *all* of your cards.

   To add more fields to a category, click the green button to the left of the field name.

   To remove fields, click the red button to the left of the field name.

Add or remove fields from the card template.

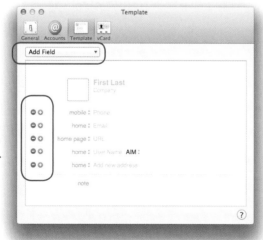

Check Out the Options

There are lots of hidden options in the Contacts. For instance, single-click the labels to the left of the fields on a card—you'll get little menus, depending on what you click on. Try it: click an email label, then choose "Send Email." Select "FaceTime" from the little pop-up menu and your Mac makes a video call to the contact's iPhone 4 (or newer). The FaceTime option is also available in the email label, so you can make a FaceTime video call to the contact's computer. FaceTime uses email addresses to call FaceTime users on their computers, and it uses mobile phone numbers to call FaceTime users on FaceTime-capable iPhones and iPads.

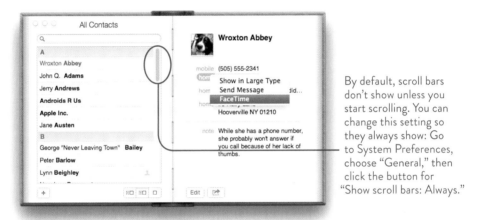

By default, scroll bars don't show unless you start scrolling. You can change this setting so they always show: Go to System Preferences, choose "General," then click the button for "Show scroll bars: Always."

Map It

You can instantly get a Google map of any address in your Contacts (you must be connected to the Internet, of course).

Click the label to the left of an address in Contacts. A little menu pops up where you can choose "Map this Address." Safari opens to Google Maps and displays the location of that address.

Create a Group

When you make a Group mailing list, you can **send email to the name of that Group** and your message goes to everyone in the Group.

To make a new Group:

1 Click the View menu and choose Groups to show Groups on the left-hand page. When you select a Group on the left-hand page, the group members appear on the right-hand page.

2 Click the File menu and choose "New Group" or the Groups view button (shown below).

3 A new "untitled group" is created. Rename it ("Friends," for example).

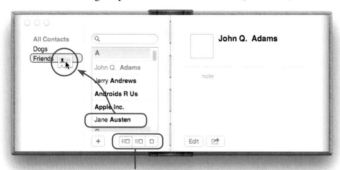

Drag a card over a Group name, then drop the card when the Group turns blue.

Switch between views: Groups, List and Card, or Card only.

4 Now select the "All Contacts" group, then drag contact names from the right-hand page and drop them on the new Group name. You can put the same name in many different Groups.

To open a Group: Click the Group name in the Group list.

To create a Group from a selection: Select multiple contacts, then from the File menu, choose "New Group From Selection."

To delete a Group: Single-click its name and hit the Delete key.

To email a message to a Group: On the Group page, Control-click (or right-click) a Group name, then choose "Send Email to *group name.*" **In Mail,** type the name of the Group in the "To" field of an email message.

To prevent all the addresses from appearing in the "To" field of everyone's email:

1 Open Mail (not Contacts).

2 From the Mail menu, choose "Preferences…," click "Composing" in the toolbar, then uncheck the box "When sending to a group, show all member addresses."

Create Smart Groups in Contacts

A Smart Group is a list of contacts that automatically updates itself as new contacts are created that meet its criteria or as information for other contacts changes. For instance, you might want a Smart Group that automatically adds people who work for a certain company or who are part of your writing group. You can create a Smart Group that tells you when birthdays or anniversaries are approaching. Or you might want to gather a list of everyone in a particular city without having to find them all in your Contacts—a Smart Group will automatically collect them.

Most of these searches require, of course, that you have a particular field on your card and that it has data in it. For instance, you can't have a Smart Group that tells you when a birthday is coming up if you don't have the Birthday field on your cards. For directions on how to **add new fields,** see page 114.

To create a Smart Group:

1 From the File menu at the top of the screen, choose "New Smart Group...."

2 In the sheet that drops down, choose your parameters.

3 If you need more parameters to narrow or expand the possible items in the Group, click the **+** button in the sheet (circled, above-right).

4 Click OK.

> TIP —— To discover which Groups a contact is in, select a contact name, then press the Option key. The selected contact is included in every Group that turns blue.

Search Your Contacts

You can do a standard, simple search for anyone or any information in your collection of contacts. And you can do a Spotlight search of anyone in your Contacts that searches your entire hard disk for everything related to that person.

To search Contacts:

1   **To search your entire database of contacts,** select the "All Contacts" group. **To search within a specific Group,** select that Group.

2   Single-click in the search field, or press Command F.

3   Type any letters in the person's name or any other data you want to find. As you type, results appear in the list of contacts on the right-hand page.

This search also looks at any words or comments you've entered in the "note" section at the bottom of a card.

4   Type more letters to narrow your search, or single-click one of the contacts on the search results page.

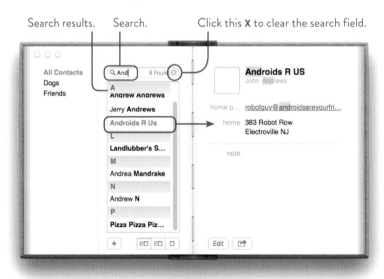

Search results.   Search.   Click this **X** to clear the search field.

5   **To show all of your contacts again,** click the **X** in the search field to clear it.

To search for a person or business in Spotlight:

1 Find the person you want to Spotlight, as explained on the previous page.

2 Control-click (or right-click) the person's name. From the pop-up menu that appears, choose "Spotlight: *This Person*" (where *"This Person"* is the name of the contact you just searched for; that name automatically appears in the menu, as shown below).

3 A Finder window of Spotlight search results opens, as explained in Lesson 21. It shows every file on your computer that is connected with this person, such as email she's sent you, files she's mentioned within, documents she has created and sent to you, images of her, and more.

Send a Contacts Card to Others

 So easy: Just click the "Share" button on any contact card. You have three options for sending the vCard: email it, use Messages to send it, or Airdrop it to other people nearby (see Lesson 23). Email the card by choosing "Email Card". This opens Mail with an email message ready to send that includes the vCard of this contact in the body.

Merge Duplicate Cards

This happens all the time: Somehow you have more than one card for a contact; one card has partial information, whereas another card has duplicated information or different kinds of information. You can merge these disparate cards into a single card, and keep all the information that's unique to each one. The cards you want to merge have to be in the same account, such as "On My Mac" (the contacts on your Mac), CardDAV, Exchange, iCloud, LDAP, or Yahoo! accounts.

Merge all duplicates

1 If you have accounts other than "On My Mac," select an account in the Group list.

2 From the Card menu, choose "Look for Duplicates...."

   An alert tells you if duplicate cards are found, or cards that have the same contact name but different information. The alert also tells you if information is duplicated on a single card, such as the same email address twice.

3 As an option, you can click the checkbox to "Also merge cards that have the same name but contain different information (such as phone numbers and addresses)". This option only appears if such duplicates are found.

4 Click Merge. Contacts merges the unique information from each duplicate into a single card.

Merge selected duplicates

Command-click to select the cards you want to merge, then from the Card menu, choose "Merge Selected Cards."

Contacts creates a single card, merges the unique information from each card, and uses the name and picture of the card that appeared first in the list.

Invite Contacts to a Calendar Event

Invite specific contacts or an entire Group to an Calendar event, such as a cookout for your friends or a meeting for business associates.

1   Open Calendar.

2   Go back to your Contacts and select one or more contacts or Groups.

3   Drag the selection to the Calendar window and drop it on a date in a calendar.

4   iCal creates an Event. Set the time and other Event options. The contacts are listed as *invitees* in the Event window.

5   Click the "Send" button in bottom-right corner of the event window (shown below). Email notifications are automatically sent to all invitees.

To remove an invitee from the list, select the name, then press Delete.

For more information about adding events to a calendar, see Lesson 8 on Calendar.

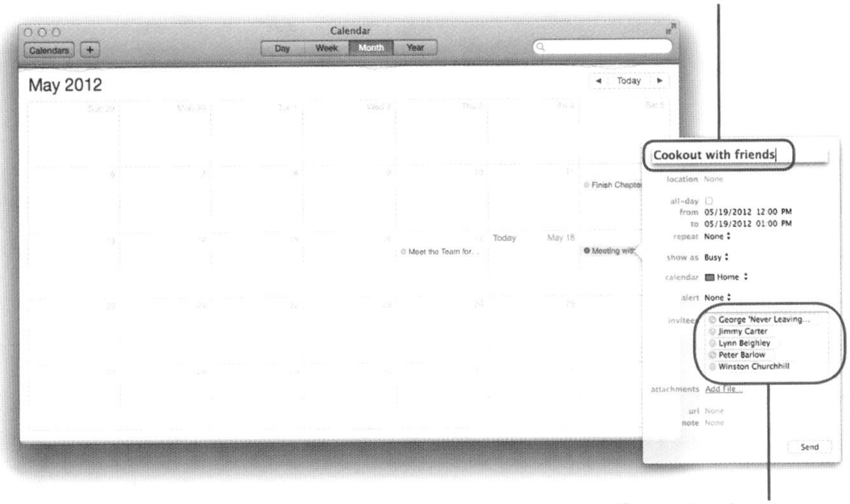

Rename the Event anything you want.

If an invitee is not highlighted with blue, it means that contact card is missing an email address.

Print in a Variety of Ways

From Contacts you can **print** mailing labels, envelopes, customized lists, and even pages that fit into a standard pocket address book.

1 First, in Contacts, select the names or the Group that you want to print.

2 Press Command P to open the Print dialog sheet, *or* from the File menu, choose "Print."

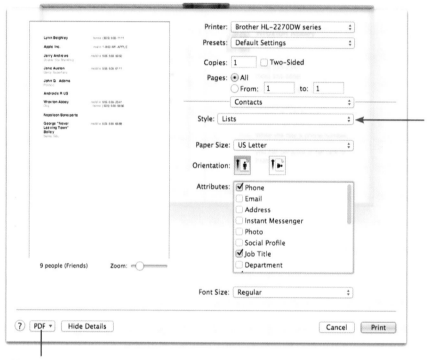

You can save the job as a PDF, then send that PDF to someone else to print.

If you don't see the full print dialog pane as shown above, click the "Show Details" button in the bottom-left corner. After you click the button, it changes to say "Hide Details" (shown above).

3 From the "Style" pop-up menu, choose what you wish to print—envelopes, lists, mailing labels, or pocket address book. Each style has different parameters to experiment with. Whatever you choose displays in the preview.

4 In the "Attributes" pane, check the information you want to include.

5 Click "Print."

Spend some time poking around this dialog box so you know what all your options are. As you can see below, you can add an image to your return address, choose different fonts and colors for the text, choose different envelope sizes, and so much more that it's just amazing.

To print a return address, check the "Print my address" box. Contacts automatically uses your "Me" card for the return address. If you want it to use another card, go back to the Contacts, select that other card, go to the Card menu, and choose "Make This My Card." You can switch it back when you're done printing. Of course, you can uncheck the box so it doesn't print any return address at all.

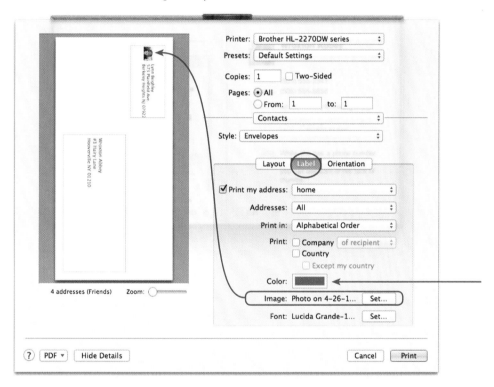

To add an image or logo to your return address, click the "Label" tab (above), then click the "Set…" button next to "Image." You can also change the font, text color, and more.

Back Up Your Entire Digital Database

There are few things more annoying than losing your entire Contacts that you have carefully created over the past year or two. You have a couple of options for backing up your entire Contacts.

- One way is to press on the "All Contacts" group name, then drag it to the Desktop. A vCard named "All Contacts" is created on the Desktop (shown below). You can then copy the vCard to another disk for safekeeping. You can also choose any Group or a selection of specific people and drag it to the Desktop to create a vCard that contains just those contacts.

All Contacts

  You can send this vCard to someone else on a Mac; she double-clicks it and the addresses automatically get entered in her Contacts.

- *Or* go to the File menu and choose "Export," then "Contacts Archive...." Your Mac will make a file for you and ask you where to store it.

  To restore your Contacts, double-click this file. Or, from the File menu, choose "Import," then select this Contacts archive.

Contacts -
05-11...abbu

  Remember, a backup is only useful if it's not in the same place as the original. That is, don't keep it on your hard disk—if your hard disk goes bad or your laptop gets stolen, both the original and the backup will be gone! Copy the file onto an external disk, upload it somewhere, or email it to a colleague for safekeeping. An even easier solution is to sync your addresses with iCloud, (which you learn about in Lesson 23).

View Multiple Contacts with Exposé

Double-click a contact name to open it in its own floating window. You can open as many contacts as you want and have them all visible on the screen at the same time.

To keep the cards separate and accessible, you can minimize them (click the yellow dot) behind the Contacts icon in the Dock: Go to System Preferences, choose "Dock" preferences, then check the box "Minimize windows into application icon."

To access the minimized cards, *press* (don't click) on the Contacts icon in the Dock until a menu appears that lists the minimized cards. Select a card from the list, or to bring forward all minimized cards, choose "Show All Windows."

Or use Dock Exposé, if you have a Magic Mouse: Position your pointer on top of the Contacts icon in the Dock, then double-tap with two fingers on a Magic Mouse. This shows the Exposé view of Contacts, shown below. Click one of the card thumbnails to bring that card forward, or Option-click one of the thumbnails to bring all minimized cards forward.

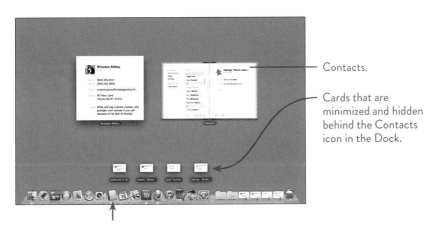

Contacts.

Cards that are minimized and hidden behind the Contacts icon in the Dock.

7

GOALS

Safari for Web Browsing

Safari is Apple's beautiful web browser for viewing web pages on the Internet. You've probably already used it, but you might be surprised at the tips and tricks it offers that you haven't taken advantage of yet.

Safari's got a few tools that make your browsing more pleasant. It can save your passwords for you and automatically fill in forms for you. It can also block obnoxious pop-up windows.

Safari offers you a tool called a Reading List. It's an easy way to save Internet content to read later whether you're online or not. Safari saves the stories you are interested in and displays a list of them.

Safari Web Browser

Below is a brief overview of the main features of the Safari window. Although it looks simple, it holds a lot of power in subtle ways.

Customize the **Toolbar:**
Control-click on it.

Reload
a web page.

Click to enter
full-screen mode.

Bookmarks Bar.
If you don't see
this bar, go to the
View menu and
choose "Show
Bookmarks Bar."
See close-up,
below.

Type a
search term
and single-
click the
magnifying
glass to send
your search
phrase
to Bing
or Yahoo!
instead of
Google.

Status Bar. If you don't see this bar, go to the
View menu and choose "Show Status Bar."

Drag any edge or the corner
to resize the window.

Add a bookmark for the current page.

Previous/Next page.

Show Reading List.

Show Bookmarks Cover Flow view.   Show **Top Sites.**

Bookmarks Bar.

Browse in Full-Screen Mode

To enter full-screen mode and fill your screen with the current web page, click the *full-screen* icon in the top-right corner of a Safari window.

To exit full-screen mode, move the pointer to the top edge of the screen. When the Mac's menu bar appears, click the blue double-arrow icon on the far right.

Quickly Access Your Top Sites

Safari keeps track of your top sites, based on how often and how recently you visited them. **To display your top sites as a wall of previews,** click the *Top Sites* icon in the Bookmarks Bar. The top sites change, depending on your browsing activity.

To open a top site in the browser window, click its preview.
To open a web page as a tab (see page 132 about tabs), Command-click the preview.
To search your browsing history, enter a keyword in the "Search History" field.
To edit your Top Sites display, click the Edit button.

Show Top Sites.

This symbol means the page has changed since you last viewed it.

Enter a keyword or phrase to search previously visited sites.

Click "Edit" to modify the Top Sites content (shown below).

Click a thumbnail to select it, then drag it to any position.

Preview size determines how many sites (up to 24) show in the display.

Click "Done" when you finish editing Top Sites.

Click the **X** to remove a site from the display.
Click the **pushpin** to prevent the site from being replaced by another site.

Bookmarks

The bookmarks in Safari are powerful and easy to use.

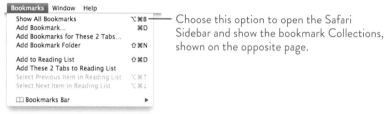

Choose this option to open the Safari Sidebar and show the bookmark Collections, shown on the opposite page.

The **Bookmarks Menu,** above, drops down from the menu bar at the top of the screen.

The **Bookmarks Bar** is the horizontal strip in the Safari window, just below the address field, shown on the opposite page. To show it (if it isn't already showing), go to the View menu and choose "Show Bookmarks Bar."

The **Bookmark Collections** are the various folders *you create* to organize lots of bookmarks. With Collections (folders), you don't have to put everything in the Bookmarks menu. Click the "Show all bookmarks" button (📖) at the far-left edge of the Bookmarks Bar when you want to open the Bookmark Collections and make **new folders for organizing.**

When you hit Command D to **create a bookmark** (*or* click the plus sign on the left side of the web address field), a little sheet drops down and asks where you want to store it. You can rename the bookmark at that point and choose to store it in any folder *you have already made* in the bookmark Collections.

Organize your bookmarks with folders (Collections)

1 From the Bookmarks menu, choose "Show All Bookmarks," *or* click the book icon on the far left of the Bookmarks Bar.

2 In the bottom-left of the window, click the **+** sign. This puts a new bookmark folder (named "Cool sites" in the example on the opposite page) in the Sidebar.

3 **To put this new folder in the Bookmarks Menu** or the **Bookmarks Bar** so you can access it easily, click "Bookmarks Menu" or "Bookmarks Bar" in the Collections list in the Sidebar. Now drag the new folder from the Sidebar and drop it into the bookmark pane on the *right.*

   A folder in the Bookmarks Bar displays a small triangle to its right, which is your *visual clue* that the item is a folder full of bookmarks.

Drag bookmarks or folders up and down in the list to rearrange them. You can also drag them directly from the Sidebar and drop them onto the Bookmarks Bar.

Bookmarks in Cover Flow View

First of all, if the Bookmarks Bar isn't visible, go to the View menu and choose "Show Bookmarks Bar." **To show a Cover Flow view of all your bookmarks** (the Bookmarks Library), click the *Show all bookmarks* icon on the left side of the Bookmarks Bar (the book icon, shown to the left and circled below).

To search a Bookmark Collection listed in the Sidebar *or* a specific folder of bookmarks you've created and organized: Select the item in the Sidebar, then enter a keyword or phrase in the search field located in the top-right corner.

Search field.

Safari
Bookmarks
Sidebar

To get rid of
the Cover
Flow view,
drag this tab
all the way to
the top.

Create and
name a new
folder (such
as "Cool sites,"
shown above).

Search results.
To open a found page,
click the large thumbnail
in the top pane, or
double-click the file
name in the bottom pane.

This lower pane ordinarily shows a list of items
in the *currently selected* Collection in the Sidebar.
Right now it shows the search results.

To create a new subfolder in a Collection, select the
Collection name and then click the *plus* button.

131

Auto-Click to Open Entire Collection in Tabs

Safari has a nifty feature called "Auto-Click" that lets you load all the web pages in a Collection into different tabs with the click of a button. Instead of going to each individual page one at a time and losing the previous page, you can open and peruse them all, each in its own tab. This only works when the folder (the collection) is stored in the Bookmarks Bar (as explained on page 130).

To view all pages in tabs automatically:

1 Click the tiny book icon in the far left of the Bookmarks Bar.

2 In the Sidebar, select the "Bookmarks Bar" collection.

A square indicates that all bookmarks in this collection will open in separate tabs (shown below).

3 In the main pane, folders that you've put in the Bookmarks Bar have an "Auto-Click" checkboxes (circled above). Put a check in one or more of the "Auto-Click" boxes. Instantly you'll notice that the tiny triangle in the Bookmarks Bar next to the folder name has changed to a tiny square. Click the tiny book icon to leave the Bookmarks pane and go back to a web page.

4 When you click a folder with the tiny square, every page in that folder opens, each in a different tab (shown below). Single-click a tab to go to that page. Drag a tab left or right to change its position in the Bookmarks Bar.

To close a tab, hover over it, then click the **X** that appears on the left.

To close all tabs, Option-click the **X.**

Click to close the tab.

Fill in Forms and Passwords Automatically

Safari can **fill in online forms** with the information you have entered into your Contacts; it takes the data from the card you have designated as "My Card" (use the Card menu in Contacts to do that; see Lesson 6). You can also tell Safari to remember your **user ID and password** for specific sites, which is great if no one else uses your Mac (or if you have set up different users; see Lesson 20).

To enable Safari to fill in forms and passwords, go to the Safari Preferences and click the "AutoFill" icon. Check the appropriate boxes.

Edit the information in your Contacts card.

Delete your password information from websites if it's no longer needed.

Next time you start to fill in a form, Safari will fill it in for you. Next time you go to a page that needs an **ID and password,** go ahead and fill them in, then Safari will ask if you want to save that information.

To delete saved user names, passwords, or forms, go back to the AutoFill preferences, above. Click the "Edit…" button next to the items you want to remove. In the sheet that opens, select one or more specific sites, then click "Remove." Or click "Remove All."

AutoFill is turned off when you turn on private browsing, explained on page 142.

Block Pop-Up Windows!

Go to the Safari menu and choose "Block Pop-Up Windows." Woo hoo! Only pop-up windows that you click on will appear—none of those obnoxious ads.

Occasionally, however, this can cause a problem. You might run across a web site where you click on a link for extra information and nothing happens. This might be because the extra information appears in a pop-up window. If so, go back to the Safari menu and choose "Block Pop-Up Windows" again to remove the checkmark.

Search with the Address (and Search) Bar

Previous versions of Safari contained a separate bar in the toolbar just for using to search. Now it's integrated in the Address bar. To search, type a term in what is now known as the Address and Search Bar. Safari will recognize that it isn't a URL and conduct a search.

By default, the search is done using Google. You can search with other search engines. Go to the Safari menu, choose "Preferences…," then click the "General" icon and choose from the "Default search engine" dropdown.

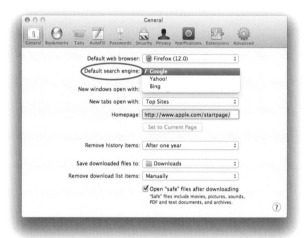

Quickly Enlarge or Reduce a Web Page

Safari can scale entire web pages, both text and graphics, to show the page elements larger or smaller. This technology is called "resolution independent scaling."

To make a web page larger or smaller, use the keyboard shortcut Command + (plus sign, larger) or Command − (minus sign, smaller). You don't have to select anything before you use the shortcut.

You can also add a "scaling" shortcut button to your Toolbar: From the View menu, choose "Customize Toolbar…." From the sheet that opens, drag the "Zoom" buttons to Safari's Toolbar. **To enlarge a web page,** single-click the larger "A"; **to reduce a web page,** single-click the small "A."

Tabbed Browsing

When you click a link, Safari takes you to another page and thus you lose track of the one you were on. You can choose to open web pages in **tabs**. Instead of losing your original page, a tabbed page gets loaded and displays as a tab, as shown below.

To use tabbed browsing, first go to the Safari menu, choose "Preferences…," then click the "Tabs" icon. Spend a few minutes to sort out the options. For instance, if you check the second box, shown below, the tabbed window will immediately come to the front instead of lining up behind the current page.

Also see page 132 about "Auto-Click": display all bookmarks in a folder as individual tabs, all at once.

To open any link into a tabbed page, Command-click the link (hold down the Command key and click the link). You can also right-click and choose from a number of options.

Command-click on a number of links and they will all load themselves into individual tabs. Then when you're ready, click any tab to display that page, while leaving your original results page still available (as a tab).

Hover your pointer over a tab to show this **X** symbol. Click the **X** to close the tab.

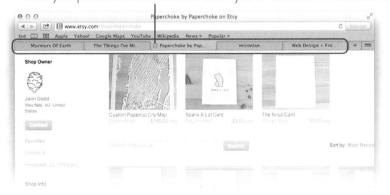

Click a tab to display that page.

Option-click the **X** to close all open tabs except the one you clicked.

Drag a tab left or right to change its position.

135

Show All Tabs

You're not limited to clicking on each tab to see each page. You can use the **Show All Tabs** button and get a scrollable view of all your tabs.

To activate the Show All Tabs view, open at least two tabs and click the button on the right (shown below).

Your tabbed pages are all open and you can navigate by clicking the small dots beneath them to view them.

- **To navigate forward or back through tabbed pages with a Magic Mouse,** swipe left or right with *one finger.*
- **To navigate with a trackpad,** swipe left or right with *two fingers.*

Click a page to display that page and return to tab view.

Click the **X** to close a tab.

Click the dots to navigate through the pages.

Find a Word or Phrase on the Current Page

To find a word or phrase on the *page* you are looking at (as opposed to searching the Internet for it), press **Command F**. Then just type—Safari knows to put the search term in the search field that appears in the top-right corner.

To make it easy for you to see the found word or phrase, Safari dims the rest of the page and highlights every instance of what you're looking for, as you can see below. Just click on the page to return it to normal.

To make Safari highlight the next found instance with yellow, press **Command G**. Each time you press Command G, Safari highlights the next found instance of the search term you typed.

Safari holds onto that search. You can go to another page and hit **Command G** again—Safari will search for the last word or phrase you requested. In fact, you can close or even quit Safari and the next time you open it, Command G will find results of the last word or phrase you were looking for.

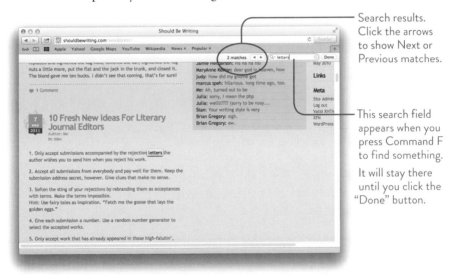

Search results. Click the arrows to show Next or Previous matches.

This search field appears when you press Command F to find something.

It will stay there until you click the "Done" button.

Message or Email a Web Page or a Link

Safari with the new Mountain Lion Share button makes it especially easy to **email an entire web page** to anyone, complete with images and links.

1   Click the Share button on the toolbar.

2   From the options, choose "Email this Page."

3   The Mail application opens with the name of the web page as the subject. The entire web page is in the body of the email. All you have to do is add the recipient's address and click the "Send" button.

Or **message just the link.** Follow the steps above, but choose "Message."

To make emailing just the *link* to a web page easy and fast, customize the Safari toolbar with a "Mail" button: Control-click on the Safari toolbar, then choose "Customize Toolbar…." From the sheet that appears, drag the "Mail" button to the Safari toolbar. Click "Done." The next time you want to mail a link, click the *Mail* button.

View PDF Documents

To view a PDF document right in Safari, just drag the PDF file and drop it into *the middle* of any Safari page.

To enlarge or reduce the size of the PDF on the screen, Control-click (or right-click) anywhere on the PDF page. From the menu that appears, choose one of the sizing options (Automatically Resize, Zoom In, Zoom Out, or Actual Size). *Or* hover your pointer over the bottom edge of the document to show controls for Zoom, Open in Preview, and Save to Downloads Folder.

If the PDF has **more than one page,** but all you see in Safari is one page, Control-click (or right-click) and choose "Next Page" or "Previous Page." You can also choose either "Single Page Continuous" or " Two Pages Continuous," then use the scroll bar to scroll through the document pages.

Save a Page and Everything on It

Safari lets you save a web page with all the images and links and text on the page. It creates one file, an archive, that you can open at any time; all the links will work (as long as the destination pages haven't changed). This is particularly handy for pages that you know aren't going to last long, such as online newspaper articles or purchase receipts. Keep in mind that some web pages can prevent you from saving items on the page.

1   Open the web page you want to save.

2   From the File menu, choose "Save As…." Or Control-click on a web page (not on an image or link), then choose "Save Page As…."

3   From the Format menu in the dialog box, choose "Web Archive," as shown.

4   Choose the folder you want to save into, then click "Save."

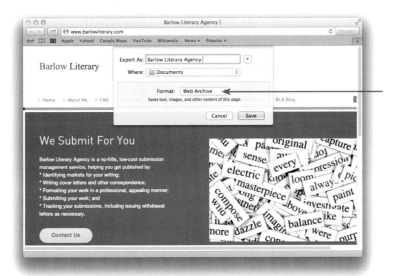

To save an image from a web page, Control-click (or right-click) the image. From the menu that pops up, choose one of the image saving options.

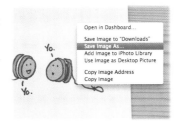

Make a Web Clip Widget

There's a button in the Safari toolbar that lets you make a Dashboard *widget* of any section of any web page. Any buttons, fields, or links that are captured in that widget will work in Dashboard. See Lesson 17 for more about Dashboard.

To make a web clip widget:

1 Put the "Open in Dashboard" web clip widget button in the toolbar: Control-click the toolbar, choose "Customize Toolbar...," then from the sheet that appears, drag the "Open in Dashboard" button (shown to the left) and drop it onto the toolbar. Click "Done."

2 Go to any web page in Safari. Click the new widget button.

3 The page turns gray, except for a clear box that follows your pointer around. Click in the area that you want to capture as a widget. Immediately eight handles appear on the clear box. You can drag any of these handles to reshape the box. Press and drag *inside* the box to move it.

4 When you like where it's positioned, click the "Add" button in the upper right.

5 Immediately Dashboard opens and displays the new widget.

  Click the tiny *i* that appears in a bottom corner to flip it over and add a fancy border, if you like.

The selected area above becomes the Dashboard widget shown to the left.

Print Web Pages

There are several specialized options when you print from Safari. You can see a preview of how the page will print, you can tell the background not to print, and you can make the web address and date appear on the page as headers and footers.

To print a web page:

1   Go to the web page you want to print, then press Command P to open the Print dialog, shown below (or go to the File menu and choose "Print…").

2   If you don't see the expanded box shown below, click the button at the bottom that says "Show Details."

3   Make sure the "Safari" option is chosen in the pop-up menu in the middle of the pane (shown circled, below). The preview appears on the left.

4   Check or uncheck the boxes to print the background and the headers and footers (the web address, page numbers, date and time), circled below.

5   If the web page needs more than one piece of paper to print, the preview will show you every page; use the arrows under the preview pane to display the previews of each page.

6   Click "Print."

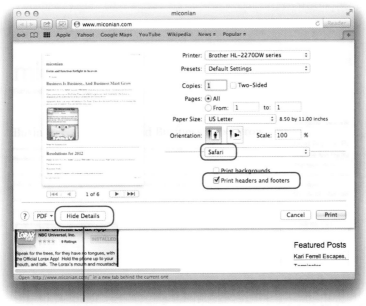

Click here to show fewer options in this print dialog. Click again (when it says "Show Details") to expand to the version shown above.

Private Browsing

You may have noticed that Safari keeps track of where you've been and what you've entered into search fields and which web pages you've asked to see. Safari's AutoFill feature even keeps track of user names and contact information you've entered on sites, as well as passwords and credit card numbers. If there are other people who use your computer, or if you are using Safari on someone else's Mac or at a school or an Internet cafe, you probably don't want Safari keeping track of all that information. That's where **private browsing** comes in handy.

When you turn on private browsing:

- None of the information you enter on any page is saved.
- Any searches you do will not be added to the pop-up menu in the Google search field.
- Web pages you visit are not added to the History menu. However, you can still go back and forward to pages you've viewed during the current session.
- If you downloaded anything, those items are automatically removed from the Download window when you quit Safari or turn off private browsing.
- Cookies are automatically deleted when you turn off private browsing or quit Safari.

To turn ON private browsing, go to the Safari menu and choose "Private Browsing." A checkmark appears next to the menu item to indicate it's turned on.

To turn OFF private browsing, go to the Safari menu and choose "Private Browsing" again to remove the checkmark.

When you **quit Safari,** private browsing is automatically **turned off,** even if you left it on before you quit. So each time you open Safari, you need to turn private browsing on again if you want to use it.

To further secure your privacy, when you are finished, go to the Safari menu and choose "Reset Safari…." You can eliminate any trace of your whereabouts from the options you see listed here. This, however, will remove *everything* from that feature in Safari, not just the ones you used today!

Parental Controls

If you have a young child (or anyone acting like a young child), you can set up some serious parental controls to limit access to web sites. It involves multiple users, which are explained in detail in Lesson 20. You'll need an admin user (you) to set up another user for the child. The child will be able to view only web sites you have placed in the Bookmarks Bar. He won't be able to enter web addresses in the Address field, modify any bookmarks, or use the Google search field in the toolbar.

To limit a young user's web access:

1 Open the "Users & Groups" system preferences to set up another user (details in Lesson 20). Click the box to "Enable parental controls."

2 Click the button "Open Parental Controls...."

3 Click the tab labeled "Web."

4 Click the button "Allow access to only these websites."

5 To remove a site in the provided list, select it and click the – button.
   To add a web site, click the + button, choose "Add Bookmark...," and type a web address of your choice.

6 Log in to that user's account, open Safari, and make sure it's what you expect. Safari puts the web sites chosen in Step 5 into the Bookmarks Bar, as shown below, and the user will not be allowed to go anywhere else.

This icon (a padlock on top of the Bookmarks icon) shows that Parental Controls are enabled.

The Bookmarks Bar contains the sites you chose in Steps 3–5.

> **Note:** This does not prevent the user from surfing the web with any other browser. If you want to limit the *applications* this user can use, do so in the "Apps" section of Parental Controls.

View the Reader Version of a Page

Safari can improve the readability of some web pages by showing only the essential text and graphics. When you see the inactive "Reader" button on the right side of the address field (circled below) turn blue and become active, click it to display the current page as text and graphics only, and hide all of the non-related clutter that's on the page. You'll see this on sites with news stories or articles when you click through to a single story. Reading a site using the Reader version is closer to reading a newspaper than a web page and I highly recommend clicking it whenever it's an active option!

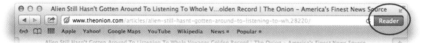

Move the cursor over the bottom edge of the page to reveal controls to enlarge, reduce, mail, or print the web page. To exit the Reader, click the **x** in the pop-up controls (below, right), or click the Reader icon in the address field again.

The original page.

The same page displayed in Reader mode.

Make a Reading List

Sometimes there's not enough time to read all the blogs and stories and articles in one sitting. Safari lets you save content to read later. You don't even have to be online when you go back to read them.

Click to hide or show the Reading List sidebar.

Click to add the current web page to the reading list.

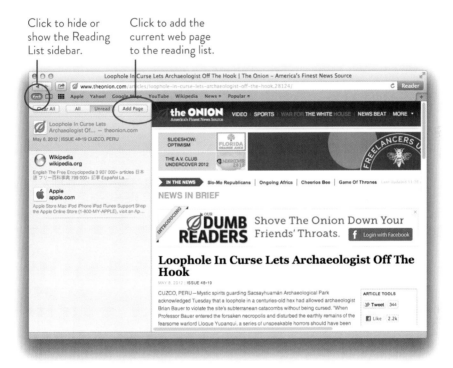

 To create a Reading List of web pages to read later, click the Reading List icon (shown on the left) that appears on the left side of the Safari Bookmarks Bar. You must be connected to the Internet to create a Reading List and to retrieve and read the items in the list.

To add the current web page to your Reading List, click the "Add Page" button (circled above) in the Reading List sidebar that opens.

To see a list of all bookmarked pages, both read and unread, click the "All" button.

To narrow the list to only unread bookmarked pages, click the "Unread" button.

To clear an individual item from the list, move the pointer over the item, then click the circle-**X** that appears in the corner of the item (circled below).

To clear all items from the list, click the "Clear All" button.

Click Clear All to empty the entire list of items.

Click to delete a single item from the reading list.

Use Multi-Touch Gestures in Safari

If you have a Multi-Touch input device that recognizes *gestures,* you can scroll or swipe through web pages with just your fingers. The Apple Magic Mouse, Magic Trackpad, and the built-in trackpad on newer Apple laptops offer this feature.

Magic Mouse:

- **To scroll up or down,** brush up or down on the Multi-Touch surface with *one finger.* A *short* brush left or right will also scroll left or right on one web page.
- **To navigate forward or back through web pages,** swipe left or right with *one finger.*
- **To enlarge the web page,** double-tap with *one finger* on the Multi-Touch surface. To return to the original size, double-tap again.

Trackpad: The movements are the same as above, but use *two fingers.*

Safari Security

Safari provides several security settings. By default, they are turned on, but you should check to make sure now and then.

1 From the Safari menu, choose "Preferences…."

2 Click the "Security" tab in the toolbar.

3 Make sure the box is checked to "Warn when visiting a fraudulent website."

   If you're going to a web site that you *know* is not fraudulent (because it's yours), contact the server of that site to let them know it's indicating a problem.

Also see page 142 to learn about **private browsing** in Safari.

Cool Safari Tips

If you have at least one tab open, you'll see the **New Tab** button (the plus symbol on the right side of the Tabs Bar). Click this to create a new tab that opens the Top Sites display. You can change that: Open Safari Preferences, click "General" in the Preferences Toolbar, then set the "New tabs open with" menu to Home Page, Empty Page, Same Page, or Bookmarks.

Use the keyboard **Arrow keys** to scroll up, down, left, and right in a web page.

From the History menu, you can **Reopen All Windows From Last Session.**

Consolidate multiple open browser windows into one with multiple tabs: From the Window menu, choose "Merge All Windows."

To create a Bookmark folder from a group of tabbed windows, from the Bookmarks menu, choose "Add Bookmark For These Tabs…." In the dialog that opens, choose a Bookmark location for the folder. Safari automatically enables Auto-Click, so a single click on the folder reopens all of the tabs in the group.

Share your tabbed windows with your other devices using iCloud, by checking the Safari option in your iCloud system preferences. Learn more in Lesson 23.

8

GOALS

Create calendars and
groups of calendars

Add Events and
get Notifications

Send email invitations to
Events

Publish your calendar
and subscribe to others

Print data in useful ways

Create Reminders

Save your Events and
Reminders to iCloud

Calendar and Reminders for Organizing Your Life

As you might guess, Calendar is a calendar program. It keeps track of Events and sends notifications to you, among other things. Calendar is a great tool for keeping track of family activities or for coordinating corporate Events. You can create separate calendars for separate parts of your life.

When you need something quick and easy and less robust, use Reminders. This feature keeps a checklist of tasks you need to accomplish, stored on a calendar in the app. As with Calendar, Reminders can send you notifications and emails.

Better still, iCloud, Apple's automatic and free storage and syncing solution, keeps your Calendar and Reminders synced to all of your computers and mobile devices.

The Calendar Window

The Calendar window is in a familiar paper calendar format, but because it's digital you can switch to different views with the click of a button. View a month at a time, a week, or a day; go back in time or forward into the future. Set recurring Events to happen every first Friday or every three months. Create Reminders that are attached to certain calendars. Turn calendars on or off so you can view just individual ones, or view several at a time to see how your events overlap.

Create a **Quick Event.**   Choose a **view mode.**   Change **date** shown.

To show the
**list of your
calendars,**
click this
button.

Your
Calendar List.

To turn the page with a Magic Mouse, swipe left or right on the surface with *one finger*.
On a Multi-Touch trackpad, swipe with *two fingers*.

Drag any edge to
resize the calendar.

Set Up Google, Yahoo!, or Exchange Calendars

You can set up those calendars in Calendar.

1 Open Calendar's Preferences and click "Accounts."

2 Click the Add (**+**) button in the lower-left corner to create a new account.

3 Enter your Google or Yahoo! email address and password, then click "Create." Calendar finds any calendar accounts associated with the email address you entered.

Create Calendars

You can have many different calendars—one for each of your kids, one for work, one for your partner, one for home life, one for the charities you volunteer for, etc. Choose to see all the calendars and events at once and you'll have a visual display of just how crazy your life is.

To create a new calendar, go to the File menu, choose "New Calendar," then choose "On My Mac." Give the calendar a relevant name, then click anywhere.

Click here to show the Calendars list. ———

To hide a calendar's Events and ———
Reminders, uncheck its box.

To change the color of a calendar or to give it a description, Control-click (or right-click) the calendar name, then choose "Get Info." A sheet slides down so you can change the calendar color, type a description, or publish the calendar.

To delete a calendar, Control-click (or right-click) the calendar name in the list, and choose "Delete."

Create a Group of Calendars

Create calendar **Groups** to organize related calendars. You might want to group together the calendars that all have to do with your children. Or perhaps a particular project has several different calendars associated with it.

To make a Group, go to the File menu and choose "New Calendar Group."

Name the new Group, then drag other calendars into it. If a Group name is *selected* when you create a new calendar, the calendar is automatically added to that group.

Click the disclosure triangle to hide
or reveal a Group's contents.

Create Events

An Event is what you'd expect it to be—something that happens on a particular day. You can **create Events** in a variety of ways.

First select the calendar (from the Calendars list) in which you want the Event to appear. Then:

- In the "Month" view, double-click a day to create a new Event. Type the name of your Event, press Return, and double-click the entry. A *New Event* Info pane opens so you can add more information; click "Done" to put it away, or click anywhere outside the Info panel. Calendar arranges multiple Events on one day according to the times you enter.

- In the "Week" or "Day" view, double-click or press-and-drag on the time grid for your Event. Double-click the Event to open the Info panel and add information; click "Done" or click anywhere outside the Info panel to put it away.

- To stretch the Event out across multiple days, be sure to click the "all-day" checkbox in the Info panel, then enter the Event's dates in the "from" and "to" fields.

- To create a recurring Event, use the "repeat" feature in the Info panel. Calendar automatically repeats the Event at a time interval you specify. For instance, my writing group meets on the third Saturday of each month.

Info panel.

To view Event details, as shown above-right, double-click the Event.

To open the Info panel for a selected Event, ready to edit, press Command E.

Event invitations

From Calendar you can send someone an invitation to a Calendar Event. The invitee can send a response back to you that shows up in that Event's Info panel.

To send a Calendar Event invitation:

1 Create a new Event, or double-click an existing Event in Calendar.

2 In the Info panel that opens (click "Edit" if it's an existing Event), click "Add Invitees...," then type contact names that are in your Contacts.

3 Edit other Event information if necessary, and add any comments you want in the "note" area.

4 Click the "Send" button. *Or* Control-click (or right-click) an Event in Calendar, then choose "Mail Event."
   An email form appears; address the message and send it.

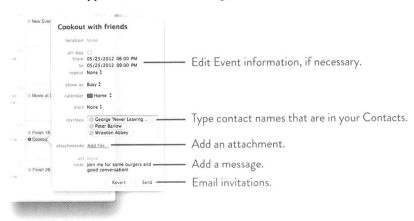

— Edit Event information, if necessary.

— Type contact names that are in your Contacts.

— Add an attachment.

— Add a message.

— Email invitations.

To respond to an email notification:

1 When you receive an email that contains a Calendar Event attachment, click the attachment icon (below) in the message to automatically put the Event in Calendar.

2 Go to Calendar and double-click the Event that was added automatically. In the Event Info panel that opens, respond with an option: *Accept, Maybe,* or *Decline.*

The organizer of the Event receives an email with a Calendar attachment. When he clicks the attachment, the response is added to the Event in *his* Calendar. He can double-click the Event in Calendar to open the Event Info panel and see the responses of invitees.

Sync Calendar with iCloud

You learn more about iCloud in Lesson 23. Here's the quick scoop on getting your Calendar synced with iCloud so it works with your other Apple devices. Be aware that as soon as you sync with iCloud, all the calendars currently existing on your Mac will be automatically moved to the iCloud. If you change your mind and want to keep everything locally again, you may lose your Calendar data.

1 Open Calendar's Preferences and click "Accounts."

2 Click the Add (**+**) button in the lower-left corner to create a new account.

3 For "Account Type," choose iCloud. Enter your Apple ID and Password.

4 Click "Create" to finish.

Your Calendar data will now sync with Calendar apps on every other iCloud enabled device you use.

Choose how frequently you want your Calendar to send updates to the iCloud.

Get Calendar Event Notifications

As with iCloud, there's an entire lesson on Notifications (see Lesson 18). You can, and do by default, get Notifications from your Calendar Events as soon as the time and date of the event arrives. You can control whether or not you receive Calendar notifications and how many you receive.

1 In Calendar, go to the Apple menu and choose "System Preferences."

2 Click the "Notifications" icon (under the "Personal" section).

3 Click on "Calendar" on the left under "In Notifications Center".

4 Make sure "Show in Notification Center" is checked, and choose the number of Calendar items you want to appear in your Notifications at any given time.

Automatic Birthdays Calendar

Calendar can work with your Contacts to create a Birthdays calendar that automatically updates itself.

1 First you must add the Birthday field to your Contacts, as explained in Lesson 6.

2 Then, in Calendar, go to the Calendar menu and choose "Preferences…."

3 Click the "General" icon.

4 Check the box "Show Birthdays calendar."

The calendar will appear in the "Subscriptions" group of the Calendars list (below, right). If you don't see a Subscriptions group in your calendar list yet, don't worry—Calendar will put it there for you when you subscribe.

Close the Preferences pane.

Now you can double-click any birthdate event in the calendar to open its Info pane. There you can click the link to go straight to that person's contact information in Contacts, from which you can send a birthday email.

You can't make any changes to the Birthdays calendar in Calendar; in fact, you can't even add alarms to notify you of upcoming birthdays. You could, of course, manually create a birthday Event and add an alarm to it. Or you can create a Smart Group in Contacts that notifies you a designated number of days before the birthdate of any of your contacts; see Lesson 6.

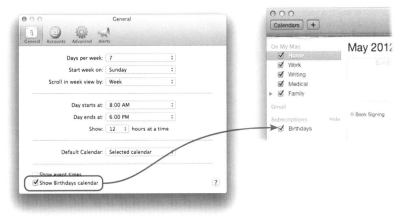

Publish Your Calendar

You can **publish** your calendar to Apple's iCloud (free storage and syncing on Apple servers) if you choose, and anyone in the world on any computer can view it. It's really remarkable.

To publish, select a calendar in the Calendars list (click the "Calendars" button to see it). Control-click (or right-click) the calendar name in the list, and choose "Publish." A sheet drops down (shown below). Make your choices, then click "Publish."

A new message appears telling you the web address where the calendar can be viewed or subscribed. Click the "Send Mail" button to get an email form ready to send to anyone you like.

To notify others later about your published calendar, select the calendar as described above, go to the Calendar menu, and choose "Send Publish Email…."

To unpublish follow the steps above to choose a calendar, then from the Calendar menu choose to unpublish or stop sharing.

Subscribe to Calendars

To subscribe to a private calendar, go to the Calendar menu in Calendar and choose "New Calendar Subscription…." Enter the web address you have been given. If you received an email invitation to subscribe to a published calendar, click the link in the email invitation.

Use Calendar in Full-Screen Mode

 To make Calendar fill your entire screen so it's easy to see and work with, click the *Full-Screen* button (the double-arrows icon) in the top-right corner of the Calendar window.

To access the menu bar across the top of the screen while in full screen mode, just push the pointer up to the top edge of the screen, and the menu bar appears while you need it.

 To exit full-screen mode, push the pointer to the top edge of the screen. When the Mac menu bar appears, click the blue double-arrow icon in the top-right corner.

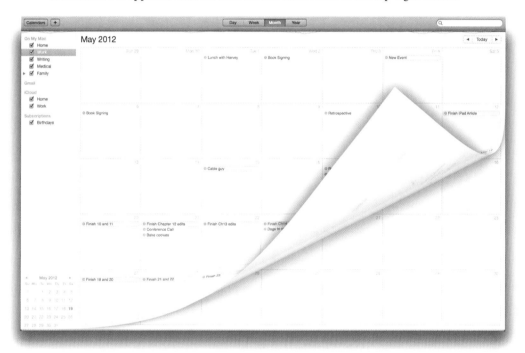

To swipe through the pages in any view, use a one-finger horizontal swipe on a Magic Mouse or a two-finger horizontal swipe on a Multi-Touch trackpad. Only the Month view gives you the page flip effect shown above.

Back Up the Entire Calendar of Information

If you don't use iCloud, you may want to back up your information. To make sure you don't lose the valuable information you have entered into your calendars, go to the File menu, choose "Export," then choose "Calendar Archive…." You will be asked where to save the file. If you have a lot of information you don't want to lose, you should save that file onto a separate backup disk, along with your other important files.

Preview Files Attached to Events

Use Quick Look to preview Event attachments: Double-click an Event to open its Info pane, single-click the attachment name, then tap the Spacebar. Almost any kind of file will preview. Tap the Spacebar again to put it away.

Print in a Variety of Ways

Check out the great features in the Print dialog box. Each "View" (Month, Day, Week, or List) you choose changes the options, so spend a few minutes exploring the possibilities for each view. You can choose to print the data from as many or as few calendars as you like. All calendars are color-coded, so you can see how Events in different calendars overlap.

To print from Calendar:

1   From the File menu, choose "Print."

2   In the "Print" dialog that opens (below) choose a time range, calendars to print, and other options provided as checkboxes.

3   After you customize your settings, click "Continue" to open the usual Print dialog where you select a printer and start the print process.

Change the view here; the preview will immediately change. | Whatever the preview displays is what will print.

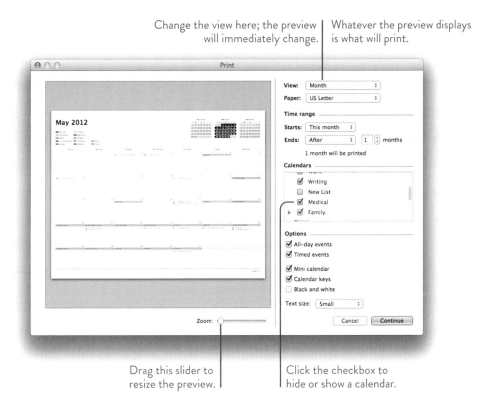

Drag this slider to resize the preview. | Click the checkbox to hide or show a calendar.

Reminders

When you need to make a quick list of tasks to get done, Calendar might be overkill. The Reminders app lets you quickly create lists of things to get done, or Reminders. Like Calendar, you can configure it to send you Notifications and sync with iCloud.

You'll find Reminders under the Launchpad in the Dock or in the Applications folder in the Finder.

The Reminders window

The Reminders window is fairly simple. Reminders are organized in lists. Clicking a list brings up its Reminders. You can create Reminders that are due by a certain date. Hide the list and calendar view with the buttons under the calendar.

Search through all your lists and reminders.

Add new reminder to list (or just start typing under the last item in the list).

As you check off items on your list, they show up in this list.

Your **Reminders Lists**.

Days on the calendar with reminders are indicated with dots.

Click to hide or show the lists or calendar.

To move between lists with a Magic Mouse, swipe left or right on the surface with *one finger*. On a Multi-Touch trackpad, swipe with *two fingers*.

Drag any edge to resize the calendar.

Create Lists and Reminders

To create a list, go to the File menu and choose "New List." Or you can click the button with the Plus sign below the calendar. Type the name of your list. If you mess up, Control-click (or right-click) and choose "Rename." Once you have a list, you can add **Reminders** to it.

To create a Reminder:

1   If the Lists pane isn't showing on the left side of Reminders, go to the View menu and choose "Show Sidebar."

2   Click on the list where you want the Reminder.

3   In the Reminders panel on the right, click in a blank space. *Or* Control-click (or right-click) and choose "New Reminder" from the contextual menu. *Or* go to the File menu and choose "New Reminder."

Double-click or click on the *i* next to the Reminder to open its Info panel (above). **Prioritize** your item, add a note, give it a due date, make it notify you when you reach a destination (with location services enabled), and more.

4   When the item has been **completed,** check the "completed" checkbox.

When you check off a Reminder, it disappears from the current list and shows up in the Completed list. You can restore it by clicking on the Completed list and unchecking it. To move a Reminder from one list to another, Control-click (or right-click) and choose "Move to List" from the contextual menu and choose the List.

Location-based Reminders

Get Reminders based on where you are by checking the **At a Location** box when you create it. To enable Location Services, open System Preferences, choose **Security & Privacy,** and click on the Privacy button. (You may have to click the lock and log in to make changes.) Check E**nable Location Services** and **Reminders.app.**

9

GOALS

Messages and FaceTime for Text, Audio, and Video Messaging

With Messages you can communicate with others around the world with text messages, audio chatting, or video conferencing—free. You can text chat with one person or with a group of people, exchange files, send text messages to someone's phone, display images from iPhoto, save printable copies of your chats, and record audio or video chats. With a fast Mac and Messages, you can have audio chats with up to ten people at a time and video conferences with up to three other people. You can even have one-way video chats with someone who doesn't have a video camera attached or built-in (or vice versa).

FaceTime expands your quick and easy video communication to new iPads, iPhones, and some iPods.

Set Up Messages

When you first open Messages, it asks you to fill in certain information to get started. You need a chat account of some sort. The rest is self-explanatory.

> **Apple ID:** In the setup process, you can click the button labeled "Create Apple ID...." This opens a form. Fill it out and verify the email address you provided and get your Apple ID.

> **AIM account:** Go to www.aim.com and sign up for a free AIM account; you can use that as your buddy name. When you set up Messages and give others your AIM buddy name, do **not** include @aim.com.

> You can also chat with a **Google** account (accounts.Google.com), **Jabber** (register.jabber.org), or **Yahoo! Messenger** (login.yahoo.com).

A sample Messages Buddies panel and chat

So you'll know what to expect after you've gone through the process, below you see a typical Messages Buddies panel and text chat.

Double-click a buddy name in the panel to open a text chat.

This is a text chat with one other person.

Make the account active

Once you set up your account, make sure it is active:

1 Go to the Messages menu and choose "Preferences…."

2 Click the "Accounts" icon.

3 Select the account in the left pane, then click "Enable this account."

When you've got your accounts set up, it's a good idea to click the Messages button to control what your chats will look like and how they will behave. These settings apply to all of the accounts you add to Messages.

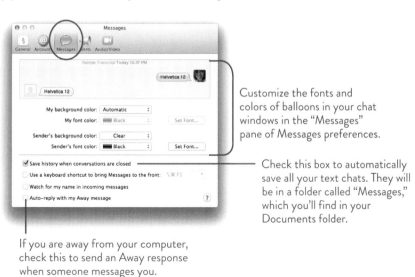

Customize the fonts and colors of balloons in your chat windows in the "Messages" pane of Messages preferences.

Check this box to automatically save all your text chats. They will be in a folder called "Messages," which you'll find in your Documents folder.

If you are away from your computer, check this to send an Away response when someone messages you.

Create a Buddies List

Set up a **Buddies** list of names to choose from when you want to chat.

1 If you don't see the Buddies window when you open Messages, go to the Window menu and choose "Buddies."

   If the title bar of the Buddies window says you are "Offline," click on the word "Offline" and from the pop-up menu choose "Available."

2 To add a new buddy, single-click the **+** sign at the bottom of the list window and choose "Add Buddy…."

   (Note that from this + menu, you can also choose "Add Group…" This helps you organize your names into categories, such as Family, Coworkers, Film Club, or whatever. A buddy can be in any number of different groups.)

3 In the dialog box that appears, enter the person's screen or buddy name in the "Account Name" field. Choose a Messages group to put the buddy in.

   Or click the disclosure button to display your Contacts (shown below), then choose a buddy from your list of contacts.

4 Click the "Add" button.

   The account gets automatically entered in Contacts (if the buddy is not already in your Contacts), and the name is placed in the Buddies window.

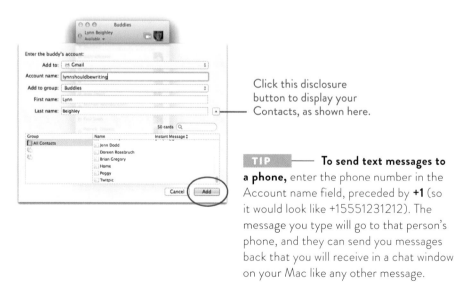

Click this disclosure button to display your Contacts, as shown here.

TIP — **To send text messages to a phone,** enter the phone number in the Account name field, preceded by **+1** (so it would look like +15551231212). The message you type will go to that person's phone, and they can send you messages back that you will receive in a chat window on your Mac like any other message.

Chat with One Other Person

To have a one-to-one **text chat** with someone in the office or on the other side of the world (or anywhere in-between):

1   If you don't see the Messages Buddies panel when you open Messages, go to the Window menu and choose "Messages Buddies."

2   Double-click the name of the buddy you want to chat with.

     Be sure to double-click the buddy *name,* any *blank space,* or the *buddy icon* in the buddy field, *not a camera or phone icon that might be visible.*

  Or single-click a buddy name, then single-click the "A" icon at the bottom of the Messages Buddies panel to open a text chat window.

3   A text chat window opens. In the text field at the bottom of the window, type a message, then hit Return.

4   To end the chat, click the red close button in the upper-left of the window.

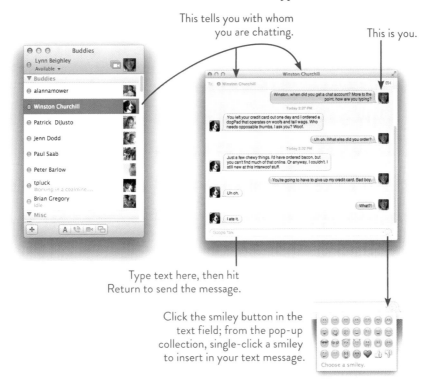

This tells you with whom you are chatting.

This is you.

Type text here, then hit Return to send the message.

Click the smiley button in the text field; from the pop-up collection, single-click a smiley to insert in your text message.

Put Multiple Individual Chats in One Window

When you want to keep multiple but separate chats going at the same time, it's easier to manage if you put the separate chats in one chat window, then switch between them. (This might be the default on your Mac, in which case this page explains what is going on!)

1 Start individual chats with two or more buddies. If they all open in the same window, then read Step 2 but don't bother going to the Window menu.

2 Go to the Window menu and choose "Messages." A pale blue Sidebar, which Messages calls a Tab Bar, opens with each buddy's name on a separate "tab."

3 To add other buddies to the Tab Bar, drag them from the Messages Buddies panel (or from any other Tab Bar you might have) and drop them on the Tab Bar. This person does *not* join the existing chat!

4 To move from chat to chat, click a buddy name in the sidebar.

5 To move a chat from the multichat window to an individual window, double-click a buddy or drag the buddy's name out of the Tab Bar and drop it on the Desktop.

6 To remove a buddy from the Tab Bar, click the **X** that appears when you hover the pointer over a buddy name. (If you're in a conversation with that person, this immediately disconnects her.)

This is the name of the person you are currently chatting with.

The Tab Bar.

Click a buddy name in the Tab Bar to switch to that particular chat.

These are still individual chats, but they are all available in one window.

None of the other buddies can see your chat with anyone else. But be careful— it's too easy to send a message to the wrong person!

Chat with a Group of People All Together

You can text chat with at least 23 different people around the world in one Chat Room.

1 From the File menu, choose "Go to Chat Room...."

2 In the window that appears, type a name that will become the name of this chat room. Make it something distinctive because if anyone else around the world types the same word, they'll end up in your chat room.

3 A Participants drawer pops out to the side of the chat room window. Click the **+** sign and invite someone.

4 Click the **+** sign again and again to invite as many people as you like.

Here I started a Chat Room named "letstalkaboutbooks" and clicked the plus sign to invite people.

Or tell people ahead of time to all meet in a chat room called, say, "jtroadrunner," at a certain time (use all lowercase). At the prescribed time, tell everyone to do this:

1 Open Messages and go to the File menu; choose "Go to Chat Room...."

2 Enter the chat room name (in this case, *letstalkaboutbooks*) and click "Go." Everyone around the world who does so will end up in the room together.

3 **To remove yourself** from the chat room, click the red close button in the upper-left corner of the window. When the last person leaves, the chat room will automatically close.

Audio Chat with One or More

Talk, **literally talk,** with other people. Make sure you have a microphone built in or connected to your Mac. Your buddies will display little telephone icons next to their pictures if they are able to audio chat with you (if he has a video camera, you can also do an audio chat).

To audio chat with someone, she has to be in your Messages Buddies list (see page 166). In the list, as shown below, you can have a one-on-one audio chat with anyone who displays a telephone icon next to her name.

If a buddy shows *multiple* telephone icons, like "alannamower" below, that means you can invite him to an audio chat that involves more than one person.

To audio chat, click directly on that person's phone icon. *Or* single-click his name, then click the phone icon at the bottom of the Messages Buddies panel.

If your Buddy doesn't have a microphone to chat back with you, select his name, then go to the Buddies menu at the top of your screen and choose "Invite to One-Way Audio Chat." Your friend will hear you but will have to send typed instant messages back.

The multiple-phone icon means this buddy can audio chat with multiple buddies at the same time.

TIP ——— If your buddy has no photo, Messages picks up his photo from Contacts; you can change the photo there; see Lesson 6.

TIP ——— If you want to replace your buddy's photo, select any buddy name and press Command I to get the Info window. Or Control-click a buddy name and choose "Show Contact Card" tab, then drag an image into the "Picture" image well. To resize and reposition it, see Lesson 6.

Open an audio chat and invite others to join you

To *initiate* an audio conference with more than one other person, you need a more powerful machine than you do to *join* an audio chat. Any machine purchased within the last few years is certainly powerful enough to initiate an audio chat.

1 Single-click directly on the multiple-phone icon next to a buddy's name.

2 That person hears a little phone ringing and sees a message on his computer; he clicks the message to see who it is, then clicks "Accept." This begins the chat. Your active audio chat window looks like this:

3 Now click the **+** button to get a pop-up menu (shown below) that lists the other people in your Messages Buddies panel who are online and capable of joining an audio conference. Single-click a person to add him or her. Add others in the same way.

Click the microphone icon to **mute** the session—the green bar turns orange and the microphone turns blue, *visual clues* that the sound is muted.

4 **To delete someone** from the audio conference, hover your pointer over his icon. When an **X** appears, click it and that person is gone.

5 **To end an audio session,** click the red close button in the upper-left corner of the Audio Chat window.

Video Chat with Up to Three Other People

See other people on your screen while you *talk* (not *type*) with them. To video chat, of course you must have a video camera attached to your Mac. All of the newer iMacs and laptops have built-in video cameras. You can use Apple's cute little iSight camera if you already have one (they're not sold anymore), or you can attach any FireWire video camera to your Mac, or a USB video camera.

With whom can you video conference?

A video conference with more than one person takes a powerful Mac and a good broadband connection. If you have a machine running Mountain Lion, then it is more than capable of participating in or initiating a video conference with four people. But perhaps you want to video conference with others who have less powerful computers—you can tell by the icons in their Buddy tab if they are capable: Any Buddy who is able to *participate* in a video conference with more than one person has a *stack* of camera icons next to his image; if there is only one camera (or none), he cannot participate.

To *initiate* a video conference with up to four people, it takes a powerful Mac and a fast broadband connection. So if it doesn't work for one of you to start the video chat, have the person with the biggest-fastest-newest Mac start it.

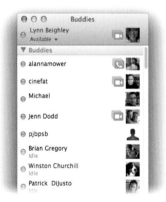

To see what Messages capabilities a Buddy has, go to the Buddies menu, choose "Show Info," and click the "Profile" tab.

Audio and video preferences

You can make some minor adjustments in the Audio/Video pane of the Messages preferences. You might try changing the "Bandwidth Limit" to see if it affects your video chat one way or another. Depending on your Internet connection and how many other people use it, a different setting can work better (or worse).

Open a video chat and invite others to join you

Just a reminder: To *initiate* a video conference with more than one other person, you need a more powerful machine than you do to *join* a video conference.

1 Single-click a buddy name that shows multiple video camera icons. That person hears a little phone ringing and gets a message on her screen inviting her to a video chat. When she clicks "Accept," she appears in your video window instead of you.

2 To add two more people to your video conference, click the **+** sign; a menu drops down with the names of the people in your Messages Buddies panel *who are online and capable of joining you.*

3 To leave the video chat, click the red close button in the upper-left of the window. The last person to leave the chat will terminate the entire session.

If your Buddy doesn't have a camera with which to video chat, select her name, then go to the Buddies menu and choose "Invite to One-Way Video Chat." Your friend will see you, and if she has a microphone attached to her Mac, you can hear her.

Video Effects

Video Effects are useless but fun. You can distort your image, add artistic touches, and even add new backgrounds so it looks like you're somewhere else.

To preview the various effects:

1 Before or during a video chat, go to the Video menu and choose "Video Preview."

2 Now from the same menu choose "Show Video Effects."

3 Select an effect from one of four Video Effects panels (two of them are shown below) to see what it will do. Click the arrows in the bottom corners to navigate all four panels. The last panel contains empty wells so you can drag and drop your own backgrounds there and use them. You can make backgrounds out of photos or movies.

Choose video effects.   Choose movie backgrounds.

Click to cycle through the
other video effects options.

To apply an effect during a video chat:

1 During a video chat, click the "Effects" button in the bottom-left corner of the chat window (shown on the opposite page). This opens the "Video Effects" panel shown above.

2 The original, non-effect version appears in the middle of the panel. Click an effect to apply it as you chat.

3 To return to the original, non-effect image, click the "Original" image in the center of the Video Effects panel.

Add backgrounds

In addition to distorting your video image with various effects, you can add a photo or a movie to replace the existing background that's really behind you (in real life). This background replacement feature works best if you have a simple, uncluttered, single-color area behind you as you sit in front of the camera. We got the best results (but not perfect) by using a background wall that was smooth and almost white. Although you can do this in the middle of chatting, you might want to get it all set up before you call someone on a video chat and surprise them.

1   In the Video Effects panel (explained on the opposite page), click the right arrow button until you get to the panel of background images. Look for background photos, not your picture.

    To add your own background photos or movies, click through the effects until you find an empty well. Drag your image or movie into that well.

2   Click a background image to select it. A text prompt appears and asks you to move yourself out of the video frame (do what it says). The prompt notifies you a few seconds later with a "Background Detected" message.

3   Move back into the picture. Messages replaces the original background with the photo or movie you selected and places you in front of it.

    If you want to change to another background, Messages will *not* ask you to step out again—it will just replace the existing one.

Someone's having her 15 minutes of fame.

Click to change video effects during a video chat.

Theater in Messages

Once you've initiated a video chat, you can use Theater to show files, photos, slideshows, or movies while you continue your chat. This is amazing.

To share a file with Theater:

1 Start a video chat with a buddy.

2 From the File menu, choose "Share a File With Theater…." Or click the **+** button at the bottom of the window, then choose "Share a File With Theater" from the pop-up menu.

3 In the Finder window that opens, select a file, photo, or movie you want to share, then click "Share." *Or* simply drag any file, photo, or movie from your hard disk and drop it onto the video chat window.

When you drag a file to the video chat window, the buddy's image minimizes to the bottom-left corner to make room for an image of the file. Your buddy sees you as a thumbnail video and sees the same file image that you see.

If the shared file is a movie, the file window displays a Play/Pause button and a scrub bar to drag the clip backward or forward (below, left).

To share *multiple* files of the same or different types, Command-click to select files on your hard drive, then drop the files on the video chat window. The files play as a slideshow. Slideshow controls are positioned under the image.

Depending on what you're sharing, these controls will vary. Theater provides controls for volume, a timeline slider that lets you drag to any part if it's a movie, or just play/pause if it's a slideshow.

To share a web page with Theater:

1 Start a video chat with a buddy.

2 From the File menu, choose "Share a Webpage With Theater...." In the dialog that opens, enter a web address, then click the "Share" button.

Share iPhoto with Theater

You can also share entire iPhoto albums as a slideshow.

1 Start a video chat with a buddy.

2 From the File menu, choose "Share iPhoto With Theater...."

3 In the iPhoto window that opens (below-left), select an album, then click "Share."

Select an album to share as a slideshow.

Theater opens a slideshow with slideshow controls and random music track.

Bonjour on Your Local Network

Bonjour is an integrated component of **Messages**. If you have two or more Macs connected through a local area network (an Ethernet network, wireless network, or a combination of both), Bonjour automatically detects and connects all of the computers on the network. You can send Instant Messages or files to Bonjour buddies on your local network. You can have audio or video chats with others on the local network (if a microphone or digital video camera is connected to your computer, of course). And you can use Screen Sharing to share your computer with others or to see another buddy's computer (see Lesson 23).

You don't have to have an AIM account or any other kind of special account—just computers that are connected on a local network, as in your Ethernet or wireless network at home or office or corporate building.

To set up Bonjour:

1 Open Messages, then from the Messages application menu, choose "Preferences."

2 Click the "Accounts" button, then click "Bonjour" in the Accounts pane on the left side of the window.

3 Check the box to "Enable Bonjour instant messaging."

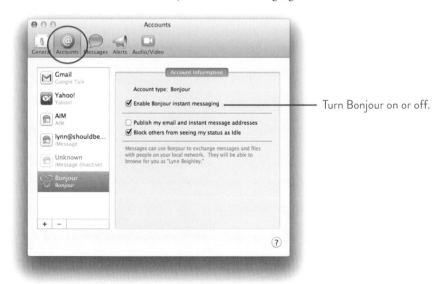

Turn Bonjour on or off.

Once you've enabled Bonjour in Messages Preferences (see the opposite page), Bonjour is listed as one of the buddy categories in the Messages Buddies panel. Click the disclosure triangle next to Bonjour to show other Bonjour users who are accessible on the local network.

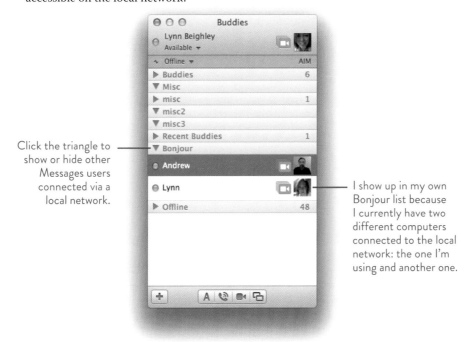

Click the triangle to show or hide other Messages users connected via a local network.

I show up in my own Bonjour list because I currently have two different computers connected to the local network: the one I'm using and another one.

Bonjour automatically detects a local network and connects you to it. If you're in a public space, such as an Internet cafe, you should quit Messages or at least turn off Bonjour when you're not using it, to ensure privacy and security.

To send a file to anyone on the Bonjour List, drop the file on a buddy name.

Or if you are chatting, **drag a file into the message field** where you type. Hit Return and off it goes. If the file is an image, the image itself appears in the chat window; your buddy can view it, drag it to his Desktop, or double-click it to open it.

TIP —— If you're interested in **sharing files** or **sharing computer screens** (where you can actually manipulate the other person's monitor wherever she is in the world), please see Lesson 23 on connecting and sharing files.

Record Chats

When an audio or video chat is in progress, you can record the chat. Recorded video Messages files require a lot of storage space, approximately one megabyte for every five seconds of video.

1 Start an audio or video chat with a buddy.

2 From the Video menu at the top of the screen, choose "Record Chat."

3 The buddy's audio or video chat window reveals a "Recording Request" sheet (below-left). When the buddy clicks "Allow," the recording begins.

4 A red *Record* light alerts both participants that recording is in progress.

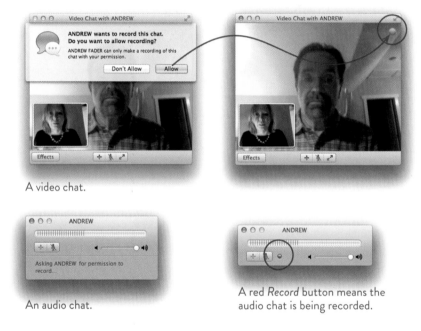

A video chat.

An audio chat.

A red *Record* button means the audio chat is being recorded.

To stop a video recording, from the Video menu choose "Stop Recording."
To stop an audio recording, click the red *Record* button in the Audio Chat window (circled, above-right).

Find recorded chats

To locate a video or audio chat file, open the Documents folder, then look in the Messages folder. The files can also found in iTunes: Look in the iTunes Sidebar for a playlist named "Messages Chats." Click that playlist to show your recorded video chats. If your recorded audio chats are not there, look in the main iTunes library.

FaceTime

FaceTime is not part of Messages, but it's similar in that it enables you to make video calls to friends. You can call anyone who has at least an iPad 2 or 3, an iPhone 4, an iPod touch, or a Mac with FaceTime installed. With FaceTime, you use a person's email addresses instead of a phone number.

1 Click the FaceTime icon in the Dock.

2 The first window (below, left) asks you to sign in with your Apple ID and password, or create a new account to activate FaceTime. If you have an iTunes account or a MobileMe account, use the ID and password from that.

3 Designate the email address you want people to use to call you.

4 Select a person from the Contacts list that appears on the right side of the FaceTime window. If you call this person often and want quick and easy access, click the "Add to Favorites" button.

5 Click the person's email address. It must be an address that the person has designated as the email address to use to call them, as in Step 3. To call an iPhone 4, use that phone number. If the person answers, she appears in the FaceTime window (below, right).

6 Click the "End" button to end the video call.

Enter your Apple ID, type your password immediately below your ID, then click the "Sign In" button. Or click "Create New Account" to get an Apple ID.

Mute.   Full-screen.

To switch to a horizontal orientation, hover the pointer over the small thumbnail image, then click the rotation symbol that appears.

10

GOALS

iTunes for Your Listening Pleasure

Import music into iTunes, create Playlists of your favorite songs, copy the Playlists to CDs so you have your own discs of customized music, or stream your music from your office down the hallway to hear it in the kitchen. In addition to buying music, you can buy or rent movies and TV shows directly through the iTunes Store with the click of a button and download them right to your computer. A multitude of podcasts are available for free from the iTunes Store, including content from many universities (click the iTunes U tab in the iTunes Store) and broadcasters.

If you have an iPhone, iPod or iPad, iTunes makes backups for you and syncs the music, apps, and data on them. If you're interested in being more social with your music interests, Ping lets you follow your favorite artists, celebrities, and friends, sharing music information.

The iTunes Window

Below is an overview of the iTunes window. This short chapter is only an overview; if you want an entire guide to using iTunes, please check one of the iLife books from Peachpit Press. There is so much to iTunes! I encourage you to explore the menus, all the buttons, and the Help files.

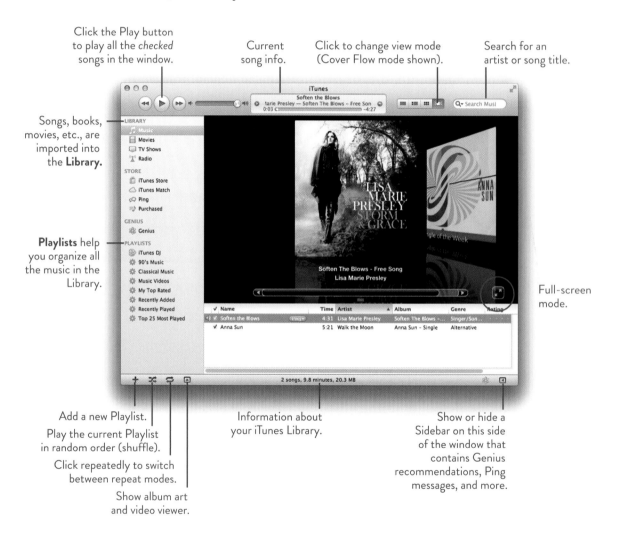

Click the Play button to play all the *checked* songs in the window.

Current song info.

Click to change view mode (Cover Flow mode shown).

Search for an artist or song title.

Songs, books, movies, etc., are imported into the **Library.**

Playlists help you organize all the music in the Library.

Full-screen mode.

Add a new Playlist.

Play the current Playlist in random order (shuffle).

Click repeatedly to switch between repeat modes.

Show album art and video viewer.

Information about your iTunes Library.

Show or hide a Sidebar on this side of the window that contains Genius recommendations, Ping messages, and more.

Buy Music, Movies, or Television Shows

To buy music, movies, or television shows, click on "iTunes Store" in the Sidebar. **To search** for something specific, use the search field in the top-right corner.

The first time you click a "Buy" button, you will be asked to set up an account with a credit card number and contact info. After you've got an account, you can buy and download music, movies, and television shows with the click of a button. **To watch a show or movie,** see page 191.

Download Album Art

When you buy music through iTunes, you automatically get the **album art** with it. If the art is not showing at the bottom of the Sidebar when you select a purchased song, click the *Show item artwork and video viewer* button (circled below).

Hide and show video or album art.

Single-click the album art preview to open a large version in its own window.

Create a Playlist

Everything you buy in iTunes goes into one of the categories in the Library. But you can create your own **Playlists,** which are collections of songs from the Music Library. You might create one Playlist for your favorite jazz songs, another of Gregorian chants, and another for a particular artist. The same song can be in any number of Playlists. This allows you, for instance, to take two songs from this CD, one from that CD, etc., to create your own personal collection, then play that collection or burn it to a CD of your own.

1 Playlists are made from songs in your iTunes Library, so first buy songs at the iTunes Store (see the previous page) or import songs from CDs (see the opposite page). You can also drag a song from your Desktop or from a Finder window to the Library pane in the Sidebar, or to a Playlist in the Sidebar.

2 Click the **+** in the bottom-left corner. A new, untitled Playlist appears in the Sidebar. Name this new Playlist.

3 Single-click the "Music" collection in the Library pane.

4 Drag songs displayed in the main window and drop them on the Playlist in the Sidebar.

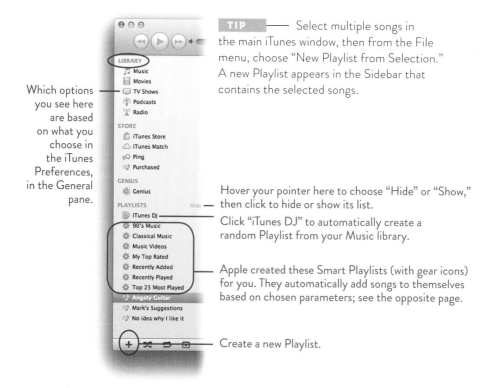

Which options you see here are based on what you choose in the iTunes Preferences, in the General pane.

TIP —— Select multiple songs in the main iTunes window, then from the File menu, choose "New Playlist from Selection." A new Playlist appears in the Sidebar that contains the selected songs.

Hover your pointer here to choose "Hide" or "Show," then click to hide or show its list.

Click "iTunes DJ" to automatically create a random Playlist from your Music library.

Apple created these Smart Playlists (with gear icons) for you. They automatically add songs to themselves based on chosen parameters; see the opposite page.

Create a new Playlist.

Import Songs from a CD

Put an **audio CD** in your disc drive and iTunes automatically opens. If you're connected to the Internet, iTunes goes to an online database and (if it can find the CD in the database) gets the artist, album title, song names, times, and more, and displays that information in the iTunes window. A message window opens and asks if you want to import the CD. If you want to import the entire CD, click "Yes."

If you want to import just specific songs on the CD, click "No," then select the songs you want to import—uncheck the checkboxes of songs you don't want, checkmark the songs you do want. You can Command-click to check or uncheck all boxes.

Click the "Import CD" button in the bottom-right corner. Only the songs you *checked* will import into the Music library.

Create a Smart Playlist

A *regular* Playlist holds the songs or music videos that you add to it by dragging items into it. A *Smart* Playlist **automatically adds certain songs from your Music collection all by itself.** It's really great.

1   Hold down the Option key—the **+** sign at the bottom of the Sidebar turns into a gear wheel; click the gear wheel.
    Or go to the File menu and choose "New Smart Playlist…"

2   In the dialog box that appears (shown below), open the menus (starting from the left) and make your choices. Click the **+** on the right to add more parameters. Click OK.

3   The Smart Playlist appears in the iTunes Sidebar, waiting for you to rename it.

This Smart Playlist will create a playlist that contains the songs of two specific artists in my iTunes library.

Share Your Music

There are two ways to share in iTunes. One, called Sharing, allows users on a local network to listen to each others' music by streaming, but not copying. The other, Home Sharing, allows you to stream or copy content to your other computers on your local network. This is handy when you've got a lot of music on one Mac, say in your office, and you want to transfer it to your laptop or other computers in your home. You can do this on Windows machines that are running iTunes as well.

Sharing (streaming) on your local network

Share your Library of music with other computers on your local network. Open the iTunes preferences (right). Click the "Sharing" tab, then select "Share my library on my local network." If you choose "Share selected Playlists," check the items you want to share.

Shared music Libraries appear in the iTunes Sidebar, under the "Shared" label. Content shared this way can be played by, but not copied to, the other computers.

Use this method when you don't have an Apple ID (required for Home Sharing, explained below), or when you don't want the other computers to be able to make a copy of your iTunes content.

Home Sharing on your local network

Home Sharing lets you stream *or* transfer (copy) your iTunes content (with the exception of movie rentals) with up to five other computers (owned by you) through your local Ethernet or Wi-Fi network. You'll need your Apple ID, such as an iTunes Store or App Store account, to enable Home Sharing on your computer; you need to use the same Apple ID to enable Home Sharing on the other computers.

Turn on Home Sharing on your Mac

1 Select the "Home Sharing" icon in the iTunes Sidebar, shown circled on the right.

(If the Home Sharing icon is not in the Sidebar, go to the Advanced menu and choose "Turn On Home Sharing." Of course, you can also turn it off here.)

2 When the Home Sharing screen appears (above), enter your Apple ID and password. If you don't have an Apple ID yet, click "Need Apple ID?"

3 Click "Create Home Share," then click "Done" in the next pane that appears. Once Home Sharing is enabled, the Home Sharing icon in the Sidebar disappears.

Set up your other computers

Use the procedure above to enable Home Sharing on your other computers. The Library names on the other computers will appear in the Sidebar under the "Shared" category.

Click this to choose categories and Playlists to enjoy.

Use Home Sharing

1 In the Sidebar, select the shared Library that you want to connect to. The contents of that iTunes Library appear in your iTunes window.

2 To *play* a song or movie, double-click its name.

3 To *manually* transfer (copy) a song or movie to your own iTunes library, drag it to the iTunes Library in your iTunes Sidebar. *Or* select it and then click the "Import" button in the bottom-right corner of iTunes.

4 To *automatically* transfer iTunes content from another computer, select the Library in the Sidebar from which you want to copy content, then click the "Settings" button in the bottom-right corner of iTunes. Check the type of content you want to transfer, then click OK.

iTunes automatically transfers new content the next time you download movies or songs from the iTunes Store.

189

Burn a CD of Your Own Collection

You can burn CDs of your own Playlists, and you can play those CDs on any computer or in any CD player. First import the songs and make a Playlist, as described on pages 186–188. You can't just select songs in the music Library to burn to a CD—you must make a Playlist. Then:

1 Insert a blank CD-R (don't use CD+R).

2 In iTunes, select a Playlist. You can only burn one Playlist onto a music CD, so make sure it's got everything you want in it. You can burn about 600 MB (megabytes) onto one CD, so add as many songs from as many different artists and albums as you like. Check the status bar at the bottom of iTunes to know how many megabytes are in the selected Playlist.

3 From the File menu, choose "Burn Playlist to Disc."

  In the "Burn Settings" dialog that opens, choose "Audio CD."
  The default speed option is probably set to "Maximum Possible"; that's good.

4 Click the "Burn" button. When it's finished, you'll see the name of the CD in the Sidebar, along with an *eject* symbol. Eject the CD and enjoy!

TIP —— It's possible to make a huge Playlist that holds many more songs than will fit on one CD. When you put in the first disc and click the "Burn Disc" button, iTunes will warn you that it will take more than one disc. Click OK; iTunes tells you when the first disc is full, ejects the completed disc, and asks you to insert another blank disc.

Watch Movies in iTunes

You can buy movies or television shows and watch them directly in iTunes. If you buy an Apple TV device and have a wireless system and widescreen TV in your home, you can stream the movies and shows from your computer to your television. (To do so, you'll have to read the directions that come with the Apple TV.)

To watch a movie or TV show in iTunes on your computer:

1 Go to the iTunes Store and buy a movie or television show. After it downloads, it appears in the Library pane under "Movies" or "TV Shows."

2 Select "Movies" or "TV Shows," then double-click the name of the movie or show. The film immediately opens in the iTunes window, as shown below.

   To view it full-screen, either click the arrows (circled below) or hit Command F.

Grid view shows resizable thumbnails of your movies.

Resize the thumbnails.

To quit the movie, click here.

These controls appear when you hover the pointer over the playing movie.

Full-screen mode.

Listen to Radio from Around the World

You can listen to radio from around the world with the click of a button. In the Sidebar, click the "Radio" icon, circled below. Double-click a category to see the variety of stations available in that genre, and double-click the radio stream you want to listen to. Amazing.

Audiobooks in iTunes

You can buy and listen to audiobooks directly in iTunes.

To buy an audiobook, go to the iTunes Store, select the "Audiobooks" tab, then shop.

To play an audiobook once you've bought and downloaded it, hover over its thumbnail, then click the "Play" button that appears (circled, below).

iTunes DJ, Genius Playlist, and Genius Sidebar

Why go to the trouble of making Playlists when iTunes will do it for you? Click **iTunes DJ** in the Sidebar. iTunes automatically picks songs from your Music collection and creates a random mix that updates after each song. You can change all songs in the list (click the "Refresh" button in the bottom-right corner), or reorder it (drag items up or down in the list) at any time.

Click the "Settings…" button (bottom-right corner) to determine how many songs appear in the list at a time. If you've downloaded the free iPhone or iPod Touch app called "Remote," you can give permission to guests to wirelessly request songs and to *vote* for songs (the vote controls when a song plays)—a good party app.

iTunes DJ Playlist.

Update the Genius Playlist.

Or instead of creating a *random* Playlist, create an automatic **Genius Playlist** of songs based on the current selection: Click the **Genius** Playlist in the Sidebar. iTunes automatically creates a Playlist of songs *from your library* similar to the current song.

The **Genius Sidebar** (which appears on the right side of iTunes) recommends songs from the iTunes Store, based on your current selection.
To show the Genius Sidebar, click the *Show Genius Sidebar* button (bottom-right).
To hear previews of recommended songs, click the button next to the song.
To buy a suggested song, click the "Buy" button.

The Genius Sidebar recommends songs for you.

Genius Playlist.   Refresh the Genius list.   Show/Hide Genius Sidebar.

Print a CD Cover Insert

You can print in a variety of ways from iTunes. This is great when you've burned your own collection of music to play in the car and want to keep your travel music discs labeled and organized.

1 Select a Playlist, then hit Command P to **print,** or go to the File menu and choose "Print...."

2 Experiment with the options in the window that opens (below). Choose a "Print" option, then choose a "Theme" for that print option.

Socialize Musically with Ping

Ping is a social network for music that's built right into iTunes. Follow your favorite artists and friends, see what music they're buying, and read their comments about albums and songs. You can also allow others to follow your own song choices and read comments that you choose to post on Ping.

To get started, click the "Ping" option in the Sidebar, then click the "Turn On Ping" button, shown below. Follow the instructions on the screen to create a new Ping account, then start following the artists, celebrities, and friends you're interested in.

Tune In to Visual Effects

To see **visual effects** that react to the music you're playing, turn on the beautiful iTunes Visualizer.

1 Choose a visualizer: Go to the View menu and choose "Visualizer." From the submenu, choose one of the options. "iTunes Visualizer" is the most current version; "iTunes Classic Visualizer" is from previous operating systems, but still impressive.

2 Go to the View menu again and choose "Show Visualizer."
Or press Command T to toggle the visualizer on and off.

3 To show the visualizer effects full screen, from the View menu, choose "Full Screen." *Or* press Command F to toggle between full-screen view and a normal iTunes window view (shown below).

For fun, from the View menu, choose "iTunes Visualizer," choose "iTunes Classic Visualizer," then tap these keyboard commands to alter the visualizer effects:

I   display track info

C   toggle auto-cycle

F   toggle freeze mode

L   toggle camera lock

N   toggle nebula mode

P   change the color palette

R   change the mode (very fun; tap it every few seconds)

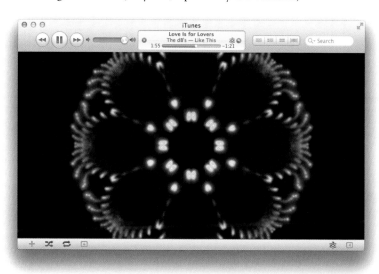

11

GOALS

Unlock and
duplicate images

Crop, color adjust,
and resize images

Make screenshots

Save files into other formats

Share images in a
variety of ways

Search PDFs

Create PDF Bookmarks
for easy retrieval of files

Copy text from a PDF
to paste into another
document as editable text

Annotate and mark up a PDF

Fill in PDF forms

Preview for Viewing Images, PDFs, and More

The seemingly small picture-viewing application called Preview does a great deal more than merely display photographs for you. It's a powerful program with which you can view images, open and annotate PDFs (even add your signature to a PDF), change file formats, crop images, adjust image color or size, make screenshots of what you see on your screen, share image and PDF files with others, and more.

As in any of the lessons in this book, we don't have room to explain every single menu command or preference. But take a few moments to explore the possibilities in the menus and preferences.

Open an Image or Folder of Images

If you haven't changed the default settings, you can just double-click images or PDFs and they open in Preview. Preview is in your Dock (if not, see Lesson 1 to put it there).

Change view and
zoom in and out.

Full-Screen
mode; see
Lesson 3.

Drag anywhere on this edge to resize the Sidebar and thumbnails.

To open an image (or multiple images) in Preview, do any of the following:

- Double-click the file.
- Drag one or more images (or PDF files) into the Sidebar.
- Drag-and-drop an image or PDF onto the Preview icon in the Dock. You can drag an **entire folder** of images to the Preview icon and they will all open and display themselves in the Sidebar, as shown above.
- Control-click an image, select "Open With," and choose "Preview."

To view multiple images as a contact sheet, click the *Contact Sheet* option under the View Options button in the Toolbar (shown below). To enlarge or reduce the image sizes in Contact Sheet view, click the **+** and **−** *zoom* buttons in the Toolbar.

View
Options.

Unlock or Duplicate to Make Versions

The moment you try to make any change to an image, a small sheet drops down asking you to unlock (or lock, if the image is already unlocked) or Duplicate the file.

If you **unlock** the image, your changes will be made to the original file.

If you choose to **duplicate** the image (unlock it first), a copy or new *version* of the image appears in front of you, as shown below-right. It *appears* to have a new name, but this is just fooling you—nothing will be saved until you press Command S (or go to the File menu and choose "Save…") and rename it.

A little message appears in the title bar whenever there are unsaved changes ("Edited"). Each time you save (Command S) this duplicate file, a new *version* is created for you. Whether or not "Edited" or "Locked" is visible, you can always single-click on the title bar (a disclosure triangle appears when you hover the pointer over it), and choose "Browse All Versions."

These are the versions you have saved, or that Preview automatically saved for you every hour. Click any title bar to bring it to the front, or use the time slider to view other versions.

Slide the cursor all the way to the top of the screen to display the Preview menu bar.

Crop an Image

You can crop any photograph or other image very easily in Preview. When you crop an image, the part you remove *is gone from the original image forever.* You might want to make a duplicate of the file before you crop (see previous page).

To crop a photograph or other image:

1 Open the image in Preview.

2 Click the "Show Edit Toolbar" button in the Toolbar and choose a Selection tool from the Edit toolbar. You can crop into a circle, oval, or rectangle, or use the lasso tool to draw a shape.

3 **To resize** the cropped area, drag any of the tiny round "handles" that you see on each corner and side (you won't get handles on a lasso selection).

4 **To move the cropped area** to a different part of the image, press in the middle of the cropping box and drag.

   To cancel, press the Escape (esc) key, or click outside the selected crop area.

5 When you are ready to crop, go to the Edit toolbar and choose "Crop to Selection." *Or* press Command K.

A selection made with the
Rectangular Selection Tool.

The cropped image.

Adjust Image Colors or Size

Preview can do some limited editing of graphic images and photos (use the Tools menu). You can **crop,** as explained on the opposite page, and also **resize, rotate,** and **resample** (change the pixels per inch). And you have some pretty powerful **color adjustments** available. The best way to learn how to use them is to experiment. Always save a duplicate of the original before you start experimenting.

To adjust the color (or the size) of an image:

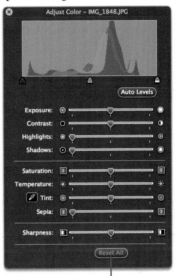

1 Open an image in Preview.

2 From the Tools menu, choose "Adjust Color…" or "Adjust Size…."; choose whether to unlock or duplicate (see page 199).
   To adjust size, fill in the fields; **to adjust color,** you'll see the panel shown to the right.

3 Move the sliders left and right to see what the options do. The image immediately changes as you adjust the sliders. You can always click the button (right) to "Reset All" and restore the image to the way it looked in the first place.

4 When you're satisfied with the changes, press Command S to save. Then you can carry on with more changes that you can choose to save or not. Don't forget that your Mac is saving various versions for you.

Reset all settings.

The original image.

The color-adjusted image.

Make Screenshots Using Preview

A screenshot is a picture of what your screen looks like at that moment. It's useful when you need to show someone a problem on your screen, or to show off something cool that's only on your Mac. Use it to show a comp of your design idea to a client or instead of a large photograph that is too big to reasonably put in email.

To make a screenshot:

1 Open Preview.

2 On the File menu, slide down to "Take Screen Shot," and choose:

   From Selection: A crosshair icon appears. Press-and-drag around an area to take a screenshot of just that area. When you let go, it takes the shot.

   From Window: A camera icon appears, circled below. As you move the camera icon on top of different windows on your screen, it highlights each one in blue. When the window you want is highlighted, single-click. It takes a picture of the entire window, whether or not you can see the whole thing.

   From Entire Screen: Preview gives you ten seconds to get your screen set up the way you want it for a screenshot. For instance, you might want a picture of a particular menu with its submenu visible. After ten seconds, Preview snaps a screenshot of the entire screen.

The screenshot immediately and automatically opens in Preview. From the File menu, choose "Save…." Choose a format, name the file, and save in a location of your choice.

Import Images from a Camera or Scanner

If you have an image device connected, such as a camera, a digital photo card reader, or a scanner, you can use Preview to import images.

From the File menu, choose "Import from Camera…" **or** "Import from Scanner…."

If your scanner doesn't appear in the "Import from Scanner…" menu, go online and search for the latest "driver" software for that scanner. After you download and install the driver, the scanner name should appear in the menu.

Save an Image As Another Format

Sometimes you need a file in another format. For instance, maybe the file is in the file format called JPG from your camera, but you need it in the format called TIFF because you need to put it in a brochure that's going to be printed on a professional press. Or maybe you have a large PNG file and you want a smaller JPG of the image.

To change a document into another file type:

1 Open the original image in Preview.

2 Make a duplicate of the file: Single-click on the title bar and choose "Duplicate," *or* go to the File menu and choose "Duplicate."

3 When the duplicate opens, go back to the File menu and choose "Save…" or "Export…."

4 In the dialog box that opens, click the "Format" pop-up menu to choose a file format. Set any necessary adjustments. Name the file. Click "Save."

Choosing different formats will provide you with different adjustment options specific to that format.

Click the disclosure triangle circled above to view the larger pane.

Working with PDFs

Everyone uses PDFs these days (Portable Document Format files). If you want a few more options in working with your PDFs, check out what you can do in Preview.

Display facing pages or continuous pages

You can display facing pages of PDF documents, as in a book (the first page will always display alone, like the first page of a book). This works whether or not the person who created the PDF saved the file in the "Spreads" format (which combines facing pages in the PDF). In fact, even if someone *did* create the PDF pages in spreads, you can view them in Preview as individual pages. This comes in very handy when you need to print the document but don't want to print two-page spreads on one page.

Thumbnails view shows page thumbnails in a Sidebar.

To switch back and forth from single pages to facing pages (above), go to the View menu, then choose "Single Page" or "Two Pages." Choose "Continuous Scroll" to show the PDF document as one long, scrolling page.

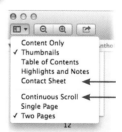

You can **open multiple PDFs simultaneously**—drag the files into the Sidebar, or drop them on top of the Preview icon in the Dock. Try viewing them in the *Contact Sheet* view; it's under the View menu button in the Toolbar.

Search a PDF

The search feature in Preview is quite amazing. Use the standard keyboard shortcut for "Find": Command F. Once you have found an instance on the page, press Command G to find the next instance. These are the same shortcuts you've probably used in Safari to find text on a web page or in TextEdit to find text in your document.

To search a PDF:

1 Open a PDF document, press Command F (or just click in the Search field), then type the word or phrase you want to find in the document.

2 The Sidebar opens to show a summary of the search results. Use the buttons at the top of the Sidebar to choose how to sort the results: "Search Rank" (number of matches per page) or "Page Order."

3 As you type, Preview starts finding and highlighting words that match. The more letters you type, the fewer matches are found.

4 In the Sidebar summary of results, click any item to go directly to that page. Click the Previous and Next buttons to cycle through the matches found. Or press Command G to go to the next match in the document.

Click here to clear all search results.

All search results are highlighted.

Search field.

Choose how to sort search results.

From the Sidebar search results list, select a page to jump to it.

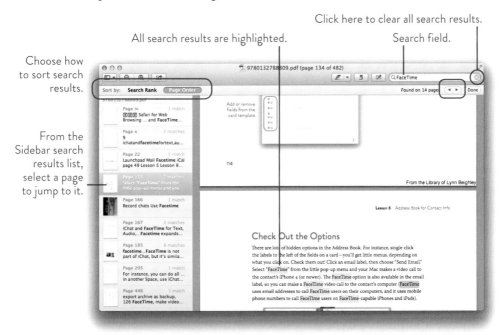

Create bookmarks in a PDF

A Bookmark puts the name of a file in the Bookmarks menu of Preview so you can open the document or photograph immediately without having to go look for it—open Preview, then choose a Bookmark listed in the Bookmarks menu (below-right), and the PDF file opens and displays that particular page. This is an easy way to quickly access important pages from different documents.

To make a bookmark, open a document or image, then press Command D (or from the Bookmarks menu, choose "Add Bookmark..." as shown below-left). You will be asked to name the bookmark. Give it a name that you'll recognize in a list.

> If the PDF is a **multipage document,** you can make several bookmarks for the same document, each one to a different page. Just make sure you are viewing the page you want to bookmark before you press Command D.

To open a bookmarked file, open Preview, go to the Bookmarks menu, and choose the bookmark name from the list at the bottom of the menu (above-right).

To edit the name or to remove a bookmark, go to the Bookmarks menu and choose "Edit Bookmarks...." The Preview preferences window opens, shown below. Click the "Bookmarks" icon in the Toolbar, then:

> **To delete a file,** single-click the file name, then click the "Remove" button.

> **To edit the file name,** double-click its name, then edit.

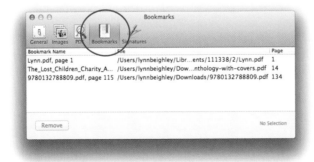

Copy text from a PDF to paste elsewhere

You can copy text from a PDF file (as long as the person who sent it to you didn't lock it) and paste it into any other document as **editable text.** Or you can copy a section of text as a **graphic** and paste it into another document as a graphic image that can be resized as a unit.

To copy text:

1 Select the Text tool under the Tools menu and choose Text Selection, or click Show Edit Toolbar and click the Test Selection button (below).

2 Press-and-drag over the text you want to select.

To select just a vertical portion of text, as in one column, hold down the Option key before you start to drag, and keep it held down as you drag.

3 From the Edit menu, choose "Copy," *or* press Command C. Open your other document and paste it in (Command V).

To copy any part of a PDF as a graphic, click the "Select" button in the Toolbar (shown below). Press-and-drag in the PDF document to select an area you want to copy. Go to the Edit menu and choose "Copy" (*or* press Command C).

Now you can go to any document in any application and paste that graphic in. To paste it, open the other document, press Command V, *or* go to the Edit menu and choose "Paste."

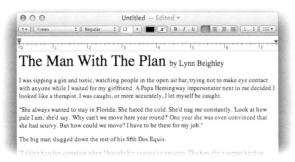

Annotate a PDF

You can add comments, highlights, shapes, and more to PDFs to call out items for other readers. The "Show Edit Toolbar" button should be in the Toolbar (if not, go to the View menu, choose "Customize Toolbar...," and drag it into the Toolbar).

To create a text note on a PDF:

1 In an open PDF, click the "Show Edit Toolbar" button in the Toolbar to display the tools. Then click the "Note" button in the editing tools.

2 Single-click on the page where you need a note or comment. Preview places a small Note symbol on the page and immediately creates a text Note in a Sidebar.

3 **To type the Note,** just start typing; the text appears in the Sidebar. By default, Preview adds your name and the date to the note (see the Preview preferences if you want to change that).

4 **To move a Note symbol,** drag it; the Note text (in the Sidebar) will align itself with the Note symbol.

5 **To delete a Note,** single-click its symbol to select it, then hit Delete.

Edit Toolbar. The "Note" button is selected.

Choose Highlights and Notes from the View menu to see this panel with your Notes.

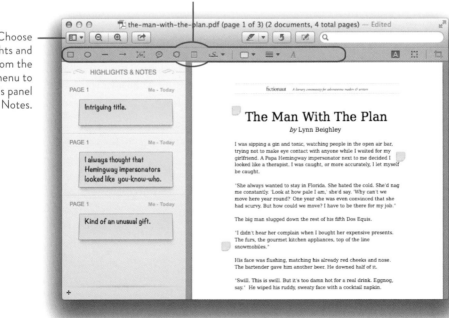

208

To draw an oval or rectangle annotation:

1   Open a PDF; click the "Show Edit Toolbar" button in the Toolbar. Notice the Shape buttons on the left side of the Edit Toolbar.

   To create an oval, select the "Oval" icon.

   To create a rectangle, select the "Rectangle" icon.

2   With the tool, drag anywhere on the page **to create a shape.**

3   **To resize a shape,** single-click to select it, then drag the handles to resize.

4   **To move a shape,** single-click the shape, then drag the shape around the page.

5   **To delete a shape,** single-click the shape to select it, then hit Delete.

Experiment with the other edit tools to highlight, underline, or strike through text.

To delete an annotation:

1   Open the Annotations Inspector by clicking the Tools menu, then choose Show Inspector. Click the Annotation Inspector icon on the right to see a list of all annotations.

2   Select an item in the list to show it in the Preview window.

   To delete an annotation, select it in this list, then hit the Delete key.

Choose "Highlights & Notes" from this menu to open the Highlights & Notes pane.

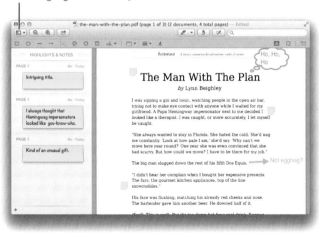

The Annotations Inspector.

Select the other tools in the Inspector Toolbar to add keywords, crop and rotate, and more.

Digitize your actual signature for PDFs

When someone sends you a PDF document that requires your signature, you can create a digital version of your real signature, size it, and place it in the document.

To create a signature:

1   Open a PDF in Preview. Go to the page that needs a signature.

2   Click the "Show Edit Toolbar" button in the Toolbar. In the bar of edit tools that opens (below, left), click the "Signature" button.

3   In the pop-up menu, select "Create Signature from *(name of your camera)."*

4   The "Signature Capture" window opens. Sign your name on a piece of white paper, then hold the paper up to the Mac's camera and align it with the blue line (below, right).

5   Click the "Accept" button (circled, below-right).

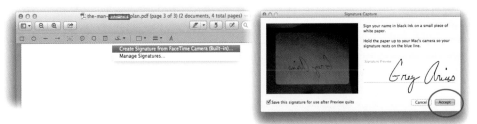

To size and place a signature:

1   Click the "Signature" button again; from the pop-up menu, select the signature you want to use. You can store multiple signatures in Preview.

2   Drag the pointer on the page. The drag determines the size of the signature, which can be adjusted later, if necessary, by selecting it and dragging the handles that appear when selected. Click and drag it to reposition it.

Fill in PDF forms

You can fill in some web forms right on your screen, if the forms have been properly created. Then you can print the fully completed form, instead of printing it first and then filling it in by hand.

The PDF must have been created and saved in such a way that it has fields ready for you to enter data. That is, you just can't start entering data into any old PDF—it must be an actual *form* format.

To fill in a PDF form:

1   Open an appropriate PDF form in Preview. The example below is a tax form downloaded from the IRS site.

2   Click on the Text tool, shown circled below on the right.

3   Click in the area where you are supposed to enter data. An insertion point appears and the text field becomes visible, as shown below.

4   Type and be sure to save regularly.

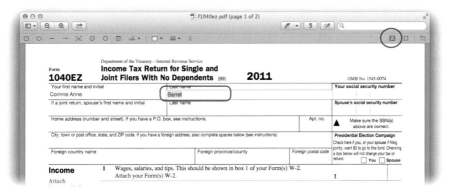

Share from Preview

While I talk about the new Share button integrated in most apps in Lesson 14, it's worth taking a look at it here in Preview. You can share an image or PDF in a variety of ways from Preview.

To share an image or PDF:

1   Open an image or PDF in Preview.

2   Click the Share button, shown circled in the examples on the next page.

3   If you are sharing a PDF, you'll see the options Email, Message, and Airdrop. If you're sharing an image, you'll see those options, as well as Twitter and Flickr (if you've set up your accounts, see Lesson 14), and Add to Airdrop.

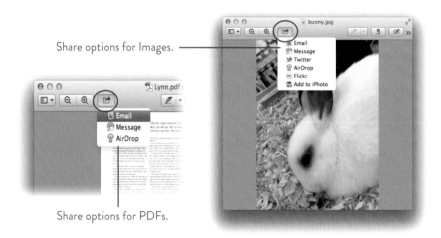

Share options for Images.

Share options for PDFs.

Print or Fax from Preview

You can print or fax any image or document from Preview.

To print an image or document:

1 If you have multiple images open in Preview, select the ones you want to print: Command-click to choose them from the Sidebar or from the Contact Sheet view.

2 From the File menu, choose "Print…."

A Print dialog sheet slides down from the title bar, shown on the opposite page. Spend a few minutes looking through all the options; click on the menu that says "Preview" to see more options. You can experiment with different settings and see how they affect the preview on the left.

3 When you're satisfied with your settings, click "Print."

Click here to collapse this Print dialog sheet
to a smaller, less detailed dialog sheet.

To fax an image or document:

Not many computers today have an internal (or external) modem installed, and you
can't fax without one. You must have a modem to fax, and it must be connected
with a phone cable to a telephone outlet—you can't fax over the Internet.

If your Mac has a modem that is connected to a phone line, it is automatically
configured to send faxes.

1 From the File menu, choose "Print...."

2 Click the "PDF" button in the bottom-left corner of the Print dialog sheet.

3 Choose "Fax PDF...."

4 Enter the fax number you want to send this to.

5 Click the "Fax" button.

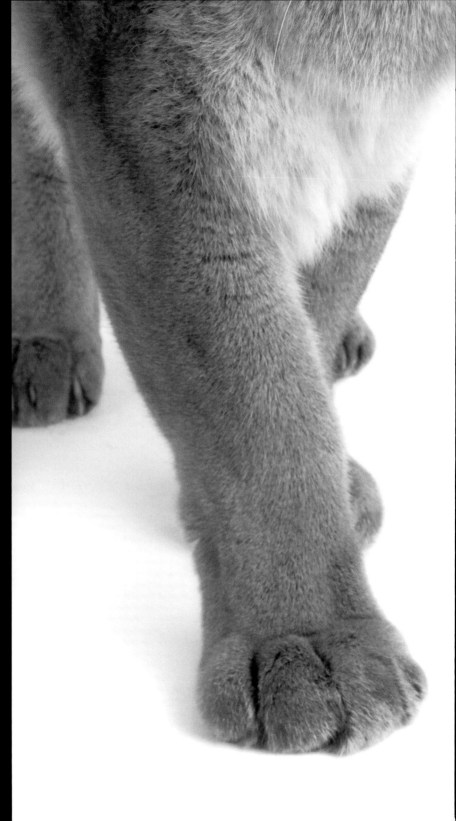

12

GOALS

Game Center for Playing with Friends

You're getting used to using your Mac to make you incredibly productive. Calendar, Contacts, Preview, and TextEdit save you lots of time. They might save you too much time. Perhaps you now have a bit of free time, and you're not sure what to do with it. Or maybe you're ready to have a little fun.

Lucky for you, there's Game Center. Game Center is an app that manages your collection of Mac games, keeping track of them and giving you an easy way to boast about your prowess to others. But it's much more than that. Use Game Center to connect with friends, and see what games they're playing and how well they are doing. Let's play.

The Game Center Window

Open Game Center from the Launchpad. The first time you start it up, you're prompted to enter an Apple ID and password. You'll need an Apple ID so that Game Center can keep track of your accomplishments in Game Center–enabled games and also to help you connect with friends.

To get started, enter your Apple ID and password and click "Sign In." Or create an Apple ID by clicking "Create Apple ID." There's nothing else you can do with Game Center until you're signed in.

These are the main site navigation buttons. But they're inactive until you've signed in.

Enter your Apple ID and password and click **Sign In**.

Drag any edge to resize.

Set Up Your Game Center Account

You've logged in, now what? It's time to set up your Game Center account so your friends can find you and be awed by your gaming prowess.

1 After you sign in, you have to agree to a very long set of terms and conditions (see below). Read them and, if you agree, check the "I have read and agree to these terms & conditions" checkbox. Whew. Click the "Accept" button.

Type in your **Nickname**. This will be the name all your friends see.

Check only if you want players you don't know to be able to see your profile.

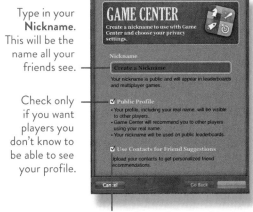

Read the terms and if you accept them, check the checkbox and click **Accept**.

If you check this, Game Center will look through your **Contacts** for other Game Center players you might know and suggest them as friends.

2 After you Accept, a new form opens. You need to select a nickname (above, right).

3 Decide if you want to allow all Game Center players to be able to see your profile. If you only want your friends to be able to see it, don't check the "Public Profile" box.

4 If you check the "Use Contacts for Friend Suggestions," Game Center finds any email addresses in your **Contacts** assigned to other Game Center players and suggests them as friends for you. If you don't mind Game Center looking through your contacts, check this box.

5 Click "Done." Your profile has been created.

Your user profile has been created. On mine, shown on the next page, I have a photo and a status message set. You can edit these and a few more items.

Edit your user profile:

- Much like a Facebook status message, Game Center lets you set a status. Enter one by clicking and typing on the brown rectangle just above the "Change Photo" banner.

- Change your photo by clicking the "Change Photo" banner. You can take a new snapshot of yourself with the camera, or use your Finder to find and drag a photo into the thumbnail.

- If you want to change your Account settings, click the "Account:" banner. You'll have to enter your password and then you'll be taken back to the screen where you selected your nickname.

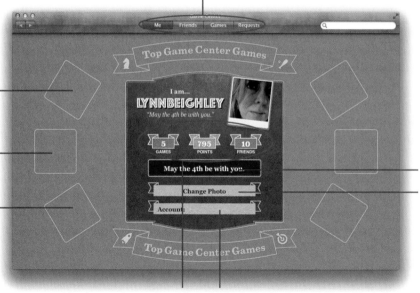

Now that you've set up your account and signed in, you can navigate Game Center with these buttons. To get to this screen at any time, click the "Me" button.

These yellow squares are used to highlight the most popular games currently being played in Game Center.

(Unfortunately, at the time of this writing, no Game Center games are available. By the time you're using Mountain Lion, you should see lots of games in these boxes.)

This is your current **Status**. To change it, type in this box.

Click the **Change Photo** banner to change your profile image. Or you can simply double-click your current image to open the Change Photo dialog.

Here's a quick summary of your Game Center activity.

Your email address will appear here. Click this banner to edit your account settings.

The profile displays your username, your image, a summary of how many Game Center games you play, your total points, and how many friends you have. The page contains two banner links: "Change Photo," which lets you modify your profile image, and "Account:<youremail>," which allows you to change your account settings.

Connect with Friends

The point of Game Center is to see and share game scores and achievements with your friends. Adding friends is easy. Open the Friends screen by clicking on the "Friends" button at the top of Game Center (see below).

This is your currently selected friend's stats. Click on each of these to see more specific information about what **Games** he plays, where he's earned **Points**, and who his **Friends** are.

Just like it says, click this banner to **Add Friends**.

Click to sort your list of friends three different ways: alphabetically, how recently they've used Game Center, or how many points they have.

This is the list of all your friends. Information about your currently selected friend (highlighted in blue) is displayed on the right.

Add a friend:

1 Click the "Friends" button to open the Friends screen.

2 Click the yellow "Add Friends" banner on the left. A window opens (see next page).

3 Type in your friend's email address or Game Center nickname. Customize the message if you wish.

4 Click Send. Your friend will be notified and will have to accept the request.

After you click this
Add Friends banner, the
Friend Request form opens.

Enter your friend's email
address or Game Center
username.

You can type in here to customize
the message your friend will receive.

Click Send and your friend
will get a request in his email.

Of course, other players may send you Friend requests. You'll get emails letting you know. It's also easy to find them in Game Center at any given moment so you can accept or ignore them.

You get an email message
like this when someone
sends you a Friend request.

Accept or ignore Friend requests:

1 Click the "Requests" button to open the Requests screen.

2 Any pending requests will show up on the left (see opposite page). Click on one and the details show up on the right.

3 Choose to "Accept" or "Ignore."

This is the list of all open friend requests. There's only one in this image. Information about the currently selected request (highlighted in blue) is displayed on the right, along with clickable banners to accept or ignore the request.

Click here to send out your own requests with the **Friend Request form** (previous page).

When you accept, your new friend appears in the list of your friends on the left side of the Friend page. Should you wish to remove a friend, click the friend's name in the friend list to open her information page and click the "Unfriend" banner link on the bottom of her page on the right.

Click on this rectangle to see a screen full of recommended potential friends, chosen for you based on your friends' friends and the games you play.

If you ever want to remove someone from your **Friends** list, select that person and click here.

Find recommended friends:

You're not limited to friends you invite or who invite you. You can view a list of recommended friends and consider sending them invitations if they play some of the same games you do.

1 Click the "Friends" button to open the Friends screen.

2 Click the "Friend Recommendations" block on the upper left. A window opens (see below).

3 Click through the list of potential friends on the left. Each listing shows how many friends you have in common and how many of the same games you play.

4 To send an invitation, click the "Send Friend Request" banner. Your potential friend will be notified and will have to accept the request.

Click here to navigate back to the main **Friends** page.

Click here to send this person a **Friend Request**.

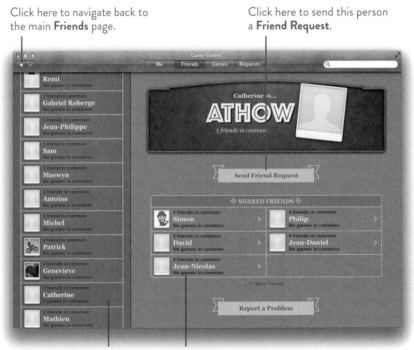

Click one of the people in this list to see her details on the right.

These are the friends you have in common.

Find and Buy Games

You've got your account and your friends. Now you're ready to play. There are many ways to find Game Center–enabled games to play. Here are a few:

- Click the "Games" button at the top of the Game Center (shown below) to see recommendations and top games. Or click "Find Game Center Games" at the bottom of the page. *Keep in mind* that at this moment, Game Center for OS X is brand new, and there aren't any games yet. By the time you reach this screen on your Game Center, you'll see lots of recommended games.

- Click the "Friends" button and select one of your friends. Click the button labeled "Games" to see what she plays and how well she's doing. Click on one of the games to see more details about it (image on right).

- On the "Me" page, you'll see all kinds of game icons scattered in the yellow squares. Click one to see details about that game and purchase it in the App Store.

There aren't any OS X games for Game Center just yet! This is why there are no recommendations and no games listed under the **OS X GAMES** section.

These are games you are currently playing. In my case, these are only iOS compatible (for example, iPhone or iPad). You'll soon see a list like this in the OS X rectangle of Game Center games you are playing on your Mac. **Be careful.** Don't buy any of the iOS games and expect to be able to play them on your Mac!

13

GOALS

Use the App Store
to get more tools!

Use the Burn Folder
to collect files for burning
to a CD or DVD

Create bookmarks in DVDs

Create a PDF from any file

Use Font Book to preview
and install fonts

Keep track of your life
with Stickies and Notes

Take photos and movies of
yourself with Photo Booth

Create and share movie
clips online with QuickTime

Share your display on
Apple TV with AirPlay

Miscellaneous Tools on Your Mac

Your Mac has a number of great tools in the form of small applications, some of which get overlooked. This lesson introduces you to some features and possibilities that you might not be taking advantage of yet.

Burn Folders make it easy to keep track of items you want to burn onto discs at a later date. The DVD Player has some great features that may surprise you, especially if you teach a class and use DVDs as part of your presentation. You'll be pleased how easy it is to create a PDF from any file. Font management is simple when you use Font Book. Applications like Stickies, Notes, and Photo Booth are both useful and fun. QuickTime Player makes creating, editing, and sharing video and audio files easy and fast, and AirPlay Sharing lets you view your media on any TV with Apple TV. Take a look at what you may have been missing!

The App Store: A Shop in Your Dock

The App Store icon in the Dock puts you a click away from Apple's online App Store where you can shop for all kinds of applications, browse app categories, read reviews and view average ratings, update an app, or buy a new one and download it directly to your Mac. Downloaded apps are automatically installed and appear in Launchpad, ready to go.

Click here to connect to the App Store.

Click Launchpad to access apps you downloaded from the App Store.

You need an Apple account and an active Internet connection. If you don't already have an Apple account, you can create one after you click a "Buy" button, or click the "Account" link in the "Quick Links" section of the App Store window (circled, below).

Click to exit the App Store.

Choose how to view the App Store.

Review purchases or download app updates.

Search for apps.

To select an app and learn more about it, click the price button, the app name, or the app icon.

When you find the app you want and go to its page, and you're ready to purchase, click the "Buy" button. Your credit card will be charged (the credit card you used to set up an Apple account), and your app will begin to download immediately. Careful, you'll get no confirmation screen!

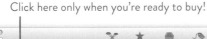

Click here only when you're ready to buy!

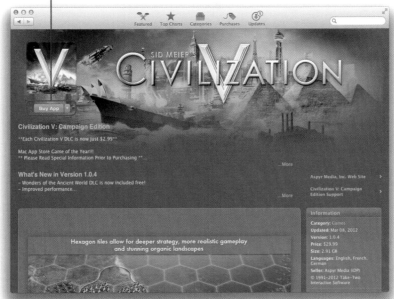

The download process places the new app in your Applications folder, and it is also accessible from Launchpad. Third-party apps (those not from Apple) appear in Launchpad on a secondary screen, not the first screen (reserved for Apple applications) that appears when you enter Launchpad.

To access the additional screens in Launchpad, first click the Launchpad icon in the Dock, then do one of the following:

- On a Magic Mouse, swipe left with one finger on the mouse surface.

- On a Multi-Touch trackpad, swipe left with two fingers on the surface.

- Click one of the small dots that appears near the bottom of the Launchpad screen but above the Dock. The white dot indicates which Launchpad screen is currently visible.

- Tap the right arrow key to go to the next Launchpad screen; tap the left arrow key to return to the previous screen.

Use a Burn Folder to Burn a CD or DVD

You need to make backups of your important work, as well as any applications, fonts, or other files that you download straight from the Internet.

The steps to burn data files (not music CDs or DVD movies) onto a disc are below (to burn a music CD, see Lesson 10). A CD holds about 650 megabytes; a single-layer DVD holds about 4.3 gigabytes, even though the package might say it holds 4.7.

Using a **Burn Folder** makes it very easy to collect your files over a period of time and then to burn a disc when you're ready. You just drop items into this special folder; your Mac puts **aliases** of the files in the Burn Folder and leaves the originals in their original locations. This means that after you burn the disc, you can throw away the entire Burn Folder without destroying any original files.

The great thing is that you can collect items you want to burn without having to actually burn the disc at that moment—you can collect files over the span of a project and when finished, you have a folder ready to back up onto a disc.

To create a Burn Folder, put files inside, and burn it:

1   Open a Finder window. Select the folder in which you want the Burn Folder to appear (you can move it at any time).

2   From the File menu, choose "New Burn Folder."

3   A folder with the "Burn" symbol on it (below) appears in the selected window.

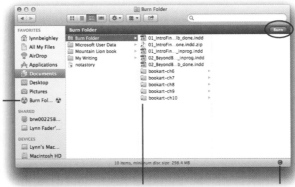

I put this Burn Folder in my Documents folder. Then I dragged it into the Sidebar so it's accessible no matter which folder I'm viewing.

The files in the Burn Folder are all aliases—you can tell by the tiny arrows in the bottom-left corner of each icon.

Click this refresh button to keep track of how much storage space you need for the files.

4 **To put a file or a folder in the Burn Folder** for later, just drag the original file or folder and drop it into the Burn Folder, either in the Sidebar or in its real location. Your Mac puts an *alias* of the file into the Burn Folder and the original stays right where it was, safe and sound.

5 **To burn the folder onto a disc,** first insert a blank CD or DVD.

6 **Then** select the Burn Folder, either the Sidebar icon or the actual folder that you made earlier. A dark gray bar across the top of the window appears with a "Burn" button, as shown circled on the opposite page.

Click that "Burn" button to start the process. You will be asked to first name the disc.

TIP —— As mentioned, to make the whole process easier, drag the Burn Folder into the Sidebar of any Finder window; you can drop files directly on that folder while it's in the Sidebar. The folder displays a burn icon next to it—you can single-click that burn icon to start the process.

TIP —— You can make as many Burn Folders as you want. Rename them like any other folder. This makes it easy to have a separate Burn Folder for each project.

To check the amount of storage space used in the folder:

1 Single-click the Burn Folder icon.

2 Press Command I to display the Info window.

3 Click the disclosure triangle next to "Burning."

4 Click the "Calculate" button to see how much you have collected in the folder.

You can also check the status bar at the bottom of the Burn Folder window. The text in the status bar tells you how many items are there and how much disc space will be required. (If the status bar isn't showing in the window, go to the View menu and choose "Show Status Bar.")

TIP —— If you change your mind and want to take an unburned disc out of the Mac, Control-click (or right-click) on the disk icon and choose "Eject *disk name.*"

DVD Player

 Besides playing your DVDs and allowing you to control viewing as you do on a DVD player connected to your television, this DVD Player has several special tricks.

Display the thumbnail bar and controls

When a video plays in full screen mode (Command F), do the following:

To see the DVD playback controls, move your pointer anywhere on the screen and they appear.

To see the thumbnail bar that displays chapter markers, bookmarks, and video clips, move your pointer near the top of the screen.

To show the DVD application menu bar, move your pointer all the way to the top of the screen.

These same controls can be found in the floating DVD player, in the Window menu, and in the Controls menu (important to know if you're not using full-screen view).

Create bookmarks to find specific points in the video

A bookmark lets you skip immediately to certain points in the video that you choose. That is, you are not limited to the chapter markers that were created when the DVD was made. These bookmarks are *not* stored with the DVD; they are stored only on the Mac on which they were made. If you loan the DVD to anyone, it will not include your bookmarks.

To create a bookmark:

1 Start a DVD.

2 Go to the Window menu and choose "Bookmarks." The Bookmarks panel opens. When you get to the point in the DVD where you want to insert a bookmark, click the **+** button at the bottom of the "Bookmarks" panel.

   Or go to the Controls menu and choose "New Bookmark...."

3 In the dialog sheet that opens, name the bookmark, then click "Add."

Once you have created bookmarks, use the Go menu and skip straight to any bookmark you made, *or* open the Bookmarks pane from the Window menu and double-click the thumbnail that represents the bookmark you want.

DVD region codes

A commercial DVD, such as a Hollywood movie DVD, usually has a *region code* assigned to it in an attempt to fight piracy of worldwide releases of movies. The first time you use DVD Player to watch a DVD that has a region assigned to it, you will get a dialog (shown below) in which to set a "region" number for your DVD drive (not for the disk). Different regions of the world have different numbers assigned to them, so if you don't assign the code for your area, you won't be able to watch DVDs from that area.

If in the future you insert a DVD that uses a different region code than the one you have assigned, a dialog appears asking if you want to change your DVD drive's code to match it. Be aware, however, that this can be changed only five times (including the first setting), and the fifth time is permanent.

To see your DVD drive's current region code,
go to the File menu, choose "Get Disc Info," then click the "Regions" icon in the toolbar.

To change your DVD drive's region code,
click one of the numbered regions on the map. North America is Region 1.

Make DVD video and audio adjustments

To adjust DVD settings for video zoom, audio equalizer, and video color, go to the Window menu, then choose the adjustment you want to make. Use the sliders to make adjustments. Each set of controls provides a pop-up menu of presets in the top-right corner.

Create your own personal disc jacket on the screen

This is great—you can add your own image to the DVD so whenever you stop the DVD, it displays the image of *your* choice.

To add your own image to the disk:

1 Open a DVD in the DVD Player.

2 Go to the File menu and choose "Get Disc Info."

3 Click the "Jacket Picture" icon in the toolbar, shown circled below.

4 Drag any image from your hard disk and drop it into the well. Click OK. Cool.

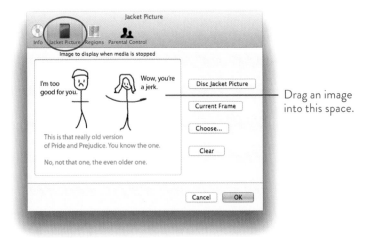

Remember, changes like this don't really apply to the actual DVD—they are stored on your Mac. So the disc jacket will only appear if you show this DVD from the computer on which you added it.

Go back to the Finder

When a DVD is playing full-screen, there are several ways to exit full-screen mode without interrupting the DVD playback:

Press Command F (Command F toggles you in and out of full-screen).

Or push your pointer to the top of the screen until the top menu appears, then go to the Go menu and choose "Switch To Finder." *Or* press Command Option F (both of which put the movie *behind* any open Finder windows).

Or tap the Escape key (esc).

Or go to the View menu and choose one of the size options there (including "Exit Full Screen").

Create PDF Files

A PDF (Portable Document Format) is a file created in such a way that most people can open and read it, no matter what kind of computer they use. The graphics, the images, the fonts, and all the formatting are held intact in the document. And it's usually compressed into a smaller file size (not physical size) so it can travel through the Internet quickly or be stored efficiently.

To make a PDF in most applications:

1 Open a document.

2 From the File menu choose "Print…."

3 Click the "PDF" button in the bottom-left corner of the Print dialog.

4 Choose "Save as PDF…."

"Save as PDF…" saves a regular PDF that you can share with others. The graphics are at full resolution and the fonts are embedded.

You can **password-protect a PDF file.** When you choose to save as a PDF, you'll see a "Security Options" button. Click it to open a dialog where you can create a password so no one can open, copy, or print the document without it.

When someone tries to open a password-protected PDF, this password dialog opens.

—continued

Open PDF in Preview

This comes in handy when you want to annotate the document, create links, etc., before sending it to someone else. See Lesson 11.

Save as PostScript

This saves the document as a PostScript Level 2 file in ASCII format, meaning that if you open it, you'll see a lot of code. But you can send it directly to a PostScript printer or run it through Acrobat Distiller. Don't choose this option unless you know you need it.

Fax PDF

If you have set up your fax specifications, then your Mac will make a PDF of the document and open the fax dialog box where you can enter the fax number and a message. Remember, you must have a phone modem attached to the Mac with a phone line connected.

Add PDF to iTunes

This adds the PDF to the Books section of iTunes. If you use iTunes to sync an iPhone or iPad, the PDF will be available on those mobile devices in the iBooks app. If you have PDF documents you need to read while on the go, this is a great way to make them available on your mobile devices.

Mail PDF

This creates a PDF of the file, opens Mail, creates a new message, and puts this PDF in the message ready to send. This is a great time-saver, but we've noticed that people using AOL or PCs often can't read these.

Save PDF to Web Receipts Folder

I love this. Have you ever bought something on the web and you got that page that says, "This is your receipt"? And you know you should print it but maybe the printer isn't turned on at the moment or it's three pages long and you know they're going to send you an email receipt anyway, but what if they don't send you the email receipt and you need this web page receipt? Well, this is a great solution: The Mac saves this web page as a PDF, makes you a folder in your Documents folder called "Web Receipts," and stores this PDF (and all others you make like it) in that folder. Thank you.

Web Receipts

Be careful, though—if you make a web receipt from the same site more than once, it will probably write over itself with the same name. Some sites automatically name their receipt file something generic like "Acme Receipt." So when you create another PDF from Acme, it gets named the same thing as all the other receipts from Acme, and the newest version replaces the last one you created.

Since this method doesn't give you a chance to customize the file name, it can be safer to choose "Save as PDF" in the Print dialog (shown on page 233). You can still create a Web Receipts folder in the Documents folder, or wherever you prefer, and save your files into it.

If you're adventurous, you can search the Internet for an Applescript that will automatically append a date and time to the file name when you choose "Save PDF to Web Receipts Folder."

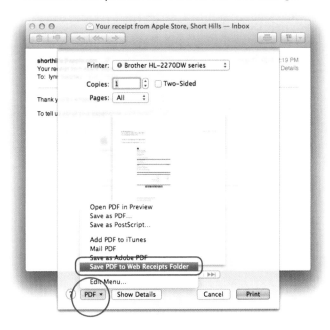

Font Book

Font Book allows you to install new **fonts** you acquire, disable fonts in your font menus that you never use, and view fonts before you install them.

Preview and install fonts

If you have some fonts or acquire new ones and you don't know what they are, double-click the font file. Font Book opens and displays the font. **To install it,** click the "Install Font" button.

Select the "All Fonts" collection to see all the fonts available to you. The other collections are subsets of "All Fonts."

Install fonts

If you have a number of fonts to install, this might be easier:

1 Open Font Book (it's in your Applications folder and in Launchpad). If you don't see the Font Book window (above-right), go to the Window menu and choose "Font Book."

2 In the "Collection" pane, Control-click (or right-click) "All Fonts." In the sheet that slides down, choose "Add Fonts...." Select fonts or folders of fonts (hold down the Command key to select multiple files), then click "Open."

3 The first time you do this, Font Book creates a new collection for you, called "User," and installs the fonts in this collection. These fonts are available only to your user account, not to other users you may have created (see Lesson 20).

4 Font Book puts a *copy* of the fonts in the default install folder. You can then keep the original fonts in their original location, store the originals in some other location, copy them to a backup disk, or put them in the Trash.

To install fonts for all users, go to the Font Book menu and choose "Preferences...." Set "Default Install Location" to "Computer."

Preview installed fonts

Single-click any typeface name in the "Font" pane of Font Book. A preview appears to the right. Use the slider to enlarge or reduce the typeface, or type in a point size.

Go to the Preview menu and choose:

- "Sample" to display the upper and lowercase letters, as well as the numbers.

- "Repertoire" to see every glyph (letter, number, punctuation, etc.) in the font.

- "Custom," and then type. Your words will display in this typeface (as shown below). Use the slider bar on the right to enlarge the font.

Click these buttons to choose *Sample, Repertoire, or Custom.*

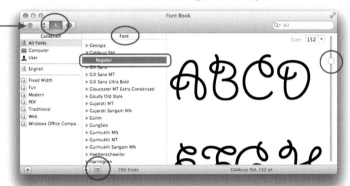

Drag the slider to adjust the text preview size. Or set a point size with the "Size" data field or pop-up menu, in the top-right corner.

To disable an individual font, find it in the Font list. Single-click to select it, then click the little checkmark button (circled, above) at the bottom of the Font list. When the checkmark is removed, the font name is dimmed and the word "Off" appears to the right of the font name.

To view only the English language fonts, click the Collection named "English."

Create your own Collections

A **Collection** is a subset of the installed fonts and is simply an easy way to look at fonts you like instead of having to grope through a lengthy font list of typefaces you don't know or want.

To make a new Collection, single-click the **+** sign at the bottom of the Collection pane, then name it. Click the "All Fonts" collection (so you can access all fonts), then drag font names from the Font pane to the new Collection name.

To disable (turn off) an entire Collection, select it in the Collection pane. Then go to the Edit menu and choose "Disable *collection name.*"

Stickies

The **Stickies** application lets you put little sticky notes all over your screen, just like you'd stick them around the edge of your monitor. Open Stickies from Launchpad. (They might be under the *Other* grouping.)

Notice in the examples above you can see these features:

- The shopping list above is a **bulleted list.**

  To make a bulleted or numbered list, click inside a note.

  Hold down the Option key and tap the Tab key once.

  Let go of the Option key and type your first item.

  To continue the list, just hit Return after each item. You can hit Option-Tab to indent an extra level.

  To end the list, hit Return twice.

  To choose from a variety of bullets and numbers, or add a prefix and/or a suffix to the bullet: Control-click anywhere in the list; from the contextual menu that appears, choose "List...." The list includes a variety of Greek and Asian characters. You can change the bullet formatting at any time. You can create a numbered list that uses such prefixes as **(1)** or **Act 1:** or **•A•** or any other combination.

- You can **change fonts, size, color,** etc., just as in any other Mac application, using the Font panel (press Command T).

- Double-click in the title bar of any Sticky note to "roll it up" so **just the title bar shows,** as you can see on the opposite page. The first line of type appears in the title bar. Double-click the title bar again to unroll the note.

- Hover your mouse over any note to display a **tool tip** of information about when the note was created and modified, as shown on the opposite page.

- Drag a **graphic** image from anywhere on your Mac and drop it into the Sticky note, as shown by the photo on the opposite page.

- A sticky can hold many pages of text and graphics. You might not see **scroll bars** until you start to scroll. **Resize a Sticky note** just as you would any other window—drag any edge or any corner.

- Notice the red dots under the name *Marcell.* This is a visual clue that the **spell checker** is on and working. Control-click (or right-click) the underlined word, then choose one of the suggested spellings from the contextual menu. To set spell-checking options, Control-click on the note, choose "Spelling and Grammar," then choose one of the options in the contextual menu.

- If you prefer working with a certain font and a certain size and a certain color note, you can **set a default** so all your notes look like that without having to select your favorite specifications for every note. Set up one note the way you like it, then go to the Note menu and choose "Use as Default."

- If you want your Sticky notes to **automatically open** and appear every time you turn on your computer, add Stickies to the Login Items for your user account (see Lesson 20).

- **To print a note,** from the File menu, choose "Print…." Set your print options as you would with any other document. If you want to print multiple notes at once, you can copy and paste them into a single note, then print.

- You can quickly **add a screenshot** of something on your Desktop and have it appear immediately in a note: Click the cursor in the note where you want to place a screenshot. Control-click the note, then from the contextual menu choose "Capture Selection from Screen." Drag across the part of the screen you want to capture. When you release the drag operation, the captured selection automatically appears in the note.

- **To discard a Sticky note,** click the tiny box in the top-left corner.

Notes

The **Notes** application is your virtual notepad. You can write quick notes to yourself and access them with iCloud on all your other devices (for more about iCloud, see Lesson 23). Open Notes from Launchpad.

Search through your notes for specific words or phrases.

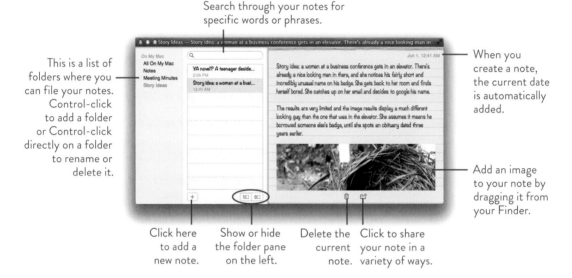

This is a list of folders where you can file your notes. Control-click to add a folder or Control-click directly on a folder to rename or delete it.

When you create a note, the current date is automatically added.

Add an image to your note by dragging it from your Finder.

Click here to add a new note.

Show or hide the folder pane on the left.

Delete the current note.

Click to share your note in a variety of ways.

Notes shares features with Sticky Notes and TextEdit.

- **To make a bulleted or numbered list,** click the Format menu and choose Lists. Or hold down the Option key and tap the Tab key once, and **to end the list,** hit Return twice.

- **Change to a different set of bullets and numbers,** or add a prefix and/or a suffix to the bullet: select the entire list and choose the "Format" menu. Mouse over "List..." and choose the list option you want. Control-clicking the selected list also works; from the contextual menu you can choose "List...."

- **Control fonts, size, color,** and other common font features by highlighting some text and choosing "Format", then "Fonts," and then choosing "Show Fonts".

- Drag a **graphic** image from anywhere on your Mac and drop it into your note, as shown by the photo on the opposite page.

- As with Sticky Notes and TextEdit, you can use **spell checker** with Notes. Set spell-checking options. From the Edit menu, choose "Spelling and Grammar" and any specific options in that menu. Also check out **dictation** (Lesson 14).

- **You can print your notes.** Open the note you want to print. From the File menu, choose "Print…."

- **To discard a note,** open the note and click on the trashcan icon at the bottom.

- **To share your notes via email or Messages,** open the note and click the Share button to see the Share Sheets menu.

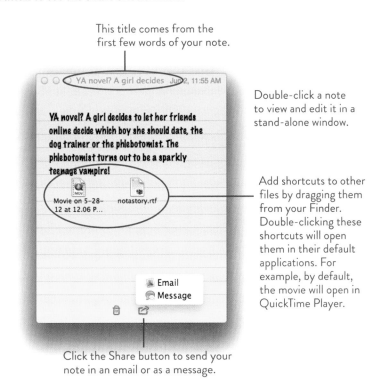

This title comes from the first few words of your note.

Double-click a note to view and edit it in a stand-alone window.

Add shortcuts to other files by dragging them from your Finder. Double-clicking these shortcuts will open them in their default applications. For example, by default, the movie will open in QuickTime Player.

Click the Share button to send your note in an email or as a message.

Photo Booth

Photo Booth is a convenient and fun way to take snapshots or movies of yourself for use as a Messages buddy picture or as your user account picture. You can email the photos or movie clips to friends, upload them to web pages, open in Preview to save in other formats, or view as a slideshow.

Take a still picture

1 Open Photo Booth (if it's not in your Dock, it's in Launchpad).

2 Click the *still picture* button (the middle button in the row of three).

3 Click the red camera button (circled, below-left). A red countdown timer replaces the toolbar (below-right) and starts a countdown, including audible beeps. Your screen flashes when the picture is taken, and a thumbnail version of the picture appears in the thumbnails pane at the bottom of the window.

When you click the red camera button . . .   a countdown begins.

4 Click a thumbnail to display it in the main window. As soon as you do this, a new button with sharing tools (shown to the right) appears. Click this button to send the photo in an email message, place it in iPhoto, tweet it, set it as your user Account photo, use it as an Messages picture, and more.

To delete a snapshot, select its thumbnail, then click the **X** on the thumbnail. *Or* select a thumbnail, then hit Delete.

Add effects to snapshots or video

Photo Booth includes a gallery of special effects that you can apply *as you take a snapshot or record a movie clip.* That is, you can't apply these effects after you've taken the photo—you have to choose an effect *before* you snap the photo.

1 Click the Effects button (circled, below-right) to show a pane of effects (below-left). The center image always shows a *Normal* preview (no effects) that you can select to remove all effects and return the image to normal.

2 Click the arrows on either side of the Effects button (below-left) to see the options.

3 Click the effect you want. A full-size preview displays in the window (below-right).

4 Click one of the snapshot buttons on the left side to choose the type of snapshot you want (*4-up, still picture,* or *movie clip*), then click the red camera button. The special effect snapshot (or movie clip, as explained on the following page) appears in the row of thumbnails.

5 Select the image in the thumbnail strip and tools appear in the Toolbar (previous page, bottom-right) so you can share it: Attach the image to an email message, add it to iPhoto, or set it as your account picture in Mail, Contacts, or Messages.

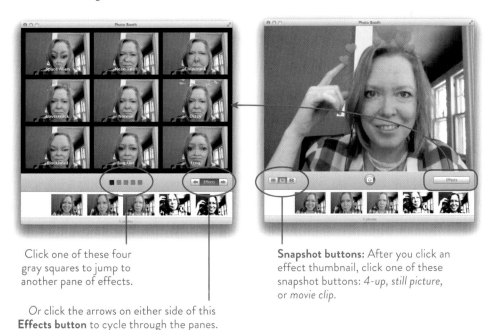

Click one of these four gray squares to jump to another pane of effects.

Or click the arrows on either side of this **Effects button** to cycle through the panes.

Snapshot buttons: After you click an effect thumbnail, click one of these snapshot buttons: *4-up, still picture,* or *movie clip.*

Create a special effects backdrop

In the gallery of special effects (previous page), the last Effects pane is full of empty "User Backdrop" spaces. You can add your own photos or movie clips to be used as a special effects backdrop for Photo Booth still photos or movie clips. It works the same as creating backdrop effects in Messages, explained in Lesson 9.

The 4-up option

The 4-up button takes four photos, much like the old photo booths that used to be in drug stores and malls, at county fairs, and almost everywhere.

To print a 4-up collection of photos, select the 4-up thumbnail, then from the File menu, choose "Print."

To view (or print) just one of the 4-up photos, select the 4-up thumbnail, then in the preview pane, click one of the four photos to make it fill the pane.

To save one of the 4-up photos to another location, first click one of the four, as described above. When it fills the preview pane, drag it from the preview pane to your Desktop, or drag it to any folder or window.

To locate any of the Photo Booth photo files or movies on your computer, Control-click a thumbnail, then choose "Reveal in Finder."

— The 4-up effect.

Don't forget all the sharing options. You can share the 4-up image or you can select one of the individual shots, then share it.

TIP ——— To **preview** all of your snapshots that are lined up in the thumbnail strip, go to the View menu at the top of the screen and choose "Start Slideshow." **To exit the slideshow,** press the Escape key.

Make a movie clip of yourself at your computer

1 Click the movie clip button (the film strip icon, shown here, selected).

2 The camera button in the center of the toolbar changes to a red video button: Click it to begin recording.

While recording, the toolbar shows a timer, and the red video button changes to a *Stop Recording* button (below). When you stop recording, a thumbnail of the movie clip is placed in the thumbnails pane at the bottom of the window.

3 Select the movie clip thumbnail and mouse over it in the view window. You have the following options:

■ To trim the movie (delete frames from the start or ending) to a smaller size, click the "Trim" button on the right side of the scrubber bar. Drag the yellow handles to a start point and end point, then click the checkmark to commit the change.

■ Click the Share button and choose "Email" to attach a QuickTime version of the clip to a message in Mail. Or click "Add to iPhoto" to send the movie to iPhoto. You may also want to get an account with Vimeo and post your video there.

■ To save the clip locally as a .mov (QuickTime) movie, drag the video thumbnail to your Desktop or to any folder on your computer.

■ To use a single frame of the movie clip for your user Account photo, Buddy photo, or Twitter profile image, select the movie thumbnail. Move your pointer over the movie preview pane to make the scrubber bar appear. Drag the playhead under the clip (circled, below) to select the frame you want, then click the "Account Picture", "Buddy Picture", or "Change Twitter Profile Picture" option under the Share button. You can also Message a single frame of the video.

The playhead.

245

QuickTime Player

QuickTime is multimedia software that you can use to play and edit movies and audio files. When you double-click a QuickTime file, it should open in the QuickTime Player—but it might not.

If the multimedia file you double-click is an older one, created or saved with QuickTime 7, you may get a message with a download link that tells you to download QuickTime Player 7 in order to play the old, dusty, ancient file from a whole year ago.

Playing a movie in the newest QuickTime Player is a much more aesthetically pleasing visual experience. The QuickTime Player provides controls to trim files (edit the movie or audio file duration), as well as menu options that can automatically send a QuickTime file to iTunes, your online MobileMe Gallery (if you have a MobileMe account), YouTube (if you have a free YouTube account), and several other options.

You can also use QuickTime Player to create a new movie recording (using your Mac's built-in camera or an external camera), a new audio recording, or a new screen recording (capture a movie of whatever is happening on your screen).

Play a movie or audio file

1 Click the QuickTime icon in the Dock or in Launchpad to open the Player.

2 From the File menu, choose "Open File..." and then select a movie (or audio) file you want to play.

An Audio file opens as a small window with playback controls (right).

A movie opens in QuickTime's elegant movie window, with a playback control bar visible (shown on the opposite page).

Click the Play button to play the audio file.

Toggle full screen.

Access sharing options.

Volume control.

Reverse, Play, Fast Forward.

Playhead.

3 Click the Play button. When you move the pointer away from the window, the title bar and control bar disappear to present the movie in an uncluttered window (shown below). To show the controls again, move the pointer over the window.

Share a movie

QuickTime can quickly and easily send movies to your YouTube, Flickr, Facebook, or iTunes, among other accounts. And you can send audio files to iTunes.

1 Open a movie file in QuickTime (as explained in this lesson, "Play a movie or audio file").

2 Click the Share button in the QuickTime playback control bar (You should be used to seeing this button by now; it appears on most of your apps!). From the pop-up menu, choose one of the options: Save your movie to iTunes, YouTube (a free YouTube account is required), or one of the many other options, such as Flickr or Facebook. You can also go to the Share menu to see these options.

Trim a movie or audio file

QuickTime makes it very easy to save or share just a partial selection of a movie or audio file.

1 Open a movie file in QuickTime (as explained as explained in this lesson, "Play a movie or audio file").

2 Go to View and choose "Show Clips."

A thumbnail movie timeline appears at the bottom of the movie window.

3 Go to Edit and choose "Trim". Or just double-click the movie timeline. A yellow border appears with handles on the left and right sides.

4 **To trim a *movie* clip:** Drag the left and right sides of the yellow border to
select the section of video you want to keep. After you make a selection, the
dark gray "Trim" button highlights in yellow (shown in the bottom example).
Click "Trim."

The movie can now be duplicated (from the File menu, choose "Duplicate"),
exported (from the File menu, choose "Export…"), or shared (from the Share
button, choose iTunes, YouTube, or other media-sharing options).

5 **To trim an *audio* file:** Open it in QuickTime. From the Edit menu, choose "Trim."
An audio waveform bar appears on the file's window, highlighted with a yellow
border. Drag the ends of the trim border to
select the section of the file you want, then
click the "Trim" button. Now you can export
or share the audio file.

Make a movie clip of yourself at the computer

If you have a built-in camera or a video camera attached, you can record a movie using QuickTime, then share it with others (explained on the opposite page).

1   Open QuickTime Player. From the File menu, choose "New Movie Recording."

2   Click the red *Record* button on the Control bar. If you don't see a Control bar, hover your pointer over the movie window to make it appear; the Control bar disappears when you move your pointer away from the window.

3   To stop recording, click the black *Stop Recording* button that replaced the red *Record* button. The Control bar changes to playback controls, so you can play the new movie.

4   If you close the movie window (click the red button in the top-left corner) without choosing to *export* or *share* it, it is automatically saved in the Movies folder in your Home folder, as a file named "Screen Recording." To export or share the movie, see the opposite page.

Click here to show options such as camera and quality settings, and where to save.

Make a new audio recording

If you have a built-in microphone or an external mic connected to your Mac, you can make audio recordings with QuickTime.

1   Open QuickTime. From the File menu, choose "New Audio Recording."

2   Click the red *Record* button in the "Audio Recording" window (shown to the right).

3   To stop recording, click the black *Stop Recording* button that has replaced the *Record* button.

To share or export your movie

Share: Go to the Share menu or Share button and choose an option.

Export: Export your movie, optimized for *syncing directly* with iPad, iPhone, Apple TV, or iPod Touch. From the File menu, choose "Export...." From the "Format" pop-up menu, choose the range of devices you want to optimize for: "iPod Touch & iPhone 3GS," or "480p."

To export a version optimized for web delivery to mobile devices (or to your computer), go to the File menu and choose "Export for Web...." A dialog opens so you can name and save the movie, and select which web-delivery option you want to create a version for: Broadband (fastest connection speed, highest quality movie), Wi-Fi (moderate connection speed, pretty good movie quality), Cellular (slow connection speed, lowest quality).

Make a new screen recording

If you want to record the activity on your screen—for instructional purposes, or perhaps to record a streaming event on the Internet, or for any other reason—use QuickTime to make a screen recording. Then share your recording as explained above.

1 Open QuickTime. From the File menu, choose "New Screen Recording."

2 In the "Screen Recording" window that opens (below), click the red button.

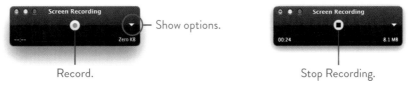

Record.

Show options.

Stop Recording.

3 The message shown below appears on the screen. Click anywhere on the screen to record the entire screen, or drag to select a specific part of the screen.

Click to record the full screen. Drag to record part of the screen.

4 **Recording starts** as soon as you click or drag. **To stop recording,** click the *Stop Recording* button that appears in the "Screen Recording" window.

If you don't choose to share or export the screen recording the movie is automatically saved in the Movies folder in your Home folder, with the default name "Screen Recording."

AirPlay Mirroring

If you have Apple TV, **AirPlay Mirroring** lets you broadcast your Mac's desktop to your TV. You no longer have to hook your computer up to a TV; you simply turn on AirPlay Mirroring and your display is up there for everyone to easily see. And that's not all. Any iTunes media or movie files can be easily shared so you can view them on your TV, complete with sound. Imagine, next time your family comes to visit, instead of making them huddle around your Mac's screen, show them your photos and movies from your trip to Mount Rushmore on your 60-inch plasma screen. George Washington never looked so good!

AirPlay your desktop

1 Make sure your Apple TV is on and linked in to the same Wi-Fi network as your Mac.

2 Click the AirPlay icon in the upper-right corner of your screen. It should be there as soon as your Apple TV is hooked up and on your network.

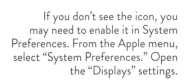

Click here to Air Play your Mac desktop to your TV.

3 From AirPlay menu, select Apple TV. Your desktop should now be visible on your TV!

4 To turn it off again, go back to the AirPlay menu and choose "Turn off AirPlay Mirroring." Easy.

If you don't see the icon, you may need to enable it in System Preferences. From the Apple menu, select "System Preferences." Open the "Displays" settings.

Set this to "Automatically" to detect when an Apple TV is on the same wireless network as your Mac. When it is, the AirPlay icon will appear in your toolbar.

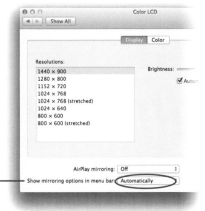

AirPlay movies and shows from iTunes

When you mirror your display, you won't hear any sound. That's not very useful when you want to watch a movie you've rented or purchased on iTunes on your TV. Fortunately, iTunes has an AirPlay control built in that sends the full-screen movie and sound directly to your TV.

1 Make sure your Apple TV is on and linked in to the same Wi-Fi network as your Mac.

2 Open iTunes and find the movie or show you want to watch. Begin watching it.

3 Find the AirPlay menu on the bottom right of the screen (see below) and select "Apple TV." When you're done, choose "Computer" from the same menu to end AirPlay.

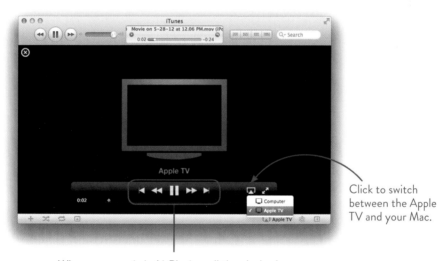

Click to switch between the Apple TV and your Mac.

When your movie is AirPlaying, all the playback controls are active on your Mac.

14

GOALS

Learn to use the tools that all Apple applications share

Dictation

Spell checker and grammar checker

Fonts panel

Data Detector

Colors panel

Speech

Preview a page before printing

Dictionary

Share Sheets

LESSON **14**

Common Tools in OS X Applications

Every Apple application that comes on your Mac uses certain tools—the spelling and grammar checker, the Colors panel, the Fonts panel, the Dictionary, and a few others. Rather than tell you how to use each one within a certain application, included here are explanations of how to use each tool regardless of which application you're using it in.

Many applications from other vendors also take advantage of these Apple tools, so look for them—they will make your computing life easier and more fun.

Spell Checker

Options for the spell checker are found at the bottom of the Edit menu in Apple applications. You can also turn these features on or off as defaults in the preferences for the application. The menu option will override the default for that document.

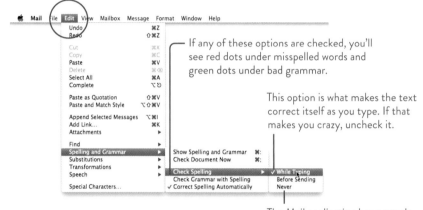

If any of these options are checked, you'll see red dots under misspelled words and green dots under bad grammar.

This option is what makes the text correct itself as you type. If that makes you crazy, uncheck it.

The Mail application has a couple of extra options that you won't find in, say, TextEdit.

Show Spelling and Grammar: This brings up the dialog box shown below. This spell checker runs through your entire document and gives you options for each word it thinks is misspelled.

If you want the spell checker to also alert you to possible grammar mistakes, click the box in the bottom-right corner to "Check grammar."

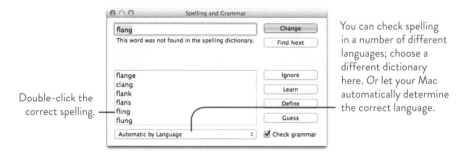

Double-click the correct spelling.

You can check spelling in a number of different languages; choose a different dictionary here. Or let your Mac automatically determine the correct language.

To replace a misspelled word with an alternative, find the word you think is correct in the lower pane, then double-click it. *Or* you can type the correct spelling yourself in the top edit box, then click the "Change" button.

Ignore the spelling temporarily: If the spell checker keeps telling you the same word is misspelled, but you like the word spelled the way it is, click the "Ignore" button when that word is highlighted by the spell checker. The spell checker will ignore it for this document, but will correct you again in the next document.

Teach your spell checker new words: Spell checkers typically don't recognize most people's names or jargon specific to different specialities (as shown below). If you often use a particular word that the spell checker thinks is a mistake (because it's not in the dictionary it's using), click the "Learn" button in the dialog box and the word gets added to the current dictionary. It will never bother you again.

Or if you're not using the spell checker dialog box at the moment, Control-click (or right-click) a word that the spell checker thinks is a mistake (it probably has little red dots under it). In the contextual menu that pops up, click the "Learn Spelling" option while the word is selected. The spell checker will add that word to its dictionary and not whine about it being misspelled again. If the word is misspelled, spelling suggestions will appear at the top of the contextual menu.

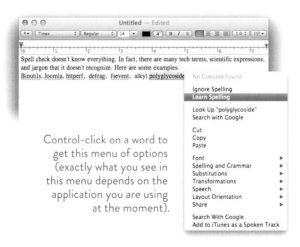

Control-click on a word to get this menu of options (exactly what you see in this menu depends on the application you are using at the moment).

Other useful commands for spelling and grammar

The following useful commands are also found in the Edit menu, under "Spelling and Grammar."

Check Document Now

Choose this command to check the document for misspelling and grammar mistakes. *Or* use this keyboard shortcut (Command ;) to skim through the spelling in your document without opening the "Spelling and Grammar" dialog box. It will stop at each word it thinks is misspelled. Well, the dictionary might think it's misspelled, but it might be your Grandmother's name, Euphemia, that you don't want to change.

Check Spelling While Typing

This marks words that are misspelled as you type them—little red dots appear beneath words it thinks are misspelled. Any words not in its dictionary are considered misspelled, such as many names of people or towns and most specialized jargon.

Check Grammar With Spelling

Choosing this option automatically selects the checkbox in the dialog box, "Check grammar." It does what it says it does—applies standard grammatical rules to your text and lets you know if you're breaking any of those rules.

Instead of red dots that indicate a misspelled word, the grammar checker puts green dots under a word or phrase. Mouse over the word, pause to the count of three, and you will see a tool tip appear that tells you what the problem is. It's up to you to fix it.

We goes to see the animal.

> The word 'goes' may not agree with the rest of the sentence.

Correct Spelling Automatically

You've probably become accustomed to this feature while texting on your phone. You can turn it on or off either from the Edit menu (which applies to the open document) or globally for all future documents (use the preferences panel from the application menu).

To change a misspelled word quickly without bringing up a dialog box:

1 Control-click (or right-click) a misspelled word (you don't need to highlight the word first).

2 A contextual menu appears, as shown below. At the top of this menu is a short list of alternative spellings for the word you clicked on.

3 Just single-click the correct spelling in the menu—the word is instantly corrected and the menu automatically disappears.

If the correct word is not offered, you can either type the correction yourself, or slide down to "Spelling and Grammar" in this menu and then choose "Check Document Now" from the submenu to run a spell check.

Even if the spell checker thinks it's misspelled, use your own judgment when deciding whether or not to change it. In some cases, such as the use of an uncommon name or a slang word you use frequently, you might want to tell it to "ignore" unusual spellings, although not in this case!

Fonts Panel

Press Command T in any Apple application and the Fonts panel appears, as shown below. If yours doesn't look like the one below, it might be because the Preview pane or the Effects bar is not showing.

Preview

■ **To display the Preview pane and/or the Effects bar** if they're not already visible, single-click the Action menu button (circled, below). Then choose "Show Preview." Click the menu again and choose "Show Effects."

Or drag the dot shown below.

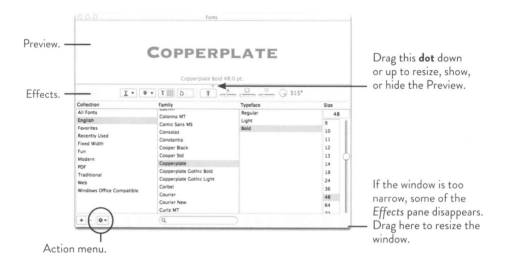

Preview.

Effects.

Drag this **dot** down or up to resize, show, or hide the Preview.

If the window is too narrow, some of the *Effects* pane disappears. Drag here to resize the window.

Action menu.

In any Apple (or Apple-compliant) application, open this Fonts panel to choose the typeface Family, the particular style (called "Typeface"), and the Size of type. Whatever you choose here will change the *selected* characters in your document. Note that you must **first select the text** you want to change, *then* choose the font and size. *Or* position the insertion point (the flashing bar in the text) where you want to start typing, then select the font and size right *before* you start typing.

Effects

You can apply **shadow effects** to selected text with these five controls, as shown below. Select text on the page, click the "Text Shadow" button (the button with the T), then drag the sliders of the other four tools (Opacity, Blur, Offset, and Angle).

When this button is blue, it's a *visual clue* that the *selected* text has a shadow effect applied to it.

Collections

The Fonts panel has a number of **Collections,** which are simply subgroups of fonts from the main list. Making a Collection does not disable or enable any fonts; it just makes it easier for you to choose a typeface—you don't have to scroll through a long list of fonts you don't care for.

To create a Collection, single-click the plus sign at the bottom of the Collection pane. Rename the Collection. Drag font families from the "Family" pane into the new Collection—drop the family name directly on the Collection name.

Favorites

If you find you often use a particular family, typeface, point size, and color, turn that combination into a Favorite and keep it in the Favorites collection for easy access. Just select the text on the page that is formatted as you like it, *or* choose your favorite combination in the Fonts panel. Then go to the Action button and choose "Add to Favorites."

When you want to use that typeface, single-click the collection called "Favorites" to display the combination. Select your text, then choose your favorite.

Action button options

Color: See page 264.
Characters: This displays the Characters viewer; see the next page.
Typography: Choose sophisticated options for certain typefaces.
Edit Sizes: Customize how font sizes are displayed in the Fonts panel.
Manage Fonts: This opens the Font Book; see Lesson 13.

Characters Viewer

Apple provides access to all sorts of **extra characters,** such as arrows; technical symbols; math and music symbols; dorky little clip art images; emoticons; currency symbols from around the world; geometric shapes; divination signs; Korean, Arabic, Greek, Cyrillic, Hebrew, and Chinese characters; and more. How do you know which characters are available? Use the **Characters** viewer.

At the bottom of most Edit menus is an option called "Special Characters...." This displays the Characters viewer, as shown below.

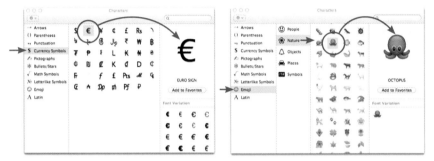

Here are two views of the Characters viewer. Click on a symbol in the Sidebar to display those characters.

To add special characters to your document:

1   Open the document in which you want to insert special characters. Type what you need in whatever font you like until you get to a point where you want to enter a special character. New characters will appear wherever the insertion point is flashing, so make sure the insertion point is in the appropriate place.

2   From the Edit menu, choose "Special Characters...."

3   To add more palettes of special characters (including many languages, ancient scripts, musical symbols, and much more), click on the Action menu (the gear icon in the Toolbar) and choose "Customize List...." Put checkmarks in all the palettes you want to display. Click "Done."

4   Single-click the various icons in the Sidebar to find the palette you need. Scroll through the characters to find the character.

5   Single-click on the character you want to see on your page. Even though it's in a different font from what you're typing in, as you continue to type, the font goes back to what you started with.

Data Detectors

Many Apple applications take advantage of Data Detectors. You might have noticed them already—when you mouse over a street address or a date or an email address, the item gets selected and a little arrow appears. This is the Data Detector.

As your pointer detects data, it gets highlighted, as shown above.

Command-click (or right-click) in the data to get a contextual menu that is dependent on what you click. Above, the data shows a date so the menu offers to look up that *date* in Calendar. If the data was a street address, the menu would offer to add it to your Contacts.

Single-click on the little triangle and an appropriate info panel appears. In this example, since the data is a date, the info panel is for Calendar.

Click the Edit button and you can edit the information as if you were in Calendar, but Calendar doesn't actually open.

If this were a street address, the info panel would let you edit the information and add it to the Contacts, but you don't have to actually open Contacts.

If your app isn't displaying the Data Detectors, see if you can turn them on in the application's preferences (from the application menu). Or check the Edit menu command called "Substitutions"; it might have "Data Detectors" as an option.

Colors Panel

When you click one of the color buttons (as shown directly below) in the Fonts panel *or* the "Colors" icon in a toolbar, you get a deceptively simple Colors panel. Select text in Mail, TextEdit, and other Apple applications, then choose a color.

Text color.   Paper color behind the text.

Experiment with the Colors panel:

- Click one of the icons across the top of the panel (shown below) to choose a color mode.

- Click the magnifying glass, and your pointer turns into a magnifying glass. Drag it around the screen; when you find a color you want to "pick up," click that color and it is added to the panel.

- In the "Color Wheel" mode (shown below-left), drag the dot around the circle to choose a color, and drag the slider up and down to change the color shade.

- In the "Image Palettes" mode (shown below-right), click the "Palette" menu, choose "New from File...," then choose a graphic or photo. You can also drag any image from the Finder and drop it on this palette. Move the pointer around the photo to pick up colors you need. Try it.

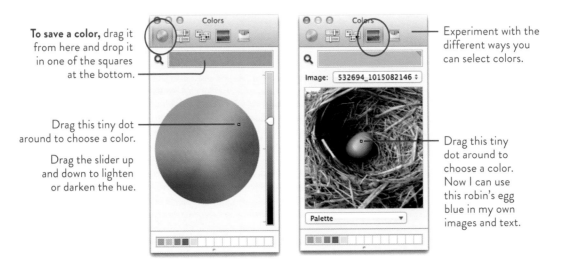

To save a color, drag it from here and drop it in one of the squares at the bottom.

Drag this tiny dot around to choose a color.

Drag the slider up and down to lighten or darken the hue.

Experiment with the different ways you can select colors.

Drag this tiny dot around to choose a color. Now I can use this robin's egg blue in my own images and text.

Dictation

Most applications that save or send blocks of text have the new Dictation tool integrated into their Edit menus. This includes any applications that accept text input such as TextEdit, Notes, Messages, Contacts, Reminders, and Mail. You can even use Dictation in Finder and copy and paste the resulting text anywhere you like.

To use Dictation: Open any application that lets you input text, for example Notes. Near the bottom of the Edit menu, choose "Start Dictation."

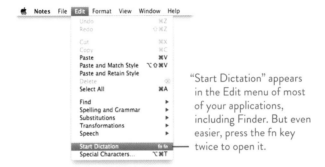

"Start Dictation" appears in the Edit menu of most of your applications, including Finder. But even easier, press the fn key twice to open it.

When you start Dictation, a dialog box with a microphone icon appears (see below). Just start talking. Everything you say at that point is recorded. When you finish, click "Done." Your words appear in the application.

This dialog pops up underneath your insertion point in your document or application when you start Dictation. Begin talking. When you're finished, click "Done." What you just said will appear at that insertion point.

While Dictation does a pretty good job of picking up your words (even if you have a bit of a Southern accent like I do), it doesn't know when you want to end a sentence, add a comma, or ask a question. But you can tell it. Speaking the name of the punctuation mark works. For example, to add a period say "period." Saying "full stop" also works. Some of the most common signs and symbols that Dictation recognizes are: period, comma, question mark, exclamation point, semicolon, colon, quote, at sign, pound sign, ampersand, parentheses, plus sign, and minus sign. Impressive!

Speech

In many applications that typically work with a lot of text, **your Mac can read selected text to you.** Depending on the application, you will find the "Speech" menu and the "Start Speaking" command in the Edit menu. Another way to access speech options is to Control-click (or right-click) selected text, then from the "Speech" option, choose "Start Speaking."

Have your email read out loud

1   Open an email message in Mail.

2   Click in the main body of text.

3   Go to the Edit menu, slide down to "Speech...," and choose "Start Speaking."

4   The entire text message will be read aloud to you.

   If you want just a portion read out loud, select that portion *before* you go to the Edit menu.

5   The voice that's used is the one selected in the "Speech" preferences.

Use Services for recording speech

In the application menu, you'll find the Services command that has options you might find useful, such as "Add to iTunes as a Spoken Track." This adds the *selected* text to the iTunes "Music" collection as an audio file named "Text to Speech." Double-click the name and rename it whatever you like.

To use the Services menu, first *select the text* in an application (or on a web page in Safari), then go to the application menu and choose the Services option.

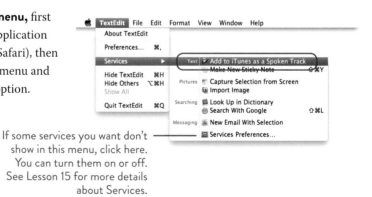

If some services you want don't show in this menu, click here. You can turn them on or off. See Lesson 15 for more details about Services.

Dictionary Panel

I keep the Dictionary application in my Dock because I use it many times a day. It's not only a **dictionary,** but a **thesaurus** and an **Apple** resource, and it links directly to **Wikipedia** (if you're connected to the Internet). The Dictionary is in Launchpad, and if you want it in your Dock so it's always accessible with the click of a button, drag its icon from the Applications folder or the Launchpad and drop it in the Dock.

Click the "All" button to display results in not only the Dictionary, but also in the Thesaurus, Wikipedia, and Apple support, if appropriate.

Single-click a result in the left pane to display its information.

This Dictionary has a special feature that extends its use out to all other Apple applications: In TextEdit, Safari, Mail, etc., Control-click (or right-click) a word you want to look up in the Dictionary. Choose the top menu item, "Look Up ...."

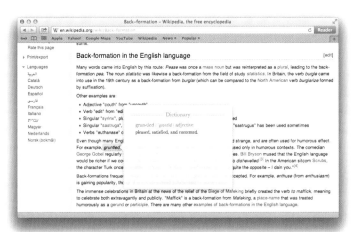

The Dictionary panel appears right on the document page. If the word is in the Thesaurus or Wikipedia, you will see entries for those.

If there are several entries, double-click on any of the entries in the panel to open the Dictionary app to that entry.

Share Sheets

You probably noticed the button with what looks like a "Send" icon on it on most of the Apple applications. This is Apple's Share Sheets feature, and it shows up all over the place, from Finder and Quick Look windows, to Calendar, Contacts, Safari, and Photo Booth.

Click this button to see your Share Sheets options. The menu items will differ depending on what kind of file or content you are trying to share.

You can also share videos from Photo Booth with a slightly different set of options.

Clicking the button opens a menu of various ways you can share the file. The actual actions you see depend on the type of file you're looking at.

Share Sheets options

Here are a few common Share Sheet options:

Email: Your file, selected text, or image appears in the body of an email message.

Message: A Messages window opens with your file in the body to send to a buddy. If it's an image, you can also choose **Set Buddy Picture.**

Twitter: If you've set up your Twitter account to work with Share Sheets, your image or text will be tweeted to your followers. If it's an image, you can also choose **Change Twitter Profile Picture.** (See the opposite page for setting your Twitter account to work with Share Sheets.)

Some apps, like TextEdit, might not have the Share Sheets button available. But that doesn't mean that you can't share content from your TextEdit files. Select what you want to share and Control-click (or right-click). Roll over the "Share" option and you see the options available to you.

Control-click (or right-click) in most Apple programs and you'll see the "Share" menu, even if you don't see a Share Sheets button.

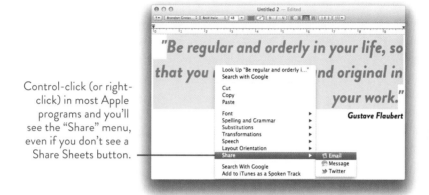

Clicking the button opens a menu of various ways you can share the file. The actual actions you see depend on the type of file you're looking at.

Set up Twitter to work with Share Sheets

It's really simple to make your existing Twitter account integrate with Share Sheets:

1 From the Apple menu, choose "System Preferences…."

2 Open "Mail, Contacts & Calendars."

3 Click on the Twitter logo on the right-hand side of the screen. A form opens where you can enter your Twitter name and password.

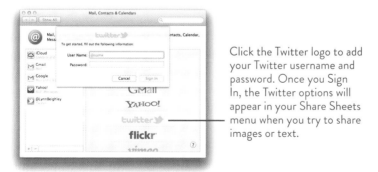

Click the Twitter logo to add your Twitter username and password. Once you Sign In, the Twitter options will appear in your Share Sheets menu when you try to share images or text.

15

GOALS

Switch between open
applications with
a keyboard shortcut

Quit or hide applications
with keyboard shortcuts

Drag-and-drop text or files
between applications

Take advantage
of the page proxy

Use Services for special
little features

Working Between OS X Applications

Now that you've had an overview of the main applications that come with OS X, let's carry it one step further and work *between* all the applications—pop between windows, drag-and-drop content and files, use Services, and more. Combine features with the use of Mission Control (Lesson 17).

Once you realize how easy it is to move data between applications and windows, you'll find more and more uses for it. Plus you'll feel like a Power User.

Work with Multiple Applications at Once

In os x, you can keep lots of applications and windows open at once so they're always accessible. You can just single-click an application icon in the Dock or Launchpad to switch to it, but there are also a couple of great shortcuts to switch between multiple applications quickly and easily.

Switch between open applications

No matter which application you are currently using, you can bring up a floating palette of open applications, like the one shown below, then select the application you want to switch to—without ever having to reach for the mouse or trackpad.

To get the Application Switcher that displays icons for all the *open* applications, press and *hold down* the Command key, then hit the Tab key once. Keep the Command key down. You'll see something like this:

Find the display method you feel most comfortable with:

To cycle through the icons from left to right, hold down the Command key and tap the Tab key (or the Right Arrow key) .

To cycle through the icons in the other direction, right to left, keep the Command key down, but also hold the Shift key while you tap the Tab key (or use the Left Arrow instead of the Shift-Tab combination).

Or press Command Tab to display the Application Switcher, release the Tab key but continue to hold the Command key while you use the cursor to select an icon (just hover over it to highlight it, then let go).

However you choose to select an icon, when the application icon you want is highlighted in the palette, **let go of the keys** and that application will come forward as the active program.

If there is no window open in that particular application, it might look like nothing happened—always check the application menu (see Lesson 1) to see which one is currently active! You might need to hit Command N to open a new window in that application once it's active.

Switch back and forth between two applications

Most of us probably spend the greater part of our time between our two favorite applications. There's a shortcut that will switch you back and forth between just those two, instead of having to bring up the Application Switcher.

First, while in one of your favorite applications, switch to the other one (just click its icon in the Dock). Now, **to switch between those two applications,** press Command Tab. I know it sounds too similar to the shortcut for switching between all applications, but the trick is to hold down the Command key, hit the Tab key *just once,* then let go of both keys right away.

Quit or hide applications

Use the keyboard shortcut Command H to **hide** all of the windows of the active application, and Command Q to **quit** the active application. Use these shortcuts in combination with the switching shortcut (above) to quit or hide selected (active) applications.

To hide all other applications except the one you're currently using, press Command Option H.

To switch to another application and hide the windows of the current one, hold down the Option key when you click the other application icon in the Dock.

Keyboard Shortcuts

Command Tab Tab Tab . . .	Select the open applications
Command Tab	Switch between two open applications
Command H	Hide the currently active application
Command Option H	Hide all the other applications *except* the active one
Command Q	Quit the active application

Switch between multiple full-screen applications

Most of the applications that come with your Mac can be run in full-screen mode. Each full-screen app occupies its own Desktop *Space* (see Lesson 17), and you can use *gestures* (the motion of one or more fingers on a Multi-Touch input device) to switch between full-screen apps (see Lesson 17).

Simplify Your Work with Drag-and-Drop

You probably have lots of applications open on your Mac. Often you'll need to move data from one open application to another. Your Mac makes this so easy with **drag-and-drop:** Drag the information you want from one application and drop it into the other application. Below are some examples. Experiment with these, and then try dragging and dropping in all sorts of other ways! If it doesn't work, nothing bad will happen—it just won't work.

Move text around in a document window

In TextEdit or Mail messages, you don't have to cut-and-paste to move text—you can simply drag-and-drop it.

1 First select the text you want to move: Press-and-drag the cursor over the text so it is highlighted. Let go of the mouse button or trackpad.

2 Once the text is highlighted, press anywhere in the selected text and hold it for a second or two, then drag.

3 Watch for the insertion point! It's that thin, flashing, vertical bar. As you drag the cursor, the insertion point moves too. When the **insertion point** (not the cursor) is positioned where you want the new text to appear, let go of the mouse. *Text will always drop in or paste in at the flashing insertion point!*

  Don't forget to use that great option in the Edit menu to "Paste and Match Style," as explained in Lesson 4.

To move a copy of the selected text to somewhere else in the same document (and leave the original text in its place), press the Option key and hold it down while you drag the text.

> **TIP** —— Often you'll find it works best to select the text or items, then **press and hold and count to three** before you drag.

Move text from one application to another

Not only can you drag-and-drop within one application, you can drag text from one application window and drop it in another. Let's say you wrote a nice essay in TextEdit—select it and drag it into an email message in Mail.

This automatically makes a *copy* of the text (instead of deleting it from the first application), so you don't need to hold down the Option key.

Make a text clipping on the Desktop

Have you ever wanted to save a quote from a web page or a statement from an email message? Just select the text, then drag-and-drop it onto the Desktop or into any folder or window. This makes a small file with an extension, called "*filename*.textClipping" (*if* extensions are set to be visible).

The clipping names itself with the first few words of the text.

You can change the name— select the text and retype.

Anytime you want to see what the text clipping says, just double-click on it. And you can drag-and-drop that clipping file into most text windows, such as TextEdit or a Mail message, and the actual text will drop onto the page.

Add email addresses to a Mail message

Drag a person's name from Contacts and drop it into any of the "To" fields in an email message to automatically address a message. You can drag addresses from one field to another.

To add more than one name at a time, select more than one name in Contacts: Hold down the Command key and click the names you want to add. Then let go of the Command key and drag *one* of the names to the email "To" field—*all* of the selected names will come along.

To add a Group name, drag the Group name and drop it into one of the "To" fields.

Send contact information through email

Winston Ch...ill.vcf (23 KB)

You can send a person's Contacts data (his card information) to anyone who uses OS X. Drag a person's name from Contacts and drop it into the body of a Mail message. You'll see a "vCard" icon, as shown to the left.

The recipient can then drag the vCard to her Address Book where it will be added automatically. *Or* she can double-click the icon in the email message and all of the Address Book data will be added to her Address Book.

Make a web location file

In Safari, you can make a web location file that will take you to a specific web page. There is a tiny icon that appears in the location field (called a "fav icon"), directly to the left of the web address, shown circled, below. Drag that tiny icon and drop it in the Dock (on the right side of the dividing bar), onto the Desktop, or into any folder. This creates a web location file, shown below. It has two different appearances, depending on where you drop it.

If you drop the icon in the Dock, it looks like a spring (below-left). You can single-click it to open Safari and that web page.

If you drop the icon on the Desktop or in a window, it looks like a document file (below-right). Double-click the icon, or drag-and-drop it into the middle of any open web page. *Or* drop the web location file on top of the Safari icon in the Dock.

A web location file as it appears in the Dock.

Apple.webloc

A web location file as it appears on the Desktop, in a window, or folder.

Save into a particular folder

When you are saving a file, first make sure the whole dialog is open (click the disclosure triangle next to the "Save As" field, if not). Drag a folder from the Finder and drop it in the center pane. The Mac saves the document into that particular folder.

Take advantage of the page proxy

You may not have noticed the tiny page icon that is in the title bar of every
document you create (it appears after you save the document). It's called the
"page proxy." You can do a lot with this tiny icon.

Make sure the document has just been saved before you experiment with any of the
following techniques (or it won't work).

To create an alias of the document on the Desktop or in any folder or window, drag
the page proxy and drop it on the Desktop, on top of any folder icon, or directly into
any window. You'll see the telltale sign of an alias's tiny curved arrow as you drag the
page proxy (below, left).

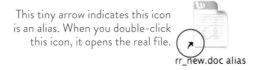

This tiny arrow indicates this icon
is an alias. When you double-click
this icon, it opens the real file.

rr_new.doc alias

To create a copy of the document, hold down the Option key and drag the proxy.
Drop it on the Desktop, on top of any folder icon, or directly into any window.
You'll see a plus sign as you drag (above, right), indicating your Mac is making a
copy of the document.

To send the document through Messages or Bonjour, drag the page proxy
and drop it on a Buddy name in your Messages Buddies list or on any name in your
Bonjour list.

Or drag the page proxy into the text field of an Messages instant message. The
recipient's message has the file attached, including a download button to click.

To email the document, drag the page proxy to an email message and drop it
anywhere in the body of the message.

Open documents in other applications

Drag documents (or page proxies, as explained on the previous page) onto application icons in the Finder or Dock to open those documents in the targeted applications; if an application is capable of opening the document, the application icon will highlight. This is great for when you want to open a document in something other than the document's default application.

For instance, **open Microsoft Word files in TextEdit**—just drag and drop the file onto the TextEdit icon, either in the Dock or in the Applications folder.

Or **drag a PDF** and drop it in the middle of a Safari window or directly on the Safari icon, and Safari opens and displays the PDF.

Take advantage of spring-loaded folders

Combine drag-and-drop with spring-loaded folders to organize the Finder. A spring-loaded folder opens as you hover your mouse over it. You can use this technique to dig down into folders with a file you are dragging: Hover over a folder, its window pops open, hover over the next folder, its window pops open, etc.

You can set the parameters for how long you have to hover the mouse to open a spring-loaded folder—use the Finder preferences (in the Finder menu).

Or use the Spacebar instead, even if the option for spring-loaded folders is unchecked: Whenever you want a folder to open instantly, hover over the folder as you drag a file, then hit the Spacebar.

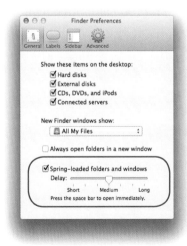

Drag content, images, or files between applications

Try dragging anything and everything!

Drag an image from the web onto a TextEdit page or an email message.

Drag a graphic file from the Desktop or a folder and drop it into the text area of your application. This works in lots of other applications, not just the ones from Apple. For instance, I'm using Adobe InDesign to create this book—I dragged the fossil image you see below from an email (and it's linked).

Drag text content and/or images from any application and drop them into other applications. Not everything will work, or it might work but not quite as you expect, but you will discover some wonderfully useful ways for working in your favorite applications.

You don't even have to open the other application first if you want to drag text from one place into a *new* file in another application. For instance, you can select and drag text from a web page and drop it on the Mail icon in the Dock—Mail will open a new message window with that text pasted in the message area. Or drag text and drop it on the TextEdit icon (which I keep in the Dock)—TextEdit will open a new window with that text in it.

Take Advantage of Services

Every application, in its application menu, has an item called "Services." Exactly which services are available at any moment depends on which application you have open and what you have selected within that application, if anything.

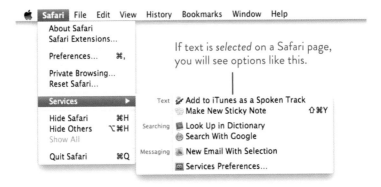

Some services also show up in contextual menus. Control-click in a window, or on a selected item in a window (text or image) to see a pop-up menu of items. The items at the bottom of the contextual menu are Services, such as "Add to iTunes as a Spoken Track," "New Email With Selection," etc.

Services let you use features of one application while you work in another. For instance, you can be browsing in Safari and make a new note in Mail from text on a web page: Select text on a web page, choose "Services" from the Safari application menu, then from the submenu, choose "New Email With Selection."

Because Services are *contextual,* only services that are relevant to the application you're using or the content you're viewing will show up in a Services menu (in both the application menu and the contextual menu that pops up when you Control-click on a selection).

You can configure the Services menus to show, or hide, the services available. Open System Preferences and choose "Keyboard"; click the "Keyboard Shortcuts" tab, then select the "Services" item in the left pane. In the pane on the right is a list of services that are available: Put checkmarks next to the ones you want to be visible in menus, and uncheck the ones you want to hide.

Make It Your Own Mac

16

GOALS

Personalize Your Mac to Meet Your Needs

Now that you've learned some of the basics of the various applications and system settings on your Mac, discover how to customize them to suit your particular way of working. Would you prefer to have your Dock on the side of the screen instead of at the bottom? Do you like a brightly colored Desktop? Do you want to customize the insides of certain windows? Color-code your files? Make the icons and text bigger? It's all doable—and more.

Customize the Dock

When you first turn on your Mac, the **Dock** is sitting along the bottom at a certain size. But as with everything else on the Mac, you can customize it to suit yourself. Would you prefer the Dock along the side of your screen? Would you like it to disappear altogether and only appear when you need it? Are the icons too small or too big? Do you want the indicator lights to tell you which applications are open? You can adjust everything.

There are three ways to customize the Dock: You can use the System Preferences, the Dock options in the Apple menu, or the secret pop-up menu in the Dock itself.

Customize the Dock using System Preferences

Go to the Apple menu and choose "System Preferences...," then single-click on the Dock icon.

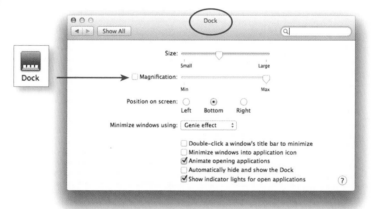

Magnification

If you turn on "Magnification," the icons in the Dock will enlarge as you hover the cursor over them, as shown below. Just how big they enlarge is up to you—move the slider (above) to "Max," then slide the cursor back and forth over the Dock (don't click) and see how big the icons get.

Minimize windows using

Choose between Genie Effect and Scale Effect to visually change how windows float down into the Dock when you click the yellow Minimize button in a window. Hold the Shift key down when you click the yellow button to see the effect in slow motion.

Minimize windows into application icon

This option sends minimized windows behind their application icon in the Dock, instead of taking up space in the Dock. To show minimized windows, press on the application's Dock icon. See Lesson 17 for more information about this feature, called Dock Exposé.

Animate opening applications

This is what makes the icons in the Dock bounce up and down when you click to open them. You can turn it off.

Automatically hide and show the Dock

Click this and the Dock disappears. It reappears whenever you move the cursor into that edge where it disappeared. As long as your cursor is hovering over the Dock, it stays visible. Move the cursor away, and the Dock hides itself again.

Show indicator lights for open applications

Apple wants us to not worry about how many and which applications are open, but we like to see the visual clue that tells us this information. If you want to turn on a little light under the open applications, check this box.

Resize the icons and the whole Dock

■ When your cursor is positioned over the dividing line in the Dock, it changes shape (shown below). Press-and-drag the line to resize the Dock and icons.

Customize the Dock with the Apple menu or Dock menu

■ **From the Apple menu,** select "Dock," then choose your options.

■ **In the Dock itself,** Control-click (or right-click) the dividing line. From the menu that pops up, choose how you want the Dock to appear and behave.

> Turn Hiding On
> Turn Magnification On
> Position on Screen ▶   Left
> Minimize Using ▶   ✓ Bottom
>   Right
> Dock Preferences…

The cursor changes into this shape to indicate you can **resize the Dock and the icons.**

Customize the Finder

There are a number of features you can customize in the **Finder.** You might expect to find these in the System Preferences, but because the Finder is actually an application (it runs the Desktop), its preferences are in the Finder application menu.

Customize the General preferences

1   From the Finder menu, choose "Preferences…." Click the "General" icon.

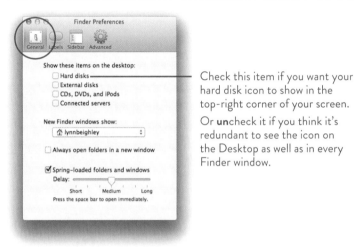

Check this item if you want your hard disk icon to show in the top-right corner of your screen.

Or **un**check it if you think it's redundant to see the icon on the Desktop as well as in every Finder window.

2   Because your Finder window can display the hard disk icons, removable disk icons, and servers in the Sidebar (under "Devices"), you can choose that these items do *not* also **show up on the Desktop.** Or if it makes you feel better to see CD/DVD icons on the Desktop when you insert them, you can choose to show only those.

3   Every time you open a **new Finder window,** it starts over—that is, the Mac doesn't remember the last window you opened. From this menu, choose the window you want to see whenever you click the Finder icon in the Dock, *or* press Command N to get a new window. For instance, I want to see my Home window every time I open a new Finder window. You might prefer to see your Hard Disk, the Documents folder, or perhaps a project folder.

Of course, this implies that your Home folder (the one with your name on it) is showing in your Sidebar. If it isn't yet, see page 289.

4   If it bothers you to have only one Finder window open to work in, you can choose to have a **new window open** every time you double-click a folder icon.

Don't forget that you can always open a separate window for any individual folder: Command–double-click it.

5   If you turn on **spring-loaded folders and windows,** then a folder will automatically pop its window open as you hover a file over that folder. That is, drag a document over to a folder that you want to put it in and just *hold* the file on top of the folder but don't click (just hover); the folder will "spring" open. This is great when you are dragging a file somewhere—you don't have to put it down to open the folder. And when you let go of the file to put it in the window, the Mac immediately takes you back to where you started.

Once the first folder opens, you can spring open another folder and another inside of that one—let go of the file, it drops into that folder, and everything closes up behind itself.

The "Delay" slider sets how long your cursor has to hover over a folder before it pops open. If you find folders popping open when you least expect it, make the delay longer.

Even if you turn off spring-loaded folders, you can always hit the Spacebar to make a folder pop open, as long as your cursor is holding a file over that folder.

Create labels for files and folders

Labels are colors that you can apply to any file or folder or application as a tool for organizing and searching.

1   From the Finder menu, choose "Preferences…." Click the "Labels" icon.

2   Change the label names for any color label you want; ignore the ones you don't.

3   **To apply the labels,** select a file, then go to the File menu and at the very bottom choose a "Label" color. As you hover over the color dot, a tool tip appears to tell you the label name.

Or Control-click (or right click) a file of any sort. From the contextual menu that pops up, choose a color label. Click the **X** to remove a label.

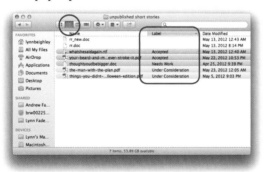

To add the "Label" column to your List View windows, right-click on any column heading; from the contextual menu that appears, choose "Label."

To rearrange the columns, drag the headings left or right (except the Name column can't move). (The columns won't move if you have an *arrangement* applied; see page 291.)

Choose what appears in your Finder window Sidebar

1 From the Finder menu, choose "Preferences…." Click the "Sidebar" icon.

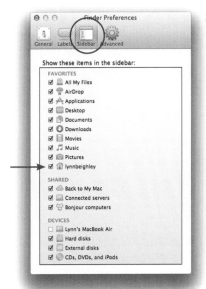

2 Check the items that you want to see in the Sidebar of your Finder windows, and uncheck the items you don't want to see. Coordinate this with the "General" Finder preferences—you don't want to eliminate the hard disk icon, for instance, from both the Desktop *and* the Sidebar!

If you find that the option to show "All My Files" is useless, you can turn it off.

I make sure to check the box to display my **Home icon** so I have easy access to my base of operations and don't have to keep everything listed in the Sidebar.

Choose file extensions and turn off the Trash warning

1 From the Finder menu, choose "Preferences…." Click the "Advanced" icon.

2 **Filename extensions** are those three- or four-letter abbreviations at the ends of file names. I like to keep them turned on because they are useful visual clues about my files. When this box is checked, you will not see the option to "Hide Extensions" in Save As dialog boxes.

3 If that **warning** you see whenever you **empty the Trash** makes you crazy, you can turn it off here.

4 **Empty Trash securely** overwrites the disk space of files in the Trash in a way that can't ever be read or recovered.

What you choose in this menu is what will appear as the default when you do a search on your Mac.

Customize the Inside of Finder Windows

Are the icons too big? The text labels too small? Do you want more columns of information available? Fewer columns? In the List View, would you like to rearrange the columns? In the Column View, do you want to turn off the preview column? You can do anything you want.

Customize the Icon View

1   Open a Finder window and click the "Icon View" button (circled below).

2   From the View menu, choose "Show View Options." The options panel shown below-left opens.

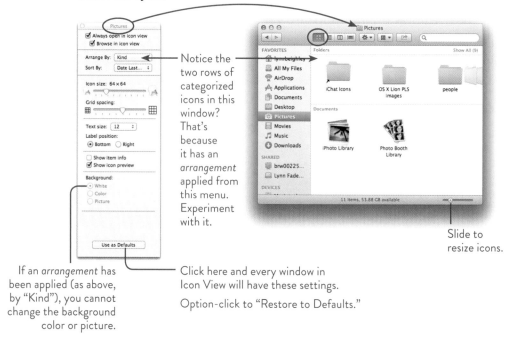

Notice the two rows of categorized icons in this window? That's because it has an *arrangement* applied from this menu. Experiment with it.

Slide to resize icons.

If an *arrangement* has been applied (as above, by "Kind"), you cannot change the background color or picture.

Click here and every window in Icon View will have these settings.

Option-click to "Restore to Defaults."

3   Choose whether you want *this particular window* to **always open in Icon View.**

Notice the title bar of the preferences pane (above-left) shows you the name of the currently active window, the one to which these changes will apply.

4   Experiment with these options.

- Use the sliders to change the **size of the icons** and how far apart they will be spaced (the underlying invisible **grid spacing**).

   TIP —— If you hold down the Command key as you move an icon in a window, it will snap to the nearest spot on this grid. Whenever you go to the View menu and choose "Clean up," the icons get arranged in this grid.

- Use the **Text size** menu to change the size of the text that labels each file.

- And use **Label position** to position the labels (file names) on the left or right side of the icons (they're generally on the "Bottom").

5   **Show item info:** This displays information about some icons. For instance, the window will display how many items are in each folder or the size (in pixels) of graphic files.

Show icon preview: This displays tiny thumbnail versions of the actual images for graphic files and photos, and even for documents.

Arrange by: *Arrange by* and *Sort by* work together. First, choose an arrangement, and you will see rows of icons grouped into those categories, as shown on the opposite page. For instance, choose "Kind" and all items will be grouped by what kinds of files they are—folders, images, text files, applications, etc.

Sort by: Then (if you like), open the "Sort By" menu and choose how you want the items in each category to be organized. For instance, choose "Name," and any file you drag or save into this window is automatically placed into its appropriate category *and* it alphabetizes itself.

"Label" is also an organizational option, but in this case it refers to the colored labels as explained on page 288, not the labels (file names) mentioned in Step 4!

   TIP —— With "Snap to Grid" chosen, you can't reposition icons— they will always jump to the nearest spot in the grid. To override this, hold down the Command key as you drag an icon.

Don't forget that you can always go to the View menu and choose **Clean Up** or **Clean Up By** (and choose a particular method) to instantly organize your files. The menu items apply to the window in Icon View that is *selected* (click anywhere on a window to select it). (If there is an arrangement applied, the Clean Up commands are not available.)

Customize the List View

1 Open a Finder window. Click the "List View" button, as circled below.

2 From the View menu, choose "Show View Options." The options panel shown below-left opens.

Enlarge the icons with this button.

Hold down the Option key and the button changes to this.

This folder, in List View, is *arranged by* Date Created, as circled in the preferences pane to the left. *You do not need to have that column visible in order to arrange by those criteria.*

3 Choose whether you want this particular folder (the Documents folder, in the example above) to always open in List View.

4 Choose the **icon size** you want, the **text size** for the labels, and which **columns** you want visible. This is where you can choose to display the "Label" column if you like to use colored labels (see page 288).

See the opposite page for the option to show "Comments."

5 **Use relative dates:** Under the "Date Modified" and "Date Created" columns, you will see "Today" or "Yesterday" instead of the actual date.

Calculate all sizes: With NO checkmark in this box, the Size column will display the file sizes of documents and graphic images, but NOT folders. Calculating the sizes of very large folders can take extra time.

Add comments and show the Comments column

This is a great feature that not many people take advantage of because few know it exists. In the List View options, shown on the opposite page, you see that you can choose to show the Comments column. But where are those comments?

You can add comments to the Info window of any file, shown below-left. You might add a reminder about what to do with this file, a committee-meeting message to someone who will be receiving it, or love notes to your sweetheart. This is the same field in which you can add keywords for Spotlight to find, as mentioned in Lesson 21.

To open the file's Info window and add comments, select a file and press Command I (I for Info). *Or* Control-click (or right-click) a file and choose "Get Info" from the contextual menu that appears. Add whatever text you want in the "Spotlight Comments" field, as shown below-left.

Once you do that, those Comments will appear in the Comments column in the List View, as shown below.

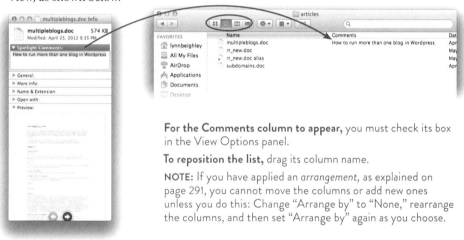

For the Comments column to appear, you must check its box in the View Options panel.

To reposition the list, drag its column name.

NOTE: If you have applied an *arrangement*, as explained on page 291, you cannot move the columns or add new ones unless you do this: Change "Arrange by" to "None," rearrange the columns, and then set "Arrange by" again as you choose.

TIP ——— If you want to add comments to more than one file, select one file and press **Command Option I.** This opens the "Inspector" window (it looks exactly like the "Get Info" window). Now when you single-click on any other file, that file's info automatically appears in the already-open Info/Inspector window.

If you like to use the contextual menus, Control-click (or right-click) a file, then hold down the Option key; "Get Info" changes to "Show Inspector."

Organize the columns in List View

Keep in mind that none of the following options will work if you have applied an *arrangement* to your window, as explained in the callout on page 293, or as chosen from the "Arrange by" menu circled below.

- **To organize the items in your list** by any column, click a column heading to organize everything by that. For instance, if you want all the different sorts of files grouped together so you can clearly see which ones are, say, Photoshop files, organize by the "Kind" column.

  The selected column heading under which everything is organized is the blue one. In the example below, the items are organized by "Name."

- **To alphabetize, or sort,** the items in the list backward or forward, click the heading triangle. That is, perhaps you want the items in the "Name" column to be listed alphabetically backward: First click on the "Name" column heading. Then single-click the tiny triangle (the "sort" triangle, or arrow) you see on the right side of the column heading.

  If you would like your items to be sorted by "Size" in ascending or descending order, first click the "Size" column heading. Then, if necessary, single-click the tiny sort arrow to reverse the current order.

- **To horizontally rearrange the order** of the columns (except the "Name" column), *press* any column heading (except "Name") and drag it to the right or left. You will see the other columns move over to make room. Drop the column (let go of the mouse button) when it's positioned where you want it.

- **To resize the width of the columns,** just *press* the dividing line between any column; the pointer changes to a double-headed arrow, circled below. Drag the double-headed arrow to the left or right.

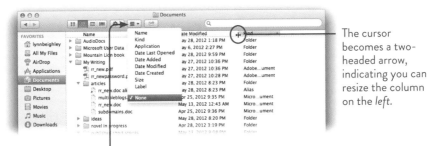

The cursor becomes a two-headed arrow, indicating you can resize the column on the *left*.

This is the "Arrange by" menu. Choose "None" when you want to resize and change the order of the columns.

Customize the Column View

1   Open a Finder window. Click the "Column View" button, as circled below.

2   From the View menu, choose "Show View Options."

The Column View is what I like best for images. I like to see the preview in the last column, and I like to see exactly where the files are stored on my computer.

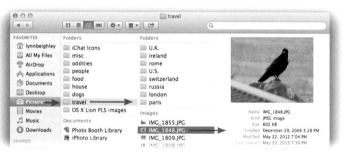

This is the same Column View as above, but I chose to "Arrange by," as you can see in the View Options, upper left. This puts files in rows according to the *Kind* of files they are. In each row, they are *sorted* by the date each was created, yet you can still see the columns showing where the files are. Experiment with the options!

You can also choose an *arrangement* from the *Arrange by* menu, as shown on the next page.

3   Choose the **text size** of the labels.

You can choose **not to show icons at all**—just a nice, clean list of items. Uncheck the box to remove the icons. (But keep in mind that the icon can tell you a lot about a file! If you can't see it, you'll miss its visual clues. This might not matter in a window that is organized by "Kind.")

If you uncheck **Show preview column,** the last column will NOT display a preview image of the selected file, such as a photograph.

Customize the Cover Flow View

1 Open a Finder window. Click the "Cover Flow View" button, as circled below.

2 From the View menu, choose "Show View Options."

3 You can't change the actual view of the covers, except to enlarge or reduce the images, depending on the window size. But you *can* choose the text size of the labels.

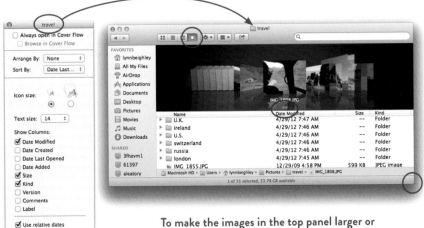

Click here, and every window in Cover Flow View will have these settings.

Option-click to restore the system defaults.

To make the images in the top panel larger or smaller, make the window itself larger or smaller (press-and-drag the bottom-right corner).

Also drag the "thumb" mark (circled in the top pane) up or down.

Customize the Desktop View

1   Click a blank spot on the Desktop to make sure no Finder window (or any other window or icon) is selected.

2   From the View menu, choose "Show View Options."

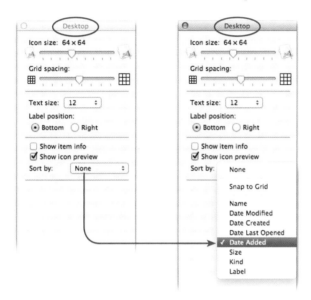

You can resize the icons or the text labels, reposition the labels, show extra file information, display an icon preview, snap the icons to a grid, or always keep the icons arranged by your chosen criteria, such as alphabetized ("Name"), Kind, Label, etc.

If you choose **Snap to Grid** (plus choose something to **Sort** them by), every file you drop onto the Desktop will snap into its appropriate place on the underlying invisible grid, keeping all those files on your Desktop nice and neat.

To override the grid-snap, hold down the Command key as you drag the file and it will land right where you let go.

If you keep a lot of files on your Desktop and it's getting messy, don't forget you can always go to the View menu (click on the Desktop first to make sure it's active), and choose **Clean Up** (which moves the files into the nearest grid space), or **Clean Up By** (which organizes them by the option you choose and lines them all up in neat rows). For some files, then choosing **Sort By** can subcategorize them.

Take Advantage of the System Preferences

The System Preferences control dozens of features on your Mac. Don't like the picture on your Desktop? Do you want your Mac to go to sleep sooner or later or never? Do you need to change the time because you moved? Would you like a whiny voice to yell at you every time you make a mistake? You can customize these and many other things through System Preferences. (Remember, every *application* has its own preferences, as explained in Lesson 3.)

To open System Preferences, click its icon in the Dock or in Launchpad. *Or* go to the Apple menu and choose "System Preferences...."

This is the System Preferences icon.

If you would rather see these preferences in alphabetical order (as shown below) instead of grouped in categories, go to the View menu and choose "Organize Alphabetically."

Global versus user-specific preferences

If you have set up more than one user, as explained in Lesson 20, individual users will discover there are some preferences they can't change because they will affect other users; these preferences are "global" and only the master administrator can change them. Individual users can change the preferences that are "user-specific" because they affect only that one user. So if you run across a System Preference that you can't change, it's probably because you are not the main administrator (please see Lesson 20 for details about users and administrators).

How to use the System Preferences

Once you open the System Preferences pane, single-click an icon to display those particular preferences. Most options are self-explanatory—poke around and see what they are (don't forget the tool tips). We'll look at a couple of examples.

1 Open System Preferences as described on the opposite page.
  Single-click the **Keyboard** icon, shown to the left.

2 In the Keyboard preferences pane, shown below, single-click the "Keyboard" tab to see the settings for that feature.

3 You can adjust how fast any **key repeats** across the page as you press it down.

  The **Delay Until Repeat** refers to how long your fingers can linger on the keys before they start repeating. If you find you type lots of double letters or spaces, choose a longer delay here. If your fingers are really heavy on the keys, slide the blue slider all the way to "Off" and the keys will never repeat automatically.

Single-click the "Show All" button to see the main window again, or *press* on this button to get a menu to choose from.

This option controls whether your keyboard shortcuts need the **fn** key held down. Experiment with it.

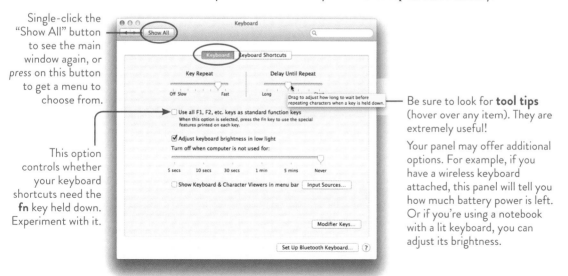

Be sure to look for **tool tips** (hover over any item). They are extremely useful!

Your panel may offer additional options. For example, if you have a wireless keyboard attached, this panel will tell you how much battery power is left. Or if you're using a notebook with a lit keyboard, you can adjust its brightness.

Open System Preferences as explained on page 298; single-click **Mouse** or **Trackpad**. Most of the controls are self-explanatory; be sure to display the tool tips and watch the little video clips.

- **Tracking** determines how far the cursor moves across the screen when you move your mouse.
- **Scroll direction: natural** means that the contents of the screen move in the same direction that your finger does.
- **Secondary click** is what you need to turn on so you can **right-click** instead of holding down the Command key and clicking to get contextual menus. (Some people prefer to use the right side as the primary button, and so a right-click is actually a left-click.)
- **Smart zoom** lets you double-tap to zoom in.

These are the mouse options for the Apple Magic Mouse. Other mouse brands will show slightly different choices.

Hover over an option; a white bar shows you it that it is selected, and a video displays to show you how to use that option.

A trackpad, either on a laptop or a wireless trackpad for your desktop computer, takes a bit of getting used to. It seems people either love a trackpad or hate it. If you have a laptop and hate the trackpad, you can always connect a mouse to it.

Spend some time getting used to the many trackpad options and what they can do for you.

This is another fun and useful System Preference—use it to **change the color or image on your Desktop.**

Desktop & Screen Saver

1 Open System Preferences as explained on page 298; single-click the "Desktop & Screen Saver" icon, then single-click the "Desktop" tab, circled below.

2 In the list on the left, select a folder so its contents display on the right.

3 Single-click any image on the right to immediately view it on your Desktop.

Experiment with the Screen Saver options.

To use your own photo, first put the photo in the "Pictures" folder that's in your Sidebar or Home folder, or put it in iPhoto. Then you can choose it from here.

Or click the **+** button, then select a folder of photos to add to this list so you can swap the photos easily.

The **Date & Time** preference is one you will use often if you travel with a laptop. Or on your desktop Mac, maybe you want to see the day of the week in the menu bar.

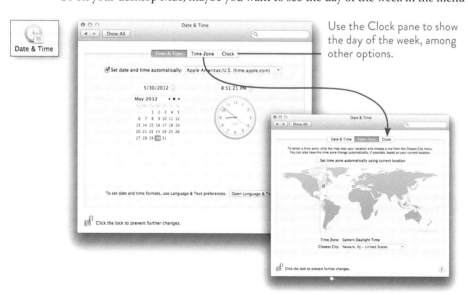

Use the Clock pane to show the day of the week, among other options.

Customize the System Preferences pane

If you don't like to see System Preferences in your pane that you never use, you can hide them. *Press and hold* "Show All" to display a menu. At the bottom is a "Customize…" command.

When you choose "Customize," each System Preference gets a checkbox, as shown below. Uncheck a box to hide the preference but not delete it.

Click "Done" when you're finished customizing.

To delete a third-party preference that might have been installed with an application, Control-click on the icon; you'll get a contextual menu with an option to "Remove" the preference, as shown above. This doesn't work for Apple prefs.

Find the right System Preferences for your task

Sometimes you know you need a System Preference to customize a particular Mac feature, but you're not sure which one has the option you need. That's where the Spotlight feature can help.

Open System Preferences (see page 298), and type what you're hoping to find in the search field (shown below). As you type, you'll see certain System Preference icons highlight, and you'll see a list of possible options. The more you type, the more specific the results will be.

Try the example shown below. I was looking for all the preferences that let me make the scroll bars visible.

Single-click on an option in the list that appears, and the appropriate System Preference will flash twice at you and then open.

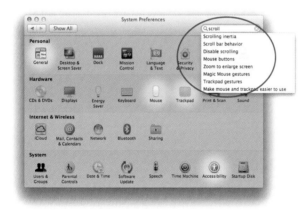

The System Preferences highlights possible results for you.

If System Preferences decides that it found exactly what you're looking for, it highlights the preference with a solid circle of light.

Don't forget about other features on your Mac that let you customize and personalize your machine! Check out "Mission Control," the "Speech" options, plus all the individual application preferences. If you need to type in another language, use the "Language & Text" preference pane. This is *your* Mac!

303

17

GOALS

Understand the concept
of Mission Control
to manage your open
applications and files

Take advantage of Spaces
to organize your work

Use Exposé to clear your
screen when necessary

Use Dock Exposé to find
open files in an application

Make your life easier with
widgets in Dashboard

Mission Control to Organize Your Space

Mission Control presents an organized view of all your open windows, enabling you to easily and quickly find anything you need on a cluttered, messy Desktop. It also lets you create different Spaces in which to work and stay organized. For instance, you can do all of your word processing in one Space, browse the web with Safari in another Space, use Messages or FaceTime in their own Spaces, and easily switch between all of the different projects.

Mission Control incorporates Exposé features to clear your screen or show open files. In addition, a Dashboard of useful widgets is accessible from Mission Control.

Mission Control

Mission Control *combines* **Exposé** (a way of showing all open windows at once), **Spaces** (multiple, alternative Desktops), **Dashboard** (a special screen full of small, specialized apps called widgets), and **full-screen apps** (applications that are in full screen viewing mode).

If your screen becomes cluttered with open documents, applications, and windows, **Mission Control** can display every application and window running on your Mac in a single organized screen view so you can select the item you want (shown below).

These are individual *Spaces*. Single-click a Space to bring it forward.

The Mission Control screen. Click any window in the center part of the screen to bring it forward.

Icons identify the applications that are open and running in the selected Space.

Mission Control shows the applications and their windows that are open. The center area of the screen shows the windows of the *selected* Space. You can assign up to 16 alternate "Desktop" Spaces, plus open, full-screen applications occupy additional Spaces. See the following pages for more about Spaces.

While in Mission Control, click any item or Space that you want to work with to bring it forward as the active item.

The currently active Space is highlighted with a border.

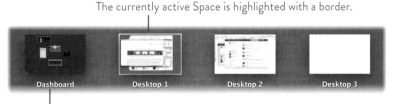

Dashboard has its own Space, assigned by Apple.

In the example above: Dashboard is a Space, and the three Desktops are each a Space for a total of four Spaces (at this moment) that are functional. The Space that is highlighted with a border is the one that is currently active and displayed in the center of the Mission Control screen.

Spaces and Mission Control are intricately interwoven, so don't worry if it's confusing at this point. You'll find it's worth the effort to learn how to control it.

To enter Mission Control, do one of the following:

- Press the Mission Control key (F3) on your keyboard, if you have one. You may have to add the fn key, as explained above.

- You may be able to press the F9 key (the default keyboard shortcut to show "All Windows").

  You may have to add the fn key (thus, press fn F9), depending on your setting in the Keyboard panel of System Preferences. You can change the F9 shortcut in the "Mission Control" preferences, shown on the next page.

- Use *gestures,* if you have a trackpad or mouse that supports Multi-Touch gestures (combinations of finger touches and swipes to scroll, flip through web pages, navigate pages or windows, and more):

  Magic Mouse: Double-tap with two fingers on the surface.

  Multi-Touch trackpad: Swipe upward with three fingers.

To exit Mission Control, do one of the following:

- Click any item in Mission Control.

- Press F9 or F3 again (or fn F9 or fn F3 on a laptop).

- Magic Mouse: Double-tap with two fingers on the surface.

- Multi-Touch trackpad: Swipe downward with three fingers.

Spaces

Spaces, incorporated as a part of **Mission Control,** is a convenient way to manage a variety of projects or just plain ol' screen clutter. The idea is to create alternate Desktops, called **Spaces,** then put certain documents or applications in their own Spaces. When you want to work with an application, switch to its custom Space.

There is always at least one Desktop Space, your default Desktop that you always see. When an application is put in full-screen mode, it automatically goes in a new Space of its own. Dashboard has been assigned its own Space. In addition to these Spaces, you can create more.

First, take a quick look at the Mission Control preferences (click the System Preferences icon in the Dock or Launchpad, then click "Mission Control"). The preferences panel has an important option that affects how you interact with Spaces.

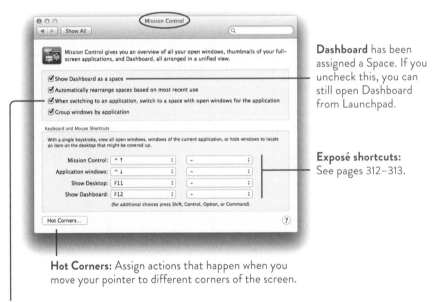

Dashboard has been assigned a Space. If you uncheck this, you can still open Dashboard from Launchpad.

Exposé shortcuts: See pages 312–313.

Hot Corners: Assign actions that happen when you move your pointer to different corners of the screen.

When this option is checked, if you click the icon in the Dock of an application that's already open in a certain Space, that Space opens on the screen.

If this box is *not* checked, the application opens in whatever Desktop Space you happen to be in at the moment, which means you can open it in multiple Spaces (perhaps you have different documents open in each Space). To cycle through those Spaces, single-click that application's icon in the Dock.

To create a new Space, do one of the following:

- Open an application, then put it in full-screen mode (click the full-screen mode button, usually in the top-right corner of the window).

Click here to create a new space that contains just this application in full-screen mode.
To get out of full-screen mode, shove the pointer into the top of the screen to make the menu bar appear; click the blue arrow icon in the upper-right corner.

- Enter Mission Control (see page 307), then hover your pointer over the top-right corner of the Mission Control screen. The *Add Spaces* button slides out from the corner (shown below); click it.

- Enter Mission Control (see page 307). Drag an item from the center section of the screen up to the top section, above the large Desktop background image. As you drag, the item becomes smaller and smaller (simulated below). Drop the item on or near the *Add Spaces* button that slides out from the top-right corner. A new Space is created for the item.

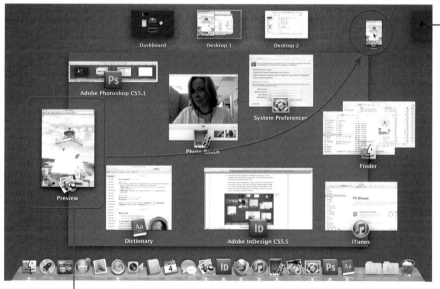

Add Space button.

Drag an item from the center section of Mission Control to the Spaces section at the top of the screen to create a new Space for that item.

To switch between all Spaces (full-screen app Spaces, the Dashboard Space, and Desktop Spaces):

> On a Magic Mouse, swipe left or right on the mouse surface with two fingers.
>
> *Or* if you have a Multi-Touch–enabled trackpad, swipe left or right on the trackpad surface with three fingers.

To switch between Spaces while in Mission Control, you have a variety of techniques available. Do one of the following:

- Single-click one of the Spaces thumbnails at the top of the screen.

- Hold the Control key and type a number key that corresponds to one of the Desktop Spaces in the top row.

- **To switch between Desktop Spaces,** not full-screen app Spaces or the Dashboard Space (you will remain in Mission Control as you switch from one *Desktop* Space to another):

  > Hold down the Control key and tap the left or right Arrow keys.
  >
  > On a Magic Mouse, swipe left or right on the surface with two fingers.
  >
  > *Or* if you have a Multi-Touch–enabled trackpad, swipe left or right on the trackpad surface with three fingers.

To remove a full-screen app from its dedicated Space, take the app out of full-screen mode: Select the Space that contains the full-screen app, then move your pointer to the top of the screen until the top menu bar is revealed (below). Click the blue *Exit Full-Screen* button that appears on the top-right side of the menu bar. The application exits the full-screen mode and returns to its original Space.

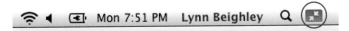

To help identify which Space you're working in, you might want to choose a different Desktop picture for each Space (see Lesson 16). You can change any Desktop picture at any time.

310

The name of a Space is located directly underneath its thumbnail in Mission Control, as shown on the previous page. However, if you add so many Spaces that the names get too crowded, the presentation changes to *magnification mode*: Space names don't appear under the thumbnails until you move your pointer over a Space thumbnail, then the thumbnail enlarges and the name appears (shown below).

To remove a Space, hover your pointer over a Space in Mission Control until a circle-**X** button appears in the top-left corner (shown below). Click the **X** button. Any windows that were open in that Space will return to their original Space or move to the default Desktop 1 Space.

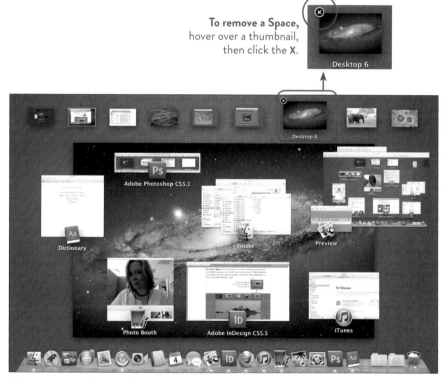

To remove a Space,
hover over a thumbnail,
then click the **X**.

When you enter Mission Control, the currently selected Desktop Space is prominently displayed (Desktop 6 in this example). Click any thumbnail or the large Desktop display to enter that Space.

Exposé

Exposé is one way to deal with a lot of open files and applications. It temporarily shows (or hides) open items so you can find what you need. This is how it works:

Let's say you've been working in TextEdit for several days and have created lots of documents. Some are open on your screen, others you have saved into their appropriate folders. Tap the F10 key to show **Application windows**. All open TextEdit files display in the top part of the screen, whereas *Recent* (and thus closed) TextEdit files and those that have been minimized to the Dock appear as a row of thumbnails. Click any document to open it.

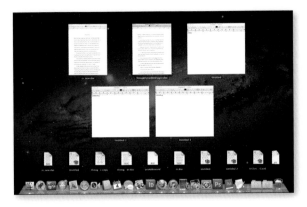

Exposé keyboard shortcut **F10** or **Control F3**: Show all the open or recent document windows from a specific application.

Sometimes you want to **get right to the Desktop/Finder.** Tap the **F11** key: All open windows temporarily move into the margins of the screen—all you can see are wee little edges. Tap F11 again to return the screen to normal. Try it. (If it doesn't work, hold down the **fn** key and tap **F11**; see Lesson 16, the Keyboard preferences.)

A cluttered Desktop.

Exposé keyboard shortcut F11: Show the Desktop.
The white arrows show the window edges that are visible.

To customize the keyboard shortcuts that control Exposé and Mission Control: Open System Preferences from the Apple menu and choose "Mission Control."

Click the "Hot Corners" button in the bottom-left corner to reveal the "Active Screen Corners" sheet (shown below). The four pop-up menus let you set an action that takes place when you move your pointer to a corresponding corner of the screen. For instance, in the example below, Mission Control is set to open when the pointer is moved to the top-left corner of the screen. To turn off the Hot Corner function for any screen corner, set the pop-up menu to show the dash option (-).

The lower section of the panel contains pop-up menus to set keyboard or mouse shortcuts for Exposé functions. In the example below, Mission Control (see pages 306-307) is set to open with a combination of the Control and up-arrow keys.

Use the left column of pop-up menus to change the default keyboard shortcut for any of the Exposé commands. Use the right column of pop-up menus if you want to set a secondary or middle mouse button click as an additional shortcut to activate an Exposé command. You cannot assign the same mouse button (the secondary or middle mouse button) to more than one Exposé command.

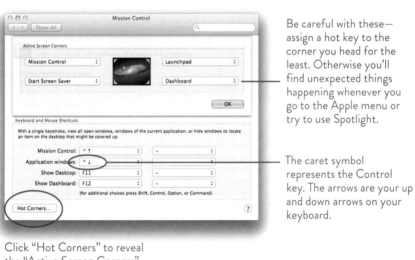

Be careful with these—assign a hot key to the corner you head for the least. Otherwise you'll find unexpected things happening whenever you go to the Apple menu or try to use Spotlight.

The caret symbol represents the Control key. The arrows are your up and down arrows on your keyboard.

Click "Hot Corners" to reveal the "Active Screen Corners" sheet, shown above.

If the Fkey commands shown above don't work, hold down the **fn** key while you tap an Fkey. See Lesson 16 to learn how you can change the Fkey settings in the Keyboard preferences.

Exposé for the Dock

Dock Exposé adds even more flexibility to managing the pile of clutter on your Desktop. In the past, you may have *minimized* open windows (by clicking the yellow button in the window's top-left corner) and sent them to the right side of the Dock to keep them accessible but out of the way. That technique certainly works, but if you minimize a lot of windows, you'll be trading a cluttered Desktop for a cluttered Dock. Dock Exposé solves that dilemma by sending minimized windows to hide behind their application icons in the Dock, completely out of sight.

To set up Dock Exposé:

1 Open System Preferences; click the "Dock" icon.

2 Check the box "Minimize windows into application icon," shown below. Then close the Preferences window (click its red button).

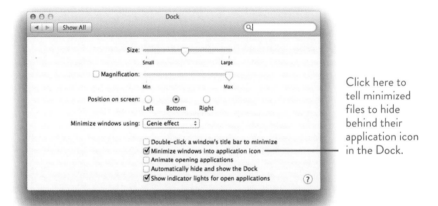

Click here to tell minimized files to hide behind their application icon in the Dock.

Now click the yellow minimize button in an open window and watch it swoop down to the Dock to hide behind its application icon and out of sight.

To show the minimized files of an application, press and hold on the application icon in the Dock (shown here). A menu pops up that shows a list of files that have been minimized to this application icon as well as recent files. Click a file name in the list to open that file on the Desktop.

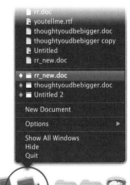

Here you can see the menu listing the minimized files hiding behind this icon.

In addition to showing a list of minimized files, the pop-up menu (shown on the opposite page) contains the "Show All Windows" command. Select this option to show thumbnails of all the minimized files for the selected application as well as Recent files (which have been closed), as shown below. The minimized files are shown in a horizontal row, just above the Dock. Files from the selected application that are open (and not minimized) appear in the top part of the screen.

To open a minimized file, click its thumbnail in the Dock Exposé view.

To show a Dock Exposé view of the next open application, press the Tab key.

If you *press* on an icon in the Dock for an application that is not open, you'll see only a pop-up menu with a limited number of commands and options.

When you move the cursor over a thumbnail, a blue highlight surrounds it (difficult to see here) and the file name is highlighted.

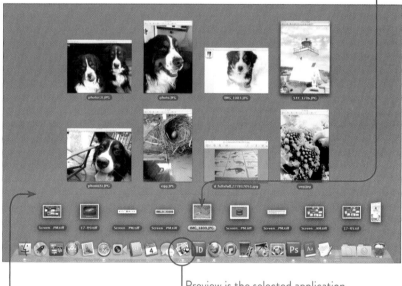

Preview is the selected application.

Thumbnails *below* this horizontal dividing line are files from the selected application that are open and minimized or closed but Recent.

Items *above* the dividing line are files in the selected application that are currently open but not minimized.

Take a Look at Dashboard

Dashboard provides quick access to information customized just for you, displayed in the form of **widgets.** Dashboard pops up in a split second, but only when you want it. With the click of a button or swipe of a finger, it goes away just as quickly. Below is an example of a **Dashboard** with the **Widget Bar** showing (the Widget Bar doesn't appear until you ask for it; see the opposite page).

When you activate Dashboard, the widgets appear *either* on top of a gray overlay on the Desktop where you can still see any windows or applications you have open in the background—*or* they might appear as shown below, in their own *Space.* You can choose how you want Dashboard to appear, and this in turn determines how you get to it; see page 318.

Each of these items is a **widget.**

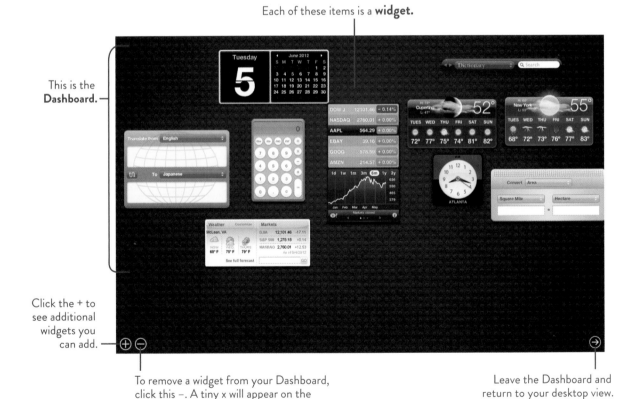

This is the **Dashboard.**

Click the + to see additional widgets you can add.

To remove a widget from your Dashboard, click this –. A tiny x will appear on the upper-left corner of each widget. Click the one you want to delete.

Leave the Dashboard and return to your desktop view.

Open Dashboard and the widgets

Dashboard is built into your Mac. If its icon is in your Dock, as shown below, just single-click on it. If Dashboard is not in your Dock, open Launchpad and single-click the Dashboard icon from there. *Or* press the F12 key (if you haven't changed the Dashboard preferences). *Or* if you have a Multi-Touch device such as a Magic Mouse, try swiping two fingers (three on a trackpad) to the right; this moves the screen into the *space* in which Apple stores Dashboard. Whew. Once you determine the best way to open Dashboard, all you have to remember is that one method.

If you're using a **laptop,** your F12 key might be used for something else, or you might need to hold down the fn key as you press F12. You can change Dashboard's keyboard shortcut; see the next page.

Add widgets to your Dashboard

To add widgets to your onscreen Dashboard, first open Dashboard. Single-click the plus sign you see in the bottom-left of your screen. (To close this screen and return to your Dashboard, click on any blank part of the screen.)

> **To add a widget,** single-click on it. The widget appears on your screen.
>
> **To see other widgets** that you can install, click on "More Widgets."

Organize widgets on the screen in any arrangement you like—simply press anywhere in a widget and drag it around. They will stay where you put them, even after you put away Dashboard.

Put Dashboard away

To put Dashboard away, single-click outside of any widget, *or* press your keyboard shortcut again (probably F12) *or* swipe to the left. When you next reopen Dashboard, your widgets are right where you left them.

Determine how to open Dashboard

The settings in the Dashboard preferences determine how you access Dashboard.
You can change this at any time.

1 At the Finder, when Dashboard is *not* active, go to the Apple menu
   and choose "System Preferences…."

2 Single-click "Mission Control."

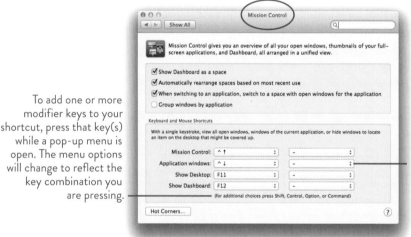

To add one or more
modifier keys to your
shortcut, press that key(s)
while a pop-up menu is
open. The menu options
will change to reflect the
key combination you
are pressing.

If you have a multi-
button mouse,
you can make the
secondary button
(or a middle mouse
button) activate
any of the Exposé
commands, in place
of (or in addition to)
a keyboard shortcut.

The default settings are that tapping the F12 key will open
Dashboard, and that Dashboard is in its own *Space.*

If the box to "Show Dashboard as a space" is *un*checked, you need to use the
keyboard shortcut or click the Dashboard icon to display it. Dashboard will
appear translucent, on top of your Desktop.

If that Dashboard space checkbox *is* checked and you have a Multi-Touch
device such as a new trackpad or a Magic Mouse, you can swipe two fingers
to the right and Dashboard appears.

If that Dashboard space checkbox *is* checked and you don't have a Multi-Touch
device, press Ctrl up-arrow (the keyboard shortcut chosen in the preferences
above) to open all windows and choose the Dashboard space. See pages
306–311 for details about working with Spaces and Mission Control.

Find more widgets

If you aren't satisfied with the pre-installed widgets, there are thousands more to choose from. Click the "More Widgets…" button that appears when you click the + in your Dashboard.

This takes you to the Dashboard Widgets page on the Apple web site (shown below) where you can download lots of free widgets that do cool things.

To make your own Web Clip widgets from Safari web pages, see Lesson 7.

There are thousands of third-party widgets for you to explore and install on the Apple web site.

18

GOALS

Understand the concept
of notifications

Use Notifications
settings to organize your
notifications

Tweet directly from
Notification Center

Manage the type of
notifications each
application sends you

Temporarily turn off all
notifications when you're
too busy to pay attention

Notification Center: Keeping You Informed

Like a personal secretary, Notification Center monitors all your incoming information and keeps you up to date when things happen. You can get notifications for important arriving emails, current calendar events, your reminders, tweets to you, and other things that you might want to be aware of.

And like a really good personal secretary, Notification Center can tell you only those only things you want to know about when you want to hear about them. You can make notifications as intrusive or private as you wish. They're always right at your fingertips.

Navigate the Notification Center

Notification Center works with many of your most useful apps, and each one can notify you, or not, in a variety of ways. You'll find yourself customizing notifications depending on the app. You'll want to experiment with the various styles of notifications so you'll know which is the most appropriate for what you need to do. Overviews of the notification settings and Notification Center follow, along with details for the various notifications options and how some specific apps you're using might best be integrated with them.

To open Notification Center, click the Notification icon in the upper right of the menu bar.

Click to open Notification Center.

This is the Twitter Sharing widget, which, when activated, lets you send out tweets by typing here without having to use a Twitter client.

If you activate Mail notifications, new emails appear in this list as they arrive.

When you click on any notification in this list, three things happen: the notification is removed from the list, the item opens in its application, and Notification Center closes.

Other apps, for example, Twitter, appear in this list as new items arrive. Click on any notification to open that item in its app and remove it from the notification list.

Click to close Notification Center.

Access to Notification Center is available no matter which application you're using—you don't have to go to the Finder to open it. When you click the Notification icon, Notification Center slides open.

To close Notification Center, either click the Notification icon or click the small icon at the bottom right of Notification Center. You can also close it by swiping two fingers to the right on a Multi-Touch trackpad, as if you're sliding the desktop over to cover it up.

Notifications Settings

The settings in the Notifications preferences determine which applications send you notifications and what kind of notifications each application will send you. You can change this at any time.

1   At the Finder, go to the Apple menu and choose "System Preferences…" or open it through its icon on the Dock.

2   Single-click the "Notifications" icon, shown to the left.

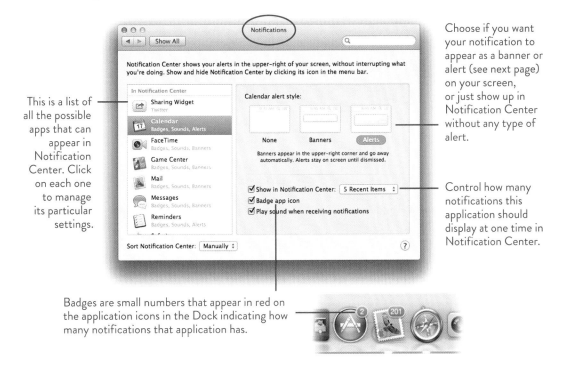

This is a list of all the possible apps that can appear in Notification Center. Click on each one to manage its particular settings.

Choose if you want your notification to appear as a banner or alert (see next page) on your screen, or just show up in Notification Center without any type of alert.

Control how many notifications this application should display at one time in Notification Center.

Badges are small numbers that appear in red on the application icons in the Dock indicating how many notifications that application has.

Notification Alert Options

You can choose from three different alert options for your notifications, as well as an optional sound that plays when a notification arrives. Your options are:

- Choose None. If you select none, a notification will still appear in Notification Center, but no indicator will pop up on your screen.

- A banner (below, left) is a small notification that appears on the upper right of your screen. It disappears after a few seconds. Clicking on a banner will open the application to the new item that triggered the alert. For example, if it's a tweet to you, Twitter will open in Safari. If it's a new email, Mail will open to that email.

- The other option is an alert (below, right). It's similar to a banner and also opens in the upper right of the screen, but it doesn't go away until you click the Close button. If you click Show, it takes you to the item and closes.

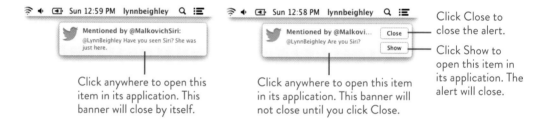

Click anywhere to open this item in its application. This banner will close by itself.

Click anywhere to open this item in its application. This banner will not close until you click Close.

Click Close to close the alert.

Click Show to open this item in its application. The alert will close.

When you've clicked on an alert or banner and seen the item in its application, the notification no longer appears in Notification Center.

To select which kind of notification you want for a specific application, do the
following:

1 Open the System Preferences through the Apple menu or the icon in the Dock.
   Single-click the Notifications icon, shown to the left.

2 Find the specific application you want to modify notifications for in the list on
   the left. You may need to scroll down. Click to select it.

3 On the right side of the screen, select the type of alert notification you want
   (see below).

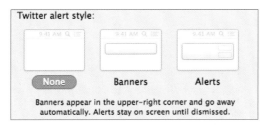

Choose which alert style you want for each
application in the Notifications settings.

You can also click the checkbox in the center of the settings to turn on or off sounds
when notifications arrive.

Notification Center Order

You can **control the order in which applications appear listed in Notification
Center** (or if they appear at all).

1 Open the Notifications settings (step 1 above).

2 Make sure the Sort Notification Center dropdown box is set to *Manually*.

3 In the list on the left, click and drag applications up and down to specify the
   order you want them in Notification Center.

If you don't want an application to ever give you notifications, you can drag it to the
bottom under the line that says "Not in Notification Center" (see next page).

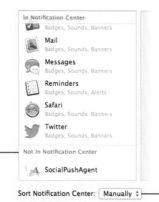

To remove notifications for any application in this list, click and drag it below into this section of the list. Drag it back up if you want its notifications to resume.

Setting the sort value to "Manually" lets you reorder this list and drag applications around. The order you see here is the order they appear in Notification Center.

The "Sort Notification Center" dropdown offers you two choices, Manually or By time. Choose **Manually** if you want to control the order (click and drag applications up and down the list). If you want to see the latest notification, regardless of application, at the top of the list, choose **By time**.

Show or hide all alerts and banners

Sometimes you're in the middle of writing a report or on a FaceTime call or maybe you're playing a game. You've got priorities, and seeing alerts and banners might not be important to you while you're busy. Sometimes it can be very distracting to see alerts every time someone tweets or emails you.

You can hide all alerts and banners at once, easily, without having to go into the Notifications settings and turning them off for each application. To **hide all alerts**:

1 Click the Notification Center icon at the upper right of your screen to open it.

2 There's a scroll bar on the right, which may not be visible. Click and drag up on the right side of Notification Center.

3 This reveals the "Show Alerts and Banners" toggle that's at the top of Notification Center. If you slide it to off, you'll quit getting alerts.

The toggle will stay switched off until you switch it back on, or until first thing tomorrow, whichever comes first.

Slide this toggle to temporarily switch off alerts and banner.

Activate and Use the Twitter Sharing Widget

For the most part, all the options in the Notifications settings are for applications. But there's also a widget you can turn on: the Twitter Sharing widget. This lets you type tweets to your Twitter account directly from Notification Center. If you have your Twitter account set up, you might find this useful.

To activate the Twitter Sharing widget:

1 Open the System Preferences and single-click Notifications.

2 Find "Sharing Widget" at the bottom of the list. If it's in the top section, it's already active!

3 Select it and click the checkbox for "Show Sharing Widget in Notification Center."

Before you close the settings, you may want to drag the widget to the top of your list of applications.

To use it, click the button and start typing.

Click to open the Sharing widget.

Type your tweet and click Send.

327

19

GOALS

Set Up Printing

Printing gets easier and more reliable with every new operating system. The Mac recognizes and automatically sets up more printers with each OS X release. Individual applications can apply more special parameters to your print jobs. Sharing one printer with many computers gets easier all the time. Mountain Lion automates one of the most troublesome aspects of using a printer: When you connect a new printer, OS X checks to see if the proper printer driver is installed. If not, it automatically goes online, finds the latest up-to-date version, and installs the driver software for you. It even periodically checks to ensure it has the latest version of the printer driver and automatically downloads new versions through your built-in Software Update application (found in System Preferences).

Set Up Your Printer Before You Print

Print & Scan

The first time you try to print, your Mac asks to set up your printer (as shown on the following pages). But you can streamline the printing process by setting up your printer ahead of time. Any time you add a new printer to your office, open the Print & Scan preferences to set it up. Occasionally you might need to use this pane to troubleshoot printing problems.

1 Make sure your printer is turned on and snugly connected to your Mac with the proper cables.

   If the printer is connected to someone else's Mac, make sure the "Printer Sharing" preferences on that Mac are turned on; see page 336.

2 Go to the Apple menu and choose "System Preferences…."

3 Single-click the "Print & Scan" icon to get the pane shown below.

This is what your panel might look like the first time you open the Print & Scan preferences.

Or you might see one or more printers listed in the left-hand pane.

4 If your printer is in the left-hand pane and shows a green light, you're good to go. Quit the System Preferences and go print.

   If you don't see the name of your printer in the list on the left, click the **+** button (shown circled, above).

   From the menu that drops down, you will probably see the name of your printer. If so, select it, then skip to Step 6.

   If your printer is not listed, choose "Add Other Printer or Scanner…" from that menu and go to Step 5 (although if it's not in the menu list, that's a clue that your Mac can't find it).

5 When you click the **+** and choose "Add Other Printer or Scanner...,"
the "Add" window opens, shown below, and your Mac searches for
and lists every printer (and scanner) that it recognizes.

If your printer shows up, single-click its name to select it, then click "Add."

If you don't see your printer listed, it has most likely lost its connection.
If you're sure it's plugged in properly, then you might want to try a different
cable—they can go bad all by themselves. Another possibility is that you didn't
install the **printer software** that came with the printer, and it's a brand that
Apple doesn't have access to. Install the software now (either from the disc that
came with the printer, or go to the printer's web site and download it, especially
what's called the "printer driver" software). Then try these steps again.

6 If you have not previously installed the software to run the printer, no worries
(most of the time). The Mac will go online (assuming you are connected to the
Internet) and get it for you and install it, as shown below.

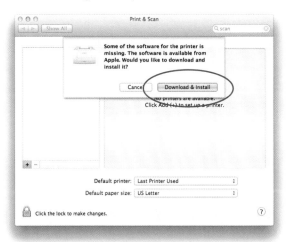

Printer driver software
needs to be updated
regularly, which is what
makes it especially great
that your Mac can go get
it for you.

—*continued*

7 If your printer is not an off-brand, your Mac will find the software it needs, install it, and you're ready to print.

If this is the printer you want to use all the time, choose its name from this menu to set it as the default printer.

The software is important

If you bought a fancy printer of some sort (meaning it cost more than a hundred dollars), be sure to install the software that came with it. What you particularly need to install is the latest "printer driver," although, as you've seen above, when you install a printer or first print a job, your Mac automatically checks for the appropriate software, and, if necessary, downloads and installs it for you.

However, if you bought an off-brand and Apple can't find what it needs, go to the web site of the printer vendor and search for the *printer driver* for that specific model that you own. Download and install it, restart your Mac, and try again.

The more expensive your printer is, the more important it is that you have the proper driver. If not, you will lose some of its most valuable features. For many printers, the drivers that Apple has access to will probably work just fine.

If your printer is really old and the vendor has stopped updating the drivers, you can try an older driver and see if it works. If not, you might have to get a new printer.

The First Time You Print to Your Printer

Your Mac automatically detects printers that are connected to the computer or on your local network. If you didn't set it up through the Print & Scan preferences as explained on the previous pages, you can do it on the fly the first time you print.

To print something for the first time in your current application, press Command P (*or* go to the File menu and choose "Print"). If you see your printer listed in the "Printer" menu in the Print dialog, then you're all set up.

Usually, however, the first time you try to print, the Print dialog tells you there is "No Printer Selected," as shown below. Your Mac just needs to be told to go find the printer and add it to its list. So:

1   Make sure the printer is connected to your Mac, that all the cables are secure, and that the printer is turned on.

   If you are printing over a wireless network, make sure the printer is turned on and that the computer to which that printer is connected is turned on and has turned on "Printer Sharing" in the Sharing System Preferences (see page 336).

2   Press the menu that says "No Printer Selected." You'll see a list of "Nearby Printers" that your Mac has found. If you see the name of your printer, select it. Your Mac will get and install the necessary software, if it can, as shown below-right. (This of course assumes you are connected to the Internet.) When the name of the printer appears in the menu, you're good to go.

   If your printer is not listed under "Nearby Printers," choose "Add Printer..." at the bottom of that menu. Go to page 331 and follow Steps 5–7.

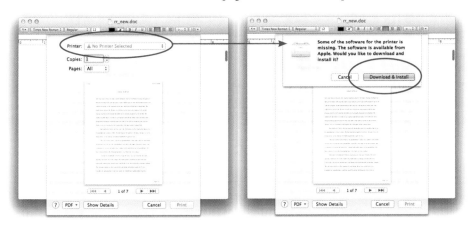

Access the Special Features of Your Printer

If you installed the software that came with your printer, then you probably have special features that allow you to choose the correct paper size, specify the quality settings, adjust the colors, and more. The quality difference in output, for instance, between a setting for inkjet paper as opposed to glossy photo paper is quite amazing.

To access the specific printer settings:

1   Start to print the job (press Command P).

2   If you see a small Print dialog box as shown on the previous page, click the "Show Details" button at the bottom of the dialog (see below) to reveal an expanded dialog.

3   In the expanded Print dialog box, click the menu circled below.

Depending on the printer you have selected, you'll see such labels as "Print Settings" or "Image Quality." Here you will have lots of options, different options for each printer you choose, and for some printers you can select specific paper/media (of course, you should have that particular paper loaded in your printer).

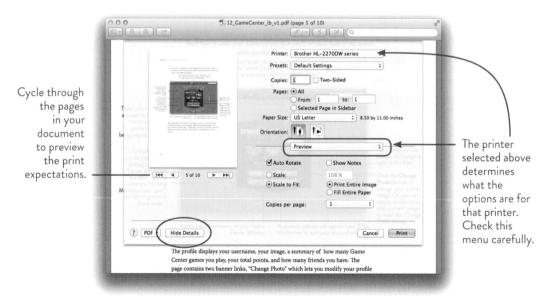

Cycle through the pages in your document to preview the print expectations.

The printer selected above determines what the options are for that printer. Check this menu carefully.

If you don't see a full window of options, this button probably says "Show Details." Click it to display more options.

Access the Special Features of Your Software

Not only does your printer offer special printing features, but most software applications also have special features.

In the Print dialog box, be sure to check the pop-up menu (circled below and on the opposite page) to view the options for the particular software you're using.

Below you see the print settings for Photo Booth, which is software on your Mac for taking photos of yourself and making movie clips (see Lesson 13).

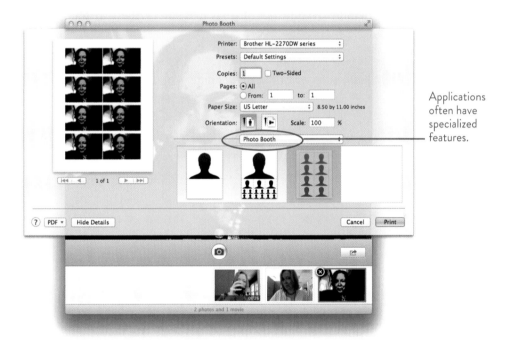

Applications often have specialized features.

Share Your Printer with Other Macs

Any printer can be set up to share, meaning any other computer in your office or home network can print to it without having to be directly plugged in to the printer. This is great because until os x came along, you had to buy a special networkable printer. Now you can have one printer in your home or office and everyone can print to it.

If the printer you want to share is plugged directly into the router or switch for your network, anyone can print to it no matter which other computers are turned on. Typically, that means it's an Ethernet printer (it uses Ethernet instead of your USB port), and probably a laser printer.

If the printer is plugged directly into a particular computer, that computer must be turned on for others to print to its connected printer.

To share a printer:

1 Turn on the printer that you want to share. If the printer is connected directly to a computer (instead of to an Ethernet hub), that computer must also be on.

2 On the Mac that is directly connected to the printer, go to the Apple menu and choose "System Preferences...."

3 Click the "Sharing" icon.

4   In the pane on the left, check the box for "Printer Sharing." Then you should see the printer that is connected to your computer in the box on the right. Make sure there's a checkmark next to the printer you want to share.

5   On the right side of the Sharing pane (shown on the opposite page), click the "Open Print & Scan Preferences…" button.

6   In the "Print & Scan" preferences, shown below, select the printer in the pane on the left. In the pane on the right, you should see a checkmark next to "Share this printer on the network." All is well.

You could also go straight to the "Print & Scan" preferences, shown here, and click the "Sharing Preferences…" button, which takes you to the preferences shown on the opposite page.

TIP —— **To put the printer icon in your Dock** so you can monitor printing easily, open the Print & Scan preferences (go to the Apple menu, choose "System Preferences…," then choose "Print & Scan"). Drag a printer icon from the left pane and drop it in your Dock. Single-click that icon at any time to open the print queue and also to access the utilities for your printer.

TIP —— If you have trouble printing and you have more than one printer connected, always check to make sure that you chose the correct printer!

The printer icon in your Dock also gives you visual clues about your job. Here you can see that one job is in the queue to print, and that the printer is on hold.

Having Trouble Printing? Check the Queue

Print & Scan

Apple applications will warn you that your printer has been paused, and this can save you a lot of time when trying to figure out what's wrong.

Having a queue can be useful—you can pause your printer intentionally, send a lot of jobs to the queue, and then when you're ready, send them all through at once.

Not all apps are so thoughtful, however, and you can end up trying to print a job over and over again, only to eventually discover they are all lined up in your print queue, waiting for the okay. Here is how to check the queue and resume printing.

1 Open the "Print & Scan" preferences: Go to the Apple menu, choose "System Preferences...," then single-click the "Print & Scan" icon.

2 Make sure the correct printer is chosen; click to highlight its name on the left.

3 On the right side of the pane, click the button to "Open Print Queue...." This brings up the list of jobs waiting to be printed on that particular printer.

Notice the icon that says "Pause." This is your clue that there are *no* jobs on hold and that the printer is *not* paused.

You can also get to this print queue by clicking on the printer's icon that appears in the Dock when you print.

4 Check to make sure the jobs are not on hold or paused. When you click the "Pause Printer" button to pause a print job, the button changes to say "Resume Printer."

There are *visual clues* that tell you all jobs are on hold until you resume printing. The documents all say "Ready to Print" but none say "Printing." The printer icon in the Dock has a *pause* symbol on it. Or the "Resume" button is visible. To resume printing, select the job/s in the list and click "Resume." *Or* select a job and click the x to the right to get rid of it, and resume printing.

Check Your Printer Utilities

Another useful feature from the Print & Scan preferences is that you can check your printer's utilities, which might include options to clean the print heads, align the colors, check the toner level, or other features, depending on your printer and its software that you installed.

Open the Print & Scan preferences as usual, and choose a printer in the left pane. Then click the "Options & Supplies..." button. What you see depends on the printer.

Some printers will give you an option to click a button to go to the Apple store and buy toner for that specific printer.

Poke around in the options that your printer supplies. Knowing what is available ahead of time comes in very handy.

20

GOALS

Understand why it's useful
to have multiple users
for one Mac

Learn to create new users

Learn how to log out
and log in

Enable fast user switching

Allow other users
to be Administrators

Teach users to adjust some
of their own settings

Learn to share files with
other users on one Mac

Apply parental controls
from mild to stringent

Delete users with
or without their files

Share One Mac
with Multiple Users

OS X is built for what's called a **multiple-user environment;** that is, Apple *expects* that more than one person is probably using the same computer, whether it's in a school, office, or home. You can set up another user so no one else can access your email or personal letters, change your sound level, poke around in your financial files, put up a dorky picture as the Desktop background, or change any of your settings.

If you are the only user who ever has or ever will use this Mac, you can skip this lesson altogether. But are you really the only user? Perhaps your kids want to use your computer. Or maybe your spouse uses your machine from time to time. Or sometimes you have relatives staying for a week who just want to use your Mac to get their email. Or you're a teacher who wants several students to have their own private spaces. If so, set up other users.

Overview of Multiple Users

First, let me explain the **concept and advantages of having multiple users** on your Mac so you can decide if you need or want to create other users.

You already have one user, **you,** which was created when you first turned on your Mac and went through the setup process. You are the main user known as the **Administrator.** The password you set up when you first turned on your new Mac or installed Mountain Lion is your **Admin password.**

You might not have noticed that you are a "user" because Apple sets a default so when you turn on your Mac, you are "logged in" without having to type in a password. Once you have other users set up, you can change this default so everyone must log in with a password. If others, like your kids, use your Mac only occasionally, you can leave it set to automatically let you in daily; then when the kids use your Mac, you go to the Apple menu and **log out,** which means they must then **log in** with their own settings, and yours will be protected.

One user, the first one (which was you, if it's your own Mac), is created as the original, main **Administrator (Admin)** of the computer. If you are the *only* user, you are still the Administrator.

Limitations of other users

So you are the **Admin** and other people are either **standard users** or **managed users.** All other users are limited in certain ways:

- Applications can be made available to everyone, *or* limited to specific users. This means you could install a game in your daughter Allison's Home folder and it won't clutter up your own Applications folder. If the game has to change the resolution of the monitor and the number of colors and Allison cranks the volume way up, it won't affect what you see and hear when you log back in. You can install your financial program in your own Home folder so others cannot use it or access your files.

  With "Parental Controls" you can create **managed users** for young kids, where you can customize their Docks so they only have access to certain programs. You can seriously limit with whom they chat and email and which web sites they visit. You can even control some Game Center settings, limiting their contact with other players.

- Even if an application is available to everyone who uses the machine, an individual user can set his own personal preferences.

- Every user can customize the Mail program, and all of a user's email is privately stored in each user's personal Library folder.

- Every user can set up her own screen effects. Fonts, window and Desktop backgrounds, Sidebar, Dock placement, Mission Control, Notifications, and preferences are individually customizable. Preferences are also individualized for the keyboard, mouse, web browser bookmarks, international keyboard settings, applications that start up on login, and QuickTime.

- The features that make the Mac easier to use for people with challenges can be customized by each user. This includes the Universal Access settings, full keyboard access, Speech preferences, VoiceOver (having your Mac talk you through doing things), etc.

- Users who need international settings for such things as date, time, numbers, or for typing other languages, etc., can customize the Mac without bothering other users. If you have a laptop that you travel with, you can set up yourself as another user, such as "Lynn in Paris," and customize those settings for that country without affecting all your settings for home.

- **Standard users cannot** change the date or time (except for the menu bar settings), nor can they change the preferences for energy saving, file sharing, networking, or the startup disk. They cannot add new users, nor can they change certain parts of the login process. And they cannot install software.

- **Managed users** have all of the above limitations, *plus* they have parental controls applied. You can seriously limit a managed user; see pages 358–361.

- The **Guest account** is a special and very temporary account. Everything a Guest user does on the Mac completely disappears as soon as he logs out. This is great for someone who says, "Can I use your Mac to check my web mail?" He can log in as Guest, use Safari to check his mail, and leave no trace.

More than one Admin

As the Administrator, you can **assign Admin status to any other user.** When that Admin user logs in, she can make system-wide changes that standard, managed, and guest users can't; she can create and delete other users, and do most of the things you can do. But your personal Home files are still protected from everyone else, including other Admins.

Guest User Is Already Created

Apple has already created a special Guest account for your guests. This is a very temporary account. It's for those times when someone comes over to your house and wants to use your Mac to check their mail or write a quick TextEdit report. As soon as this person logs out, everything she did on the computer is completely erased.

There is no password for a Guest user. As soon as you **enable login** (explained below), anyone can log in as Guest, but they have no access to any of your files.

1. Click the lock in the bottom-left corner to allow you to enable login for the Guest Account. You'll need your Admin password to unlock the screen.

If you don't enable login, a Guest can use the network to share public files, but cannot log in to your Mac.

2. Click "Guest User" in the left pane to see the screen shown here. Check the box to "Allow guests to log in to this computer."

3. Click the lock again to lock the panel (although it will automatically lock when you close the panel).

To log in as Guest, from the Apple menu, log yourself out. The login window that appears has a "Guest" button at the bottom. Single-click it.

To log out as Guest user, go to the Apple menu and choose "Log Out Guest Account." There will be a warning that all files that have been created will be deleted.

Create New Users

If you are the Admin (as explained on pages 342–343), you can create standard or managed users (also explained on the previous pages). You'll create the user in the "Accounts" pane of System Preferences, plus you'll assign a password and a login picture. In the "Login Options" pane (click the house icon that you see just above the lock icon), you can make adjustments to the login window.

To create a new user:

1 Go to the Apple menu and choose "System Preferences…."

2 In the System Preferences pane, single-click "Users & Groups." You'll get the dialog box shown below. Your user account is also the **Admin.**

3 Click the lock icon in the bottom-left corner. In the dialog that appears after you click the lock, enter the Admin password (the one you chose when you set up your Mac), then click OK. The lock in the bottom-left corner is now open, as shown below.

4 To add a new user, click the "plus" button. This makes a sheet drop down (as shown on the following page) where you will add new user information.

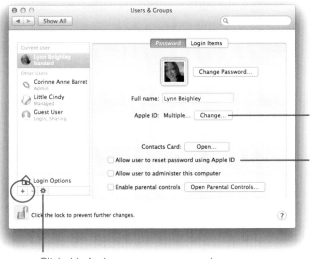

If you "set" a user's Apple ID here, that user can use her Apple ID to log in to this computer from another computer on the network.

Check this box to then allow the user to reset her own password at some point (see Lesson 24).

Click this Action menu to get an option to set a **master password.** With the master password, an Admin user can reset the password of any user.

—continued

345

5 Type the full name (or any descriptive phrase) in the "Full Name" text field. A short "Account name" is automatically created for you, but you can edit it. *You will never be able to change the Account name after you leave this pane!* The only way to "change" it is to delete the entire user and make a new one.

The Account name should be short (eight characters or fewer), you can't use spaces, and you should avoid non-alphabet characters (like * ! ? or /).

OS X can use either the short Accountname or long name. But the short name is sometimes necessary if you use FTP, Telnet, or other applications that let you log in to your Mac from some other location.

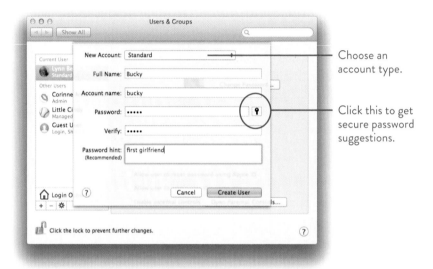

Choose an account type.

Click this to get secure password suggestions.

6 Enter a **password** for the user. **Write this down somewhere.** As you've probably seen before, you need to type in the password twice to make sure you've spelled it right, since you can't see it. If you like, click that tiny key icon to get some suggestions for passwords that are very secure.

Passwords are "case sensitive." That means capital or lowercase letters change the password: "ChoCho" is not the same password as "chocho." So be darn sure when you write down your password somewhere that you make note of any capital letters used.

It is possible to leave the password blank, but that makes the entire computer easier to get into. If privacy is an issue, be sure to assign a password.

You can, if you like, enter a **password hint.** On login, if a user enters the wrong password three times, a message appears with this hint (see page 348 to see the box that must be checked to make the hint appear).

7 Click the "Create User" button.

8 Enter the user's **Apple ID,** if she has one and you know what it is. This allows the user to log in to this computer on the network using her Apple ID and password (see Lesson 23). If you check the box to "Allow user to reset password using Apple ID," then she can, obviously, reset her own password at any time.

   If a user does not have an Apple ID and wants one, she can click the "Set..." button, then click "Create Apple ID" to go to Apple's site and get one. It's free.

9 **To choose a login picture,** do one of the following:

   ■ Single-click the existing picture you see in the window and choose another from the collection that appears.

   ■ *Or* do the step above (click the picture), then choose "Edit Picture...." Then skip to "Edit the image," below.

   ■ *Or* do the step above (click the picture), then click the button to "Take photo snapshot" with the computer.

   ■ *Or* drag a photo or other image from a Finder window and drop it on top of the existing picture.

   Now you can **edit the image:** Resize, reframe, take a new photo, or choose a different image. You can edit this at any time in the future as well.

Click "Recents" to show a selection of recent pictures. If your Mac has a camera, click "Camera" to take your photo.

Press-and-drag this image to position it within the frame.

Resize the image with the slider and use special effects on the image by clicking the round "Effects" button.

When you're happy with the image, click "Done."

—*continued*

10 To give this user admin privileges so she can change preferences, install software, reset her password, etc., check the boxes on the main pane, shown on page 345.

To enable parental controls, check the box, then click the button to "Open Parental Controls" (see pages 358-361).

11 At the bottom of the accounts pane, single-click **Login Options** (circled below; the lock must be unlocked) to assign a user the ability to automatically log in, as shown below. This pane is available only to Administrators (that is, standard and managed users will not be able to change anything on this pane). The options shown here are explained on the following pages.

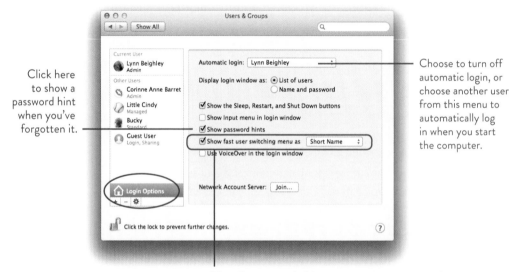

Click here
to show a
password hint
when you've
forgotten it.

Choose to turn off
automatic login, or
choose another user
from this menu to
automatically log
in when you start
the computer.

When **fast user switching** is checked, a menu list of user accounts is placed in the menu bar across the top of the screen, next to the Spotlight icon (see page 352). Users can choose their user names from that menu and log in.

If fast user switching is not activated, the current user must log out before another user can log in. See page 351.

I set up several new users, but my Mac will **automatically log in** to "lynnbeighley," meaning I do not have to go through the login screen and enter a password whenever the Mac starts or restarts. This is good for me on the Mac in my office because I work by myself; for my laptop that I travel with, I **disable** automatic login just in case someone steals it.

Only one user can be assigned the automatic login at a time. Whenever necessary, click the "Login Options" button (shown on the previous page), then choose a different user from the "Automatic login" pop-up menu.

Display login window as: The "List of users" displays icons for all accounts, as shown below. At login, click a picture, then type the password (as shown on page 351). (If you have a very young user who can't type and you feel your Mac is safe from strangers walking by, do not assign a password; she can just click her picture to log in.)

The "Name and password" option (see the previous page) displays a small log-in window with two edit boxes, one for the user name and one for the password. A user will have to type in both name and password, which makes your Mac one step more secure.

Show the Sleep and Shut Down buttons: If you choose to show these, you will be able to put the Mac to sleep or shut it down without having to first log in and wait for the computer to pull itself together.

Show Input menu in login window: This gives you access to the language options that you may have set up in the International preferences.

Show password hints: If a user enters the wrong password three times, the hint that was provided in the password pane when the user was created is displayed. *Or* go ahead and click the question mark (shown on page 351) to provide the hint immediately. If you've forgotten the password *and* if you previously enabled the user to use her Apple ID to reset it (see page 345), the question mark provides an option to do just that.

—continued

Show fast user switching menu as: This is so cool—it allows multiple users to stay logged in at the same time without having to close files or quit applications (see page 352). The fast user pop-up menu lets you choose how a user is shown in the menu at the top of the screen: as a full name, short name, or icon.

Use VoiceOver in the login window: This turns on Apple's built-in spoken user interface so a visually impaired person can log in. It reads everything on the login screen out loud to you and tells you what is highlighted so you know where to type your name and password. To disable VoiceOver, make sure this checkbox is *not* checked.

12 **To limit** what the new user can access, see pages 358–361.

To choose login items that automatically open on login, see page 355.

When done, close the Users & Groups preferences pane. You can make changes at any time. If you want to make changes to other users, they must be logged out.

Create a Group

You can create a Group account that consists of individual users who will all have access to the same files. This makes it even easier to share files with a group of people, such as students or coworkers, who are all using the same network. You must first create individual users for the people you want to add to the Group.

Then make a new user account (see page 345) and choose the "Group" option from the "New Account" menu. After you name the group, you'll get a pane in which you can add *existing* users to this new Group.

To maximize the file-sharing capabilities, use the Sharing preferences (Lesson 23) to turn on various sharing possibilities, then add this Group to the list of sharing users.

Log Out and Log In

Automatic login allows *one* selected user to use the Mac without having to enter a password. If automatic login is enabled (page 348), then you must make sure to **Log Out** (*not* restart or shut down) before another user can log in. This is because the computer will automatically log you in again when it starts up.

If automatic login is *not* enabled, then it doesn't matter how you turn off the Mac—it will always display a **Log In** screen where every user, even Admins, will have to enter a password.

When you log out, all of your documents will close and your applications will quit. If this is inconvenient, read about "fast user switching" on the next page.

To log out, go to the Apple menu and choose "Log Out *User...*," where *"User"* is the name of the currently active user. All applications will quit, the current screen will disappear, and the login window will appear, waiting for the next user to log in. *Or if* "fast user switching" is turned on (as explained on pages 350 and 352), go to the user menu on the right side of the menu bar, choose "Login Window...," and the login screen shown on page 349 appears; your applications do not close.

To log in, click your name (or type it in) and then type your password. If the password is incorrect, the login window shakes back and forth, as if it's saying "No! No! No!" After three wrong passwords, it will show you the hint you assigned (see page 346). *Or* at any point, click the question mark; the clue is displayed, plus if your account is set up with your Apple ID (page 345), you can use it to reset the password.

Click this arrow to return to the main login screen.

If your password isn't working, check to make sure the Caps Lock symbol is not in the field! If Caps Lock is on, your password will be typed in all caps and won't work. To take it off, press the Caps Lock key again.

If you checked the box to "Show password hints," click the question mark to see the hint.

351

Switch Users with a Click

The Mac has a feature called **fast user switching** that allows multiple users to stay logged in at the same time without having to close files or quit applications.

When fast user switching is turned on, all users are listed in the top-right corner of your screen, next to the menu clock. The currently active user's name appears in the menu bar.

To see other user names and to see which ones are logged in, single-click the current user name in the menu; a menu drops down showing all users (below right). Users in the list that have a checkmark next to them are already logged in. The currently active user is grayed out.

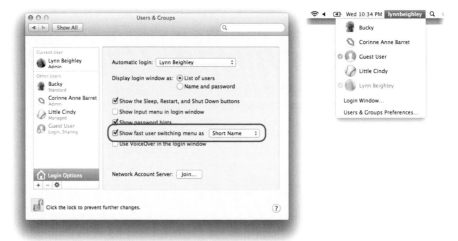

To enable fast user switching, click the checkbox "Show fast user switching menu as" in the "Login Options" pane of the Accounts system preferences (shown above-left). See page 348 for more about fast user switching.

To switch to another user, choose one from the user menu (above-right). If you (the Admin) assigned a password to the chosen user, a login window opens so the user can type a password. Enter the correct password and the user's own personal Desktop environment opens.

If a password was not assigned to a user, that user's Desktop opens immediately, without a password-protected login window. Actually, it doesn't just open like some ordinary computer; the entire Desktop rotates like a cube to the new user space.

To open the main login window, choose "Login Window…" from the list of users in the menu bar, as shown on the opposite page. This is a convenient way to leave the screen if you have multiple users. The next user who sits down at the Mac just clicks her name to log in and start work (or play).

TIP ——— If the rotating-cube effect isn't happening for you during fast user switching, the graphics card installed on your Mac might not be able to handle the intense processing that this effect requires. Fast user switching will still take place—it's just not quite as sexy.

Allow Other Users to Be Admins

An Admin can select another user and give that user Administrator privileges. Make sure that user is not logged in. In the Users & Groups preferences, unlock the lock. Select the user in the left panel, then click the button to "Allow user to administer this computer."

A standard user can give himself Admin privileges if he knows the name and password of an Administrator. All he needs to do is click the lock icon and enter the correct information.

TIP ——— Even the Admin cannot make changes to another user if that user is already logged in. So if you try to make changes and it won't let you, log out that user.

Let Users Adjust Their Own Settings

Once a **standard user** is *logged in,* she can adjust some of the login settings, even if she's not the Administrator. She can change her password (she has to know the current password before she can assign a new one). She can change the login picture, and choose which applications open when she logs in.

Below you see the applications that Bucky likes to have open automatically when he comes to visit and uses my Mac. See the opposite page for details about assigning Login Items.

Set Up Login Items

In the **Login Items pane,** any standard or Admin user (including yourself) can choose to have certain items automatically open during the login process. You can open your favorite applications, utilities, documents, even movies or music. (If you choose to have a document open, the application it was created in will have to open as well, even if you don't have it in the list.)

This pane applies only to the user who is currently logged in! No other user even has access to the Login Items pane for someone else.

To add items to the Login Items list, click the "plus" button circled below. A dialog box opens to let you choose any file or application to add to the Login Items. To add more items, click the "plus" button again.

The files will **open in the order in which they are listed.** Drag any file in the list up or down to change the order.

If you don't want to see an item right away every time you turn on your Mac, click in the checkbox to **hide** it. It will open, but its windows won't be visible on the screen.

To delete items from the Login Items list, first select the item, then click the "minus" button.

Another way to add items: Press (don't click) *or* right-click an icon in the Dock. Choose "Options," then choose "Open at Login."

To remove it, repeat the above to remove the checkmark next to "Open at Login."

Share Files with Other Users

Once users are set up, other users can only access each other's Public folders, the Drop Boxes inside the Public folders, and the Sites folders. But the Shared folder (which is in the Users folder, which is on your main hard disk) is available to everyone who uses your Mac. Here's how it works:

- Put files in your own **Public folder** that you want others to be able to read, copy, or print. They have to open your Public folder to do so.

- Other users can put files *for you* into your **Drop Box,** which is located inside of your Public folder. They cannot *open* your Drop Box, not even to see if their file transferred successfully.

- Put files in the **Shared folder** that you want everyone who uses the Mac to be able to access. This is a good way to distribute something to everyone on the Mac without having to copy it to each individual's Drop Box.

You can also change the sharing "privileges" for any folder in your Home folder. That is, you can turn *off* the sharing privileges for the Public folder and the Drop Box so no one can access them, and you can also choose to share *any* or all of your other folders, with varying levels of access. See the following page for details.

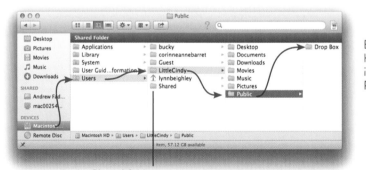

Every user has a **Drop Box** inside his Public folder.

All users can access items in the **Shared** folder.

For easy access to your Public folder, put your Home folder in the Sidebar (use the Finder preferences to do this; see Lesson 16.)

Set Permissions for Shared Files

Every file on your Mac has "permission" settings. Some of these permissions you can change, if you like. For instance, you might want to send a memo to all users of this Mac, but you don't want them to be able to edit it. So select that document and give the others a permission of "Read only." Or perhaps you don't want anyone to access a Screenwriting folder you made; give it a permission of "No Access." Maybe you want to share your Movies folder so another user can drop movie files into it; select the folder and change its permission to "Read & Write" or "Write only" (which means they can put files *into* your folder but can't take them out).

To change permissions on a file or folder:

1 Single-click a file or folder to select it.

2 Press Command I to display the Info window, as shown below.

3 Click the disclosure triangle next to "Sharing & Permissions."

4 Click the lock icon in the bottom-right corner and enter your Admin password. Click OK.

5 Click the "Privilege" menu next to user names to change the permissions.

6 When you're finished, just close the Info window.

To revert changes or to apply the permissions to all items in a folder, use the Action menu.

Add users or a Group to this list and assign Privileges (permissions).

Apply Parental Controls

Parental
Controls

There are several levels of limited user access you can create. Once you apply any of these parental controls, the user changes from a "Standard" user to a "Managed with Parental Controls" user (you cannot apply Parental Controls to an Admin user). Choose the level of access you want to control. Each of these options is explained on the following pages. Only an Admin can apply or change parental controls. You can even manage these controls from another computer.

You can limit the applications to which a user has access, the content of the Dictionary and web sites, whether or not a user can burn CDs or modify their Dock, and more. You can set time limits and check logs to see where a user has been.

Simple Finder is the most serious limitation. This is appropriate for very young children who want to use their educational software and games on your Mac and really don't know how to surf or chat anyway. It makes the Mac very easy for them to use and they can't do any damage.

Set limitations on a user

1 In the Users & Groups preferences, set up a new user, as explained on pages 345–350, if you haven't already.

2 Make sure that the user is not logged in. If she is, log her out.

3 If the lock icon in the bottom-left corner is locked, single-click on it and enter the Admin name and password. Click OK.

4 Select the user in the left-hand pane.

5 Check the box "Enable parental controls."

6 Click the button "Open Parental Controls...."

7 You'll see the window at the top of the opposite page. Make sure the account to which you want to apply parental controls is selected on the left.

8 The rest of the process is pretty self-explanatory—essentially, you're going to choose what you want to limit. Don't choose **Simple Finder** until you read page 360.

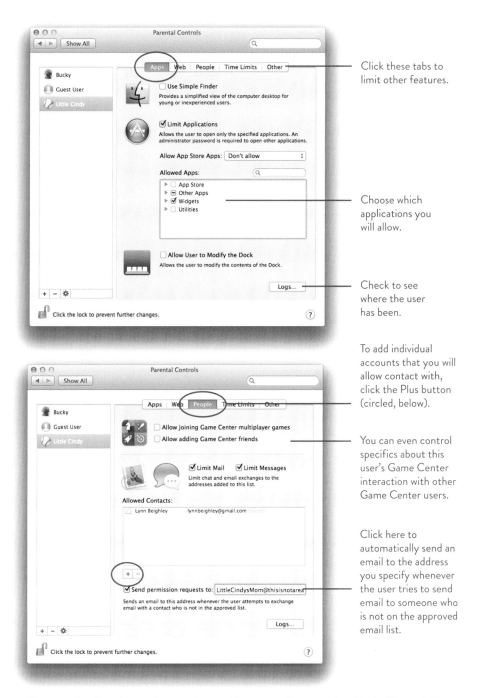

Click these tabs to limit other features.

Choose which applications you will allow.

Check to see where the user has been.

To add individual accounts that you will allow contact with, click the Plus button (circled, below).

You can even control specifics about this user's Game Center interaction with other Game Center users.

Click here to automatically send an email to the address you specify whenever the user tries to send email to someone who is not on the approved email list.

Open each tab and spend some time poking around to see what kind of boundaries you can set. You can always change them later.

Simple Finder

Simple Finder (in the Apps pane in the Parental Controls settings) provides the most serious limitation. It's great for young children. The illustration below shows what a user logged in using **Simple Finder** might see.

- The Applications and Utilities are limited to what you allow.

- The user has no access to a Desktop, hard disk, or other partitions.

- The user cannot move files from one folder to another.

- The user has three folders in her Dock: My Applications, Documents, and Shared. The Shared folder contains items placed in it by other users of the computer, as explained in Lesson 23. *Anything anyone puts into the Shared folder (shown in the Dock) will be available even to users running Simple Finder.*

- The Finder windows have no Sidebars or Toolbars.

In Simple Finder, click an icon just once to open it.

My Applications folder.　　Shared folder.

Documents folder; all saved documents will be in this folder.

To set up a user with Simple Finder:

1   Follow the steps to create a new user with parental controls (see page 358), up through Step 7.

2   Click the button "Use Simple Finder."

3   In the list of applications, uncheck the boxes to deselect applications.
    Every checked item will be available to the user in Simple Finder.

The applications list in the Parental Controls window (below) are shown in groups. Click the disclosure triangle next to an application checkbox to hide or show the individual applications in that group.

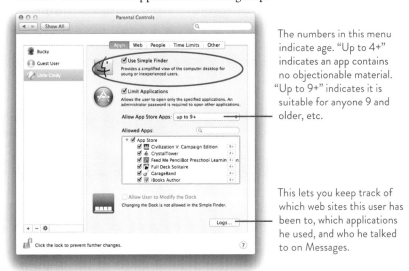

The numbers in this menu indicate age. "Up to 4+" indicates an app contains no objectionable material. "Up to 9+" indicates it is suitable for anyone 9 and older, etc.

This lets you keep track of which web sites this user has been to, which applications he used, and who he talked to on Messages.

Disable Simple Finder

To disable Simple Finder in a user account, the managed user must be logged out: From the Apple menu, choose "Log Out *user name*." An Admin user (or anyone with an Admin name and password) can then go to the System Preferences select "Users & Groups," then click the padlock in the bottom-left corner; a dialog opens that requires an Admin name and password. Select a managed account in the sidebar, uncheck "Enable parental controls." **To manage parental controls on one computer from another computer**, click the "Open Parental Controls…" button, then check "Manage parental controls from another computer."

To open the full Finder while in Simple Finder, go to the Finder menu and choose "Run Full Finder." You'll need to enter an Admin name and password. Return to Simple Finder via the same menu.

Delete a User

Any Admin can delete a user. You have three choices about what to do with all of the files that belong to a user when you delete her account:

Save the home folder in a disk image. The contents of the user's Home folder will be compressed as a disk image format (.dmg) and saved into a "Deleted Users" folder located in the Users folder. This is a nice safety net in case you need to access that user's files later—just double-click the DMG file, it opens to a hard disk icon (as shown on the opposite page), and all the files are restored in that hard disk icon.

Don't change the home folder. This stores the entire Home folder and all its contents in a folder called "*username* (Deleted)." All of the folders except Public are locked. However, you, as Admin, can open a folder's Info window and change the permissions to give you access to it, as shown on page 343.

Delete the home folder. Choose this if you're certain you don't need anything the deleted user may have in her Home folder. The user account and all of the files in the user's Home folder will immediately disappear.

To delete a user:

1 From the Apple menu, choose "System Preferences…," then click the "Users & Groups" icon.

2 Single-click the lock icon in the bottom-left corner. Enter the Admin name and password. Click OK.

3 Click once on the name of the user you want to delete. If the user name is gray and you can't select it, that means that user is logged in. She must log out before you can delete the account.

4 After you select the user, click the "minus" button at the bottom of the user account pane.

5 A sheet drops down, shown at the top of the opposite page, asking what you want to do with the files belonging to this user. Make your choice based on the information above.

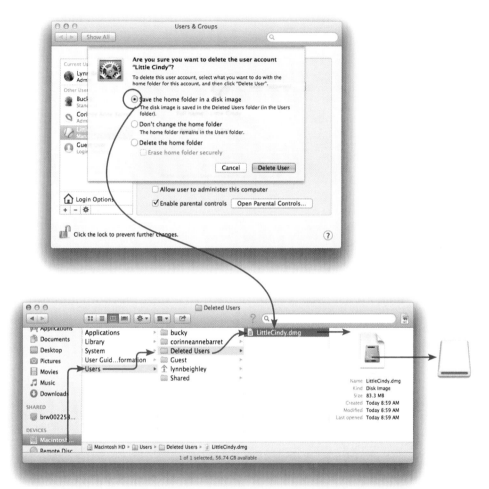

If you choose "Don't change the home folder," the deleted user looks like this: Little Cindy (Deleted). The user's files are all in this folder, but they're all locked. Use the Info window, as described on page 357, to unlock the folders.

To access the saved user files later, double-click the DMG file. It will open to a hard disk icon (shown above-right). Open the hard disk icon (double-click it) and you'll find all the files.

21

GOALS

Understand the different
ways to access Spotlight
and search your Mac

Choose or change the
categories for searching

Prevent selected folders
from being searched

Expand the search
with metadata

Add searchable
keywords to files

Create Smart Folders

Take advantage of Spotlight
in other applications

Find What You Want, Fast—with Spotlight

Spotlight is not just a search feature—it's a way of working with your Mac. Once you get accustomed to its speed, versatility, and usefulness, you'll find yourself using Spotlight regularly to find and open files instead of opening and closing folders and windows.

Spotlight searches for more than just file names. It can search for keywords and comments you type into a file's Get Info window, and it can search the content of documents, such as PDF documents, TextEdit documents, email messages, and Calendar Events and Reminders.

If you find you perform a certain search often, save it as a Smart Folder. Files that match the search criteria are listed in the Smart Folder, and the folder updates itself every time a matching file is created or changed.

The Many Faces of Spotlight

Spotlight has multiple ways of working. You'll find yourself using different options at different times. Experiment with each one so you'll know which is the most appropriate for what you need to do. Details for each option are on the following pages.

Spotlight menu

To open Spotlight, click the Spotlight icon in the upper-right of the menu bar, *or* use the keyboard shortcut, Command Spacebar.

Type your query into the field that appears and Spotlight instantly starts presenting results. As you type more letters, the search narrows and updates.

Move your pointer over an item in the Spotlight list to see a Quick Look preview of the found item. Click the item to open it.

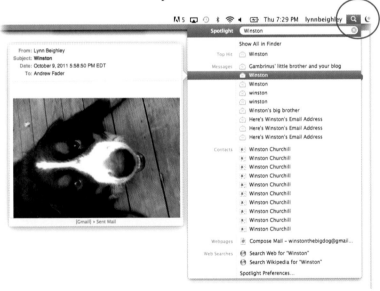

Access to the Spotlight menu is available no matter which application you're using— you don't have to go to the Finder to run a search. See pages 374–375 for details.

Spotlight windows

To show the Spotlight search results in a Finder window with more information:

Click the option "Show All in Finder" at the top of the Spotlight menu after you've made a search, as shown on the previous page.

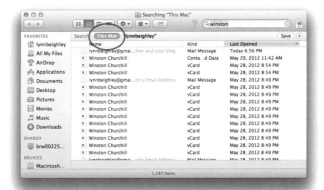

Although it claims to search "This Mac," Spotlight really only searches the active user (see Lesson 20 about multiple users).

Or use a keyboard shortcut to open a Spotlight search in a Finder window:

If you're in the Finder, press Command F.

If you're in an application, press Command Option Spacebar.

When you type into the Search field in a Finder window, Spotlight instantly kicks in and shows you simple results directly in that window. It searches in the area defined by the Finder preferences, as shown below-right.

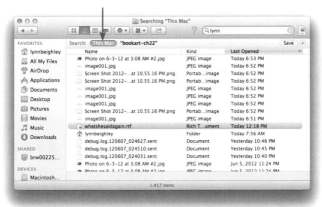

From the Finder menu, choose "Preferences…" and use the "Advanced" tab.

Spotlight-powered search in many applications

Spotlight-enabled searches are in many other applications, as shown in the examples below. Some applications also let you create other forms of Smart Folders (explained on pages 379–380).

Mail (below) and its Smart Mailboxes (Lesson 5).

Contacts (page 368) and its Smart Groups (Lesson 6).

Text in any application (below).

System Preferences (page 381).

Open and **Save As** dialog boxes (page 383).

Search field.

Search results.

Mail: The search displays results that contain either the search term (shown here); messages that have the search term in the Subject field; messages that have an attachment whose name contains the search term; etc.

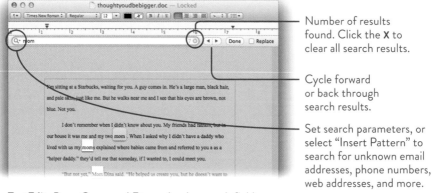

Number of results found. Click the **X** to clear all search results.

Cycle forward or back through search results.

Set search parameters, or select "Insert Pattern" to search for unknown email addresses, phone numbers, web addresses, and more.

TextEdit: Press Command F to make the search field appear. Click the magnifying glass to open the menu of options.

But Before You Begin

There are several things you might want to know before you start using Spotlight. In the Spotlight preferences, you can choose which **categories** of items you want Spotlight to search through. You can also choose certain disks and folders that you (or anyone using your machine) *cannot* search through, giving you some extra **privacy.** And on the following pages are some tips to help you make your searches more productive.

Choose the categories for searching

1 From the Apple menu, choose "System Preferences...."

2 Single-click the "Spotlight" icon.

3 Click the "Search Results" tab (below) if it isn't already highlighted.

4 *Uncheck* boxes for categories you *don't want* Spotlight to search.

5 Drag the category items up or down to change the order in which results appear in Spotlight.

369

Create some privacy

1 If you haven't already, open the Spotlight preferences, as explained on the previous page.

2 Click the "Privacy" tab.

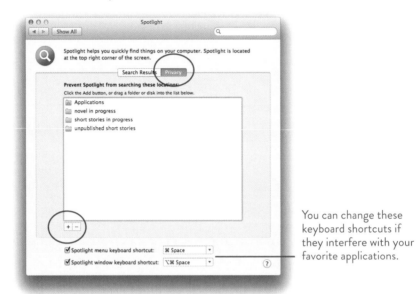

You can change these keyboard shortcuts if they interfere with your favorite applications.

3 Click the **+** sign to open a dialog box where you can choose any folder or disk on your Mac that you don't want Spotlight to search.

Or drag any folder or disk icon from the Finder and drop it into this pane.

Note: This isn't a very *safe* privacy feature because anyone using your computer can just open the preferences and remove these items (if they know how to do it). If you want more privacy, make a separate *user* because a Spotlight search only searches the files for the active user (see Lesson 21).

Keyboard shortcuts to open Spotlight

Notice in the illustration above (at the bottom of the window) that the Spotlight preferences also include options to change the existing keyboard shortcuts to open Spotlight, or to turn them off altogether by unchecking the boxes. Some applications might use those same shortcuts; Spotlight overrides the applications' shortcuts, so if it creates a problem for you, go to the preferences above and change them or turn them off.

Don't search just file names

Spotlight doesn't just search file names. It searches the senders' names and the contents of email messages; it can look through the contact information in your Contacts; it finds images and graphics, calendar Events and Reminders, System Preferences, PDF text, the contents of TextEdit pages (but not the contents of text clippings), even Messages conversations (if you previously chose to save them).

Expand your repertoire of searchable items

You're not limited to searching just for *words* that might be found in a file. In the Finder Spotlight search, you can use selected parameters to find particular categories of files. For instance, you can look for "music" to find all your music files, or choose "Image" in the pop-up menu, then add another search options bar (click the **+** button) and limit the search to "Last modified date within last 1 days" (as shown in the example below).

Type a word or phrase here.

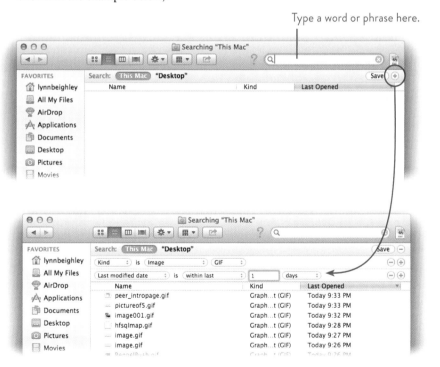

Click the *Add* (**+**) button (circled above) to add more parameter bars with pop-up menus of additional search options.

Expand the search with metadata

Spotlight also looks in the **metadata** that every file contains. Metadata includes information about who created the file, when it was created and modified, the copyright date, the file type, the color space for a photo or image, even what kind of camera a particular photo was taken with. Different kinds of files have different kinds of metadata associated with them.

To make metadata attributes appear in the parameter pop-up menus:

1   Press Command F to open a search window.

2   Click the first pop-up menu (it probably says "Kind"), and choose "Other...."

3   In the sheet that opens (as shown far below), find an attribute you want included in the lengthy list that appears; checkmark its box. Click OK.

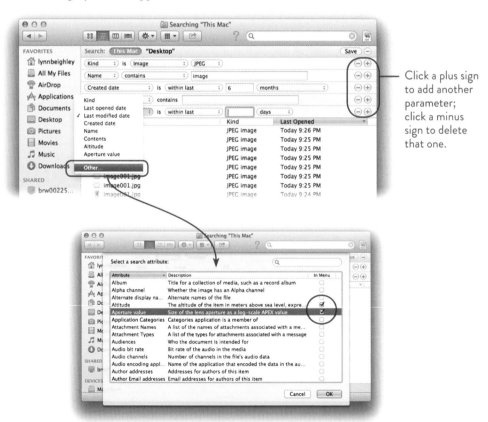

Click a plus sign to add another parameter; click a minus sign to delete that one.

Add keywords to files

There are some files that, even with all the options in Spotlight, still won't be found because there is nothing associated with them that Spotlight can decipher. For files that you want to make sure you can find later, add your own **keywords.** For instance, the example below is an image file of a cool old bright red fire alarm. I can search for "alarm" (if I remember the image's name correctly), but if I want to find images with strong red colors for use in a design where color matters, this image can't be easily found. So I added a number of keywords that I might use in a search to the Get Info window for this file and also for other images with vibrant red colors I have on my Mac. Now Spotlight can find them.

To add a keyword to a file:

1 Single-click a file to select it.

2 Press Command I to open the Get Info window.

If this field isn't showing, single-click the tiny disclosure triangle.

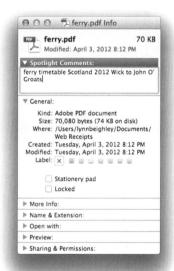

Add keywords to a file's Spotlight Comments so you can search for it later.

When a file has a forgettable name, as above, additional information or keywords in Spotlight Comments make it easy to find the file later.

3 Type your keywords into the "Spotlight Comments" area.

If you have more than one file to which you want to add keywords, select one file, then press Command *Option* I (instead of just Command I). Now as you select other files, this Get Info window displays the information for the file you select.

Spotlight Menu

The Spotlight menu is available no matter which application you're using at the moment (although this is *not* the tool to use to search within your application, such as searching the text on a visible web page or in your word processor).

To open the Spotlight menu:

1 Simply click the Spotlight icon in the upper-right of the menu bar, *or* press Command Spacebar to open it.

2 A text field appears. Start typing in it.

Results appear instantly in the Spotlight menu, as shown below. The more letters you type, the narrower the search becomes.

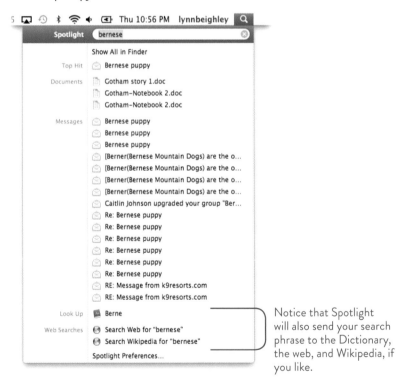

Notice that Spotlight will also send your search phrase to the Dictionary, the web, and Wikipedia, if you like.

To use the Spotlight menu:

Below are callouts of the various features of the Spotlight menu. Use the Spotlight menu for a quick search for something you think can be found easily.

Single-click the **X** to delete everything in the search field.

Single-click "Show All in Finder" to display the Spotlight window, as shown on the following page.

These are the categories that Spotlight is searching. See page 369 for a list of the categories possible.

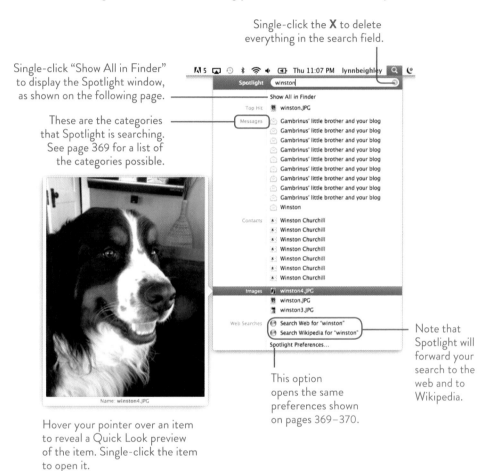

Name: winston4.JPG

Note that Spotlight will forward your search to the web and to Wikipedia.

This option opens the same preferences shown on pages 369–370.

Hover your pointer over an item to reveal a Quick Look preview of the item. Single-click the item to open it.

Spotlight in the Finder

There are two ways to open Spotlight in the Finder, both of which use your Finder window. You can do a **quick search** by simply typing in the search field that appears in the upper-right corner of every Finder window, as described below. For a **more specific search,** press Command F to go straight to an empty window with an extra Search Parameter bar already available (as shown on the opposite page).

Quick search in a Finder window

Below are the **results** of a quick search for "lynn." As soon as you start typing, results appear in the window, and a pop-up menu shows where results are being found.

In the Search Bar, choose a location for Spotlight to search—"This Mac," *or* a selected folder in the Sidebar, *or* any "Shared" drives that are connected to your computer.

Click the **+** button on the right side of the Search Bar (next to the Save button, shown on the next page) to add Search Parameter bars for narrowing your search.

Search Bar.

If I choose this option, it will narrow the results.

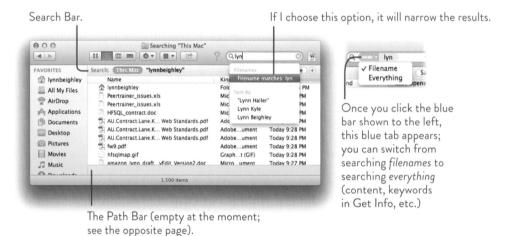

Once you click the blue bar shown to the left, this blue tab appears; you can switch from searching *filenames* to searching *everything* (content, keywords in Get Info, etc.)

The Path Bar (empty at the moment; see the opposite page).

To see where a file is located, single-click it; the path to that *selected* file appears in the Path Bar at the bottom of the window (shown on the next page). If the Path Bar is not showing, go to the View menu and choose "Show Path Bar."

To open the enclosing folder that holds the selected file, press Command R.

To open a file, double-click it.

To quickly view the file, press the Spacebar to open the *selected* file in Quick Look.

Narrow the search in a Finder window

If you've already started a search (as on the opposite page), click the **+** button (next to the "Save" button in the Search Bar) to reveal an additional Search Parameter bar.

If you have not yet started a search, press Command F; the active window switches to a blank search results window. If no window is open or active, a new one opens.

The only difference between the window below and the one on the opposite page is that this Find window provides a parameter bar for you to work with. You can add as many parameters as you need.

To add more parameters to narrow your search, click the plus sign.

To delete a Search Parameter, click its minus sign.

To change the parameters, click a parameter menu to choose a different option. The choice in any menu affects the options available in the next menu to the right, which might then create a new field in which to enter a new parameter.

Use these pop-up menus to narrow your search in specific ways.

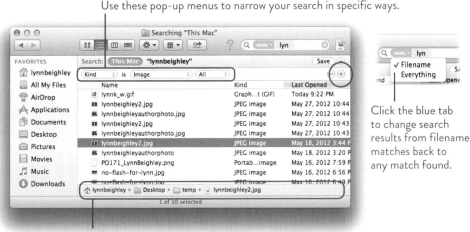

Click the blue tab to change search results from filename matches back to any match found.

The Path Bar shows the path to the selected file.

Sort Spotlight's search results

Sort search results by different criteria. Click the *Arrange by* button in the Toolbar, and choose one of the sort items (Name, Kind, Application, Date Modified, Date Created, etc.).

Arrange by options.

Use a Boolean search

A Boolean search means that you limit the search by using the words AND, OR, or NOT. As you can see below, a search for "squirrel" showed me six files. But a search for *squirrel AND dog* found exactly the one I was looking for—*only* that one. Keep in mind that booleans have to be used in all caps: AND, OR, or NOT.

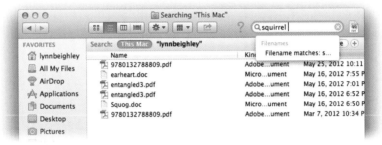

As you type a search term, a pop-up menu shows possible matches in different categories. This search found only "filename" matches.

A search for squirrel AND dog easily narrows results to the only match.

You can also use quotation marks, just as you probably do when searching the web. For instance, if you search for *knitting wool* without quotes, you'll get every document that has the word *knitting* in it and every document that has the word *wool* in it. But if you search for *"knitting wool"* in quotation marks, you will only find pages with that exact phrase. If you want to search for an exact phrase that contains "and", "or", or "not", but you don't want them interpreted as boolean terms, use quotes (for example, "peanut butter and jelly").

Smart Folders and Spotlight

Once you create a great search in the Finder via Spotlight, you might like to make a **Smart Folder** that keeps track of every file that fits that search. This folder doesn't store the original files—the originals stay in their original folders, and the Smart Folder just keeps a list of everything so it's easily accessible to you.

For instance, you might want a Smart Folder that contains all the various PDF files you've made in your Documents folder so you don't have to go looking through various project folders to find a particular one. If so, make a Smart Folder that just stores PDF files.

Your Smart Folder keeps track of all PDF files in one place for you, even though the files themselves are scattered in different locations. The Smart Folder updates automatically as PDF files are created, changed, or thrown away.

To create a Smart Folder:

1   In the Finder, press Command F to open Spotlight in a Finder window.

2   Define your parameters. Below is a search of all files that are PDFs. There is nothing typed into the search field at the top of the window because I want to find *all* PDFs regardless of their names. I selected the Documents folder because I only want to find PDFs in that folder.

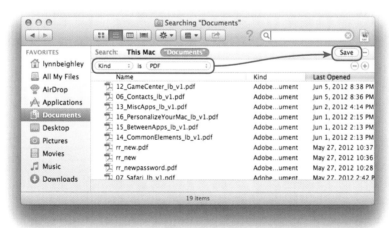

You can also create a Smart Folder by going to the File menu and choosing "New Smart Folder." The window that opens looks exactly like the one above. Set the Search Parameters.

—continued

3 Click the "Save" button below the search field (shown on the previous page). You will be asked to **name** this Smart Folder.

The default location for a Smart Folder is in a "Saved Searches" folder in the invisible Library folder, which is in your Home folder, but you can't see it. That's okay because you are not allowed to put anything in this folder yourself.

However, you do want this folder to be accessible from the Sidebar so you can open files from it, so make sure there's a check in the box "Add To Sidebar" in the Save dialog window (below). Then click the "Save" button.

4 Now that the Smart Folder is saved, all you need to do is single-click it in the Sidebar (below), and your Mac will display all the files that match the criteria you originally set.

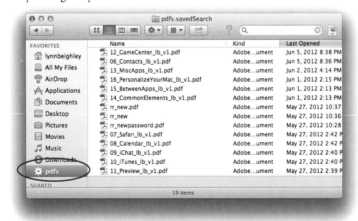

Spotlight Search in System Preferences

As explained in Lesson 16, Spotlight also works in System Preferences. This is great when you know you need a System Preference to do something in particular, but you're not sure *which* one you need.

To search in System Preferences, type into the search field. As you type, Spotlight highlights all the possible preferences that might help you.

When you click one of the options in the pop-up menu that appears, Spotlight highlights the best preference for that option in a bright white spotlight, then opens it for you.

This menu appears as you type a search term.

Spotlight Search in Time Machine

If you use Time Machine to back up your files, you can use Spotlight searches within Time Machine and find files that may not still be on your computer. See Lesson 22 for more about Time Machine.

Spotlight Search in Mail

In Mail, type a search word or phrase in the search field when you can't find a particular message in a large collection of emails. Choose a folder in the Sidebar to search, then choose one of the parameters in the Search Bar (just below the Toolbar).

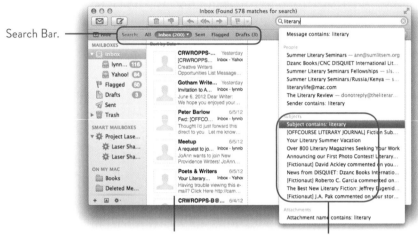

Search Bar.

These results show messages that contain the word "literary."

This menu shows results by category, such as messages with "literary" in the Subject field.

Spotlight Search in Contacts

Control-click a contact name in Contacts, then choose "Spotlight: *contactname.*" A search results window opens to show files and folders on your Mac that match the selected contact name.

Control-click (or right-click) a contact name to reveal this contextual menu.

Spotlight Search in an "Open" Dialog

When you're working in your favorite application and want to open a file to work on, Spotlight can locate all the files with your search phrase in the name that your application thinks it can open and display, plus all folders (it will also search contents of files). From the File menu, choose "Open...." In the Open dialog, as shown below, you can search for a file name or for any content.

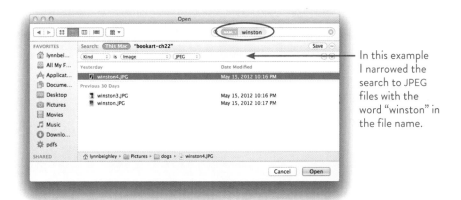

In this example I narrowed the search to JPEG files with the word "winston" in the file name.

22

GOALS

Learn about
Time Machine

Create a backup of your
entire hard disk

Find and restore files

Search in Time Machine

LESSON **22**

Time Machine Backup

You know you should back up important files every day, but really, "I just don't have time today!" Surely everything will be okay for a couple of days until you have time to make backups. Months later, you finally have some extra time and the files are nowhere to be found. Or the original version has been overwritten by a newer version with unwanted changes in it. Oh, if only you had a time machine that could go back in time and grab earlier versions of files. And wouldn't it be nice if the time machine did this without you doing anything—except maybe turning it on?

Wait . . . there *is* such a thing! And, amazingly, it's called . . . Time Machine!

Time Machine can even make backups for you without having a dedicated disk assigned.

About Time Machine

After you set up Time Machine, it backs up your computer regularly. Initially, Time Machine backs up everything, including system files, applications, etc. After that, it only backs up files that have changed. Hourly backups are stored for 24 hours; daily backups are stored for a month; weekly backups are stored until the disk is full. Because backups are stored by date, you can restore files or folders (or your entire system) exactly as they were at certain points in the past.

When the backup disk fills up, Time Machine deletes the oldest files to make room for new ones. It could take a long time to reach this point, but be prepared to either replace the Time Machine disk with another one, or to let Time Machine delete older files as necessary.

While Time Machine is a good solution for temporary storage of backups and is a great way to restore files that have been thrown away, lost, or changed, it isn't a final solution for creating permanent archives. If you plan to use the same backup disk and let Time Machine delete the oldest files, be sure to use other methods to create permanent archives of important files (burn files to CDs or DVDs, copy items to your iCloud, or copy items to other external drives). Remember, it's safest to create *multiple* copies of items that you absolutely cannot afford to lose, and store those copies in several different places—if your office burns down or floods or is burgled, it won't matter if you had 12 backups in that office—they're all gone. Keep in mind that documents printed on paper will last hundreds of years longer than anything you store on any media today.

What kind of disk to use as backup

Use a disk for Time Machine that is separate from the hard disk you work on. An extra internal hard disk is great, and external hard disks work fine too. The disk needs to be big enough to back up the drive it's assigned to. For best results, use a disk dedicated only to Time Machine backups.

Both FireWire and USB disks work with Time Machine. Time Machine backup disks must be formatted as Mac OS Extended (journaled), and have Access Control Lists (ACLS) enabled. Time Machine will erase and reformat the disk if necessary.

Create a Time Machine Backup

It's very easy to start the process. Make sure you have an appropriate disk connected.

To set up Time Machine backups:

1 Once you have an extra **internal** hard disk installed *or* you've connected an **external** hard disk, open Time Machine: Go to the Apple menu, choose "System Preferences…," then click the "Time Machine" icon.

Select this option to place a Time Machine icon in the menu bar that appears at the top of your screen.

Click the icon in the menu bar to access some helpful commands, such as "Back Up Now" and "Open Time Machine Preferences…."

2 Click the "Select Backup Disk…" button. You'll get a list of possible drives that can be used; choose one and click "Use for Backup."

3 Once a backup disk has been assigned, Time Machine switches itself On and displays information about that disk, including when the first backup will start.

4 Click the Options button to display a sheet (shown on the next page) in which you can designate items you want to *exclude* from Time Machine backups.

See the next page.

—continued

5   To add items to the "Exclude these items from backups" list, click the plus (**+**) button, circled below.

Another sheet slides down from the title bar, covering up the one shown below. Select the items (drives, volumes, files, or folders) that you do NOT want Time Machine to back up. Click the "Exclude" button. This returns you to the first sheet, shown below.

To remove items from this list so that Time Machine *will* back them up, select them and click the minus (**−**) button on the sheet shown below.

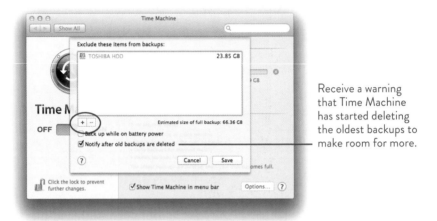

Receive a warning that Time Machine has started deleting the oldest backups to make room for more.

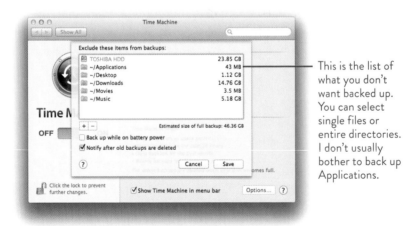

This is the list of what you don't want backed up. You can select single files or entire directories. I don't usually bother to back up Applications.

6 Click "Save."

Time Machine makes an initial backup that includes everything on your computer (shown in progress, below). This backup can be time consuming, depending on how many folders, files, and applications are on your Mac. Subsequent backups are faster since only changed files are backed up.

To stop a backup, click the **X.**

Or slide the ON button to OFF.

To recover backed-up files: Click the Time Machine icon in the menu bar or in Launchpad. Time Machine takes over the screen, as shown below. Use the forward and back arrows or the vertical timeline to go back in time to recover an earlier version of a file. The following pages explain how to do that, and more.

Vertical timeline.

Time Machine navigation tools.

389

How to Use Time Machine

Once you've got Time Machine all set up, as explained on the previous pages, you're ready to use it to find earlier versions of files that have changed (see below) or to find files that are now missing from your Mac.

To find and restore a file:

1   On your Desktop, select a file or folder.

2   Single-click the Time Machine icon in the menu bar or in Launchpad. Time Machine takes over the screen. It shows the current Finder window in the foreground, with earlier versions of that same window receding into the past. The file you selected is still selected.

Notice that the middle of the horizontal bar at the bottom of the star field is labeled "Today (Now)." In other words, the files shown or accessed through this particular window are the same as what is on your computer right now.

3   To go back in time and find *previous* versions of the selected file, click the back-in-time arrow (circled, below). Time Machine zooms back in time through the floating windows until it reaches a window where an earlier version of the selected file exists.

Click "Cancel" to exit Time Machine, or press Escape on your keyboard.

Navigate back in time to older backups, and forward again.

Notice that the bar at the bottom of the window now identifies the time that this version of the file was last saved.

If this isn't the version of the file you're looking for, click the back-in-time arrow again to find earlier versions. *Or* drag your pointer over the vertical timeline on the right edge of the screen and select a backup time or date.

4 **To restore the version of the file** you want, first make sure it's selected. Then click the "Restore" button on the right side of the horizontal bar at the bottom of the screen.

To go directly to a specific backup date and time, click in this timeline.

The windows seem to blur as you move back in time!

The backup date and time of the visible files.   Restore the selected version.

5 A message asks if you want to keep the original version of the file (instead of the backup), keep both files, *or* replace the original with the backup version.

If you choose "Keep Both," a restored copy of the backed-up file is made and put in its original location on your computer. The word "original" is added to the original file's name (right).

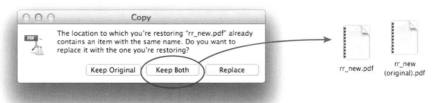

Do a Search in Time Machine

When you use Spotlight to search for items on your computer, the search naturally takes place in the "Now" time frame; in other words, it finds files in their current versions. But if you've lost or deleted files, Time Machine can zoom into the past and find the files in the various states in which it saved them.

Search in Time Machine:

1   Single-click the Time Machine icon in the menu bar or in Launchpad.

   The Time Machine screen appears, with Finder windows receding into the past. Type your search string into the Search field on the foremost Finder window, just as you would on your regular Desktop.

2   Click the back-in-time arrow. Time Machine zooms back in time until it finds the item and displays its name. To look for an even earlier version of the item, click the back-in-time arrow again, *or* click in the timeline along the right edge of the screen. Notice that the time label in the horizontal bar at the bottom of the screen shows when the *selected* item was backed up.

3   When you find the item you want, click "Restore" on the right side of the bar at the bottom of the Time Machine screen (circled below).

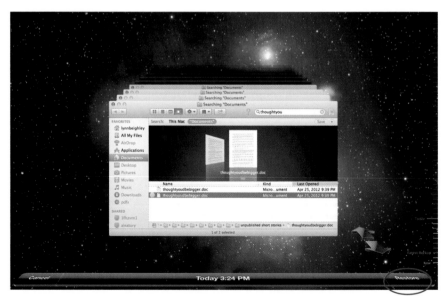

To show a Quick Look preview of a selected item, tap the Spacebar.
To close Quick Look, tap the Spacebar again.

Tech Stuff

23

GOALS

Get Connected and Share Files

On a Mac, you have various ways to connect to the Internet. You might have a dial-up account that goes through your phone line, a cable modem, a DSL modem, a wireless connection, an Ethernet office connection that plugs into a broadband setup, or some other arrangement.

And you have various ways to connect your Macs together in a home or office. Once your computers are on a local network, you can transfer files between them and even access your own Mac from another computer.

The feature that most amazes me is screen sharing, where you can connect to someone else's computer and actually see her screen and use her computer! It has been invaluable in allowing people to help friends and families on their computers across the country.

How Your Mac Connects to the Internet

When you first turned on or upgraded your Mac and walked through the setup process, you probably filled in the information for your Internet connection. The Network preferences is where your Mac stored that information and where you can change it, adjust it, or troubleshoot it.

The Network preferences lists all of the ways that your Mac might be connected and displays the current status of each option. You can configure all interfaces for all your possible connections from this one window.

To open the Network preferences, go to the Apple menu and choose "System Preferences…." Single-click the "Network" icon.

When you first open the window, it probably looks something like the one below, showing you the status of any possible connections your Mac might have access to.

The available "network port configurations" for your Mac are shown here.

This pane shows how you are connected to the Internet and to the other computers in your office.

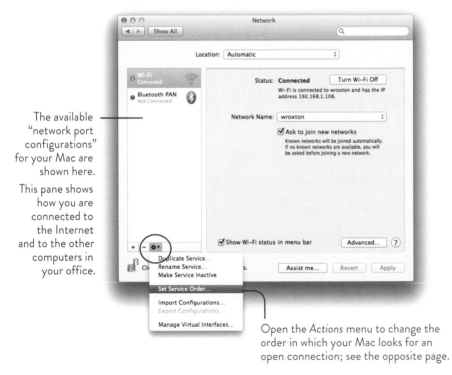

Open the *Actions* menu to change the order in which your Mac looks for an open connection; see the opposite page.

Check the port configurations

You might have several options for connecting. For instance, your Mac might recognize a modem port, if you have one (whether or not you use it), and it might find a wireless card and an Ethernet port. Every possibility it finds is listed in the Network preferences, in that pane on the left side.

As you see on the opposite page, you can open the *Actions* menu (shown circled) and choose to "Set Service Order...." This is the first place you go if there is a connection problem because the Mac goes down this list in order and chooses the first interface that works. **If you're having problems making a connection,** make sure your *preferred* connection is at the top of the list—just drag it to the top. Click ok, then click the "Apply" button to force the change.

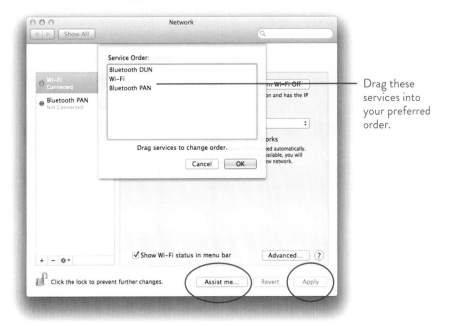

Drag these services into your preferred order.

Establish a new connection

If you didn't set up your Internet connection when you first installed Mountain Lion or turned on your brand-new Mac, you can always do it in this Network preferences pane. Just click "Assist me..." (circled above). A sheet drops down from the title bar (as shown on page 399). In that sheet, click the button labeled "Assistant...." It will walk you through the process.

Troubleshoot Your Internet Connection

If your connection doesn't work when you first turn on your Mac, perhaps the information you entered in the setup process wasn't correct. Or if you changed Internet service providers (ISPs) or changed your connection process, you might need to change the information. Most of the information is supplied automatically, but if your provider says you need to change a setting, this is where you'll do it. There is also a little trick you can do here that sometimes kicks things into gear.

Network

1 From the Apple menu, choose "System Preferences...," then click the "Network" icon.

2 In the left-hand pane, you can instantly tell whether or not your Mac thinks your connection is working. (Sometimes the Mac swears it's working, but it isn't and you know it.) Choose the connection that you need to fix or change.

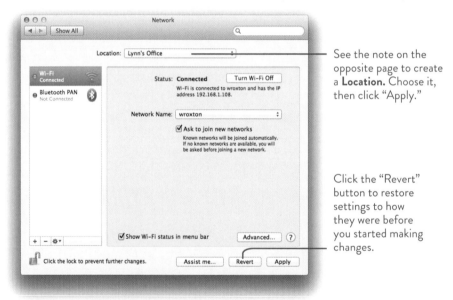

See the note on the opposite page to create a **Location.** Choose it, then click "Apply."

Click the "Revert" button to restore settings to how they were before you started making changes.

3 First, use the technique on the previous two pages to make sure the connection you want to choose is the first one in the list. Click "Apply." Wait a minute or two and see if your browser will connect to the Internet. If not . . .

4 This trick often works if all the settings are correct and there's no major problem with your modem or router (if you have one): Change any setting; for instance, if you see "Using DHCP," change it to "Manually." Then immediately switch it back. This makes the "Apply" button available. Click the Apply button. Sometimes all it needs is a kick in the pants to make it take effect.

5   If you think the settings need to change, do so here; you need to click the "Advanced…" button to get to the rest of the settings. If you're not sure what the appropriate settings are, you have two choices:

   ■ Call your **ISP** and ask them what to enter in which panes. Your ISP is the company to whom you pay the monthly fee for your connection to the Internet. Although these windows look scary, there are only two or three settings you need. If you use cable or DSL with "DHCP," it probably sets it up for you automatically. Click "Apply."

   To check, open Safari and see if it goes to a web page. If it does, you're done.

   ■ *Or* use the **Network Diagnostics tool,** as described in the following steps.

6   Click the "Assist me…" button at the bottom of the Network pane. This drops down a sheet from the title bar, as shown below. For troubleshooting help, click the "Diagnostics…" button.

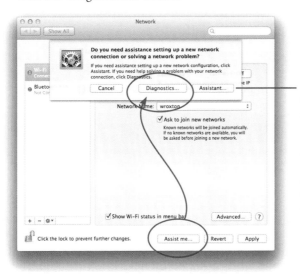

If you take your laptop to various places where the connections are different, use the **Assistant** to set up the specific settings for the various **Locations**. It saves the settings for you—choose that **Location** from the Location menu in this pane and your laptop is ready to connect in that particular place.

7   The diagnostics tool will check all the relevant settings on your Mac and ask you simple questions. If it can't fix the problem, it will at least pinpoint it so you can call your ISP with the specific issue.

Use the AirPort Utility

AirPort Utility

If your connection is through an AirPort wireless setup, use the AirPort Utility to see if it knows what's wrong. You'll find this tool in the Utilities folder, which is inside the Applications folder. Don't randomly change settings—either let it make the appropriate changes, or ask someone knowledgeable. There is an option to restore the original factory settings and set it up again from scratch.

Unplug everything and reboot

Your modem box, whether it's a dial-up, cable, or DSL, usually has a tiny **reset button.** It's often so tiny you need to poke it with a pin or paper clip. That can sometimes get things going again.

If not, do the unplug routine (I have to assume you've got all the wires in the right places). First, shut down your Mac. Then, if you have a number of devices in your system, such as a switch, a router, and a modem box, unplug the items starting with the smallest one, the dumbest one. That would be the switch, if you have one. Next, the router (which might be your AirPort Base Station). Last, unplug the modem itself. Let everything sit for several minutes.

Then plug everything back in again in the opposite order—start with the most important item first, the modem box. Let it get going and make sure all the lights are green. If the problem is in your modem box, call your provider.

Then plug in the router, if you're using one, and let it get going. Then the switch. Let everything get running, then turn your Mac back on.

Sometimes I go through all this and give up. Shortly thereafter it starts working again. Sheesh.

Call a friend, check your cables, talk to your ISP

Call a friend in your neighborhood who uses the same ISP and see if she is connected. If her connection is down as well, then just let go and wait until they fix it.

Check your cables—one might have wiggled loose or gone bad. They do that sometimes. If you're setting up your Internet connection for the first time and using Ethernet cables, make sure they're the right kind; see page 406.

If everything seems okay on your end and you still can't get connected to the Internet, call your ISP. They can check your modem from their office and help pinpoint the cause.

Troubleshoot Your Mail Account

The problems that can happen with connectivity are different for a new account setup than for a working account.

Setting up a new account

If you have problems getting your email to start working **for the first time,** first make sure your Internet connection is working, of course (check by making sure your browser can get to the Internet). Then check your account information in Mail (go to the Mail menu, choose "Preferences," and click the "Accounts" tab):

The **Description** is anything that will tell you which account this is.

The **Email Address** and **Full Name** describe your mail to those you send it to so they know who it's coming from.

- The **Incoming Mail Server** is information that you have to get from whoever hosts that particular email account. I have lots of email accounts, not one of which is with my ISP. So I need to get the Incoming Mail Server of each of the hosts where I have the email *coming from.* Typically it's something like *mail. domain.com* or *pop.domain.com.* And as I mentioned in the Mail lesson, some providers don't allow you to get your email through a mail application like this; see Lesson 5.

- Keep in mind that some ISPs have a different **User Name** and **Password** *for your account with them* than the user name and password to get your email. This is especially true if you've had the account for a long time. If your email account is not with your ISP, then of course the account information in your Mail window is definitely not the same as for your ISP. You might have to check their web site or call your email host and ask what to enter here.

—continued

■ The **Outgoing Mail Server** (SMTP, Simple Mail Transfer Protocol) is usually from your ISP, no matter where your email account is located. You *can* use a Gmail or other SMTP, but if your outgoing mail is having trouble, you are assured of being able to *send mail out* if you use your ISP's SMTP. If you don't know what the SMTP is, call and ask them or check their web site—it should be listed. Or if you want, you might be able to use your ISP's server. For example, I could use the same Comcast SMTP because that's who connects me to the Internet.

To change your SMTP setting, click on the "Outgoing Mail Server (SMTP)" pop-up menu and select "Edit SMTP Server List…." Click the **+** button to add an SMTP server. Double-click the blue bar that appears to add the SMTP name. Make sure that is the *selected* server (highlighted in blue), then click OK.

Some companies will not give you an SMTP address unless you pay an extra fee. If you don't want to pay the extra fee, you cannot use the Mail application—you must go to the company's web site and do all mail online.

Reminder: where to get the information: Your email provider's web site should include the information for the *incoming* mail server (also known as the POP address, Post Office Protocol), user name, and password. Your ISP's web site should provide the SMTP (*outgoing* mail server) address information.

If you have a **free webmail account** like Google, Yahoo, or Hotmail, and it didn't get set up automatically when you went through the setup process, go to the service's web site and search for POP mail instructions. Or go to Google and search for something like "Google POP settings Mac," or "Yahoo SMTP settings Mac," etc.

Working account (that's not working)

If you've been using Mail for a while and it stops working, try this:

■ **If an email message won't go out** and you positively know the address is correct, retype the address. Retype the whole thing, even if the automatic address appears. Retype the whole thing, and hit Return. Try sending again.

Keep in mind that when sending to a list of people, if any one address is wrong, it can stop the whole process. So check carefully.

■ Maybe your mailbox on the server is full. If you have a POP email account set up, you can tell Mail to "Remove copy from server after retrieving a message" (go to the Mail menu, choose "Preferences…," click the "Accounts" tab, then click the "Advanced" tab). This prevents your POP server from running out of storage room over time; however, sometimes Mail doesn't remove messages from the server even if you've told it to, so check the account info:

1   In Mail's sidebar, select the POP Inbox that's having trouble.

2   Press Command I to open the "Account Info" window (as shown below).

3   Click the "Messages on Server" tab to show the email messages that are on the POP mail server. Select all (or some) of the messages shown in the window, then click the "Remove from Server" button.

4   Close the Info window. Restart Mail and try again.

Someone might have sent you a two gigabyte attachment that needs to be deleted from the server. Sort your messages by size to see.

Use the Mail Connection Doctor

If your account information is correct but email still isn't working, check this utility: In Mail, go to the Window menu and choose "Connection Doctor." You'll get the window shown below; it will check your accounts. If it finds a problem, the dot is red; depending on the problem, you may be able to click the "Assistant..." button (page 397) to help pinpoint the issue further.

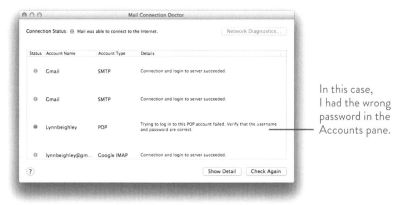

In this case, I had the wrong password in the Accounts pane.

iCloud Automatic Storage and Syncing

iCloud is a service from Apple that automatically uploads and syncs most of your apps including Mail, Notes, Reminders, Contacts, Calendar, and even your Safari tabs allowing you to share data between Macs and Apple devices. iCloud uploads content without you having to do anything and synchronizes that information to all your iOS devices (such as the iPhone 4, iPad, or iPod touch). It requires mobile devices to run iOS 5 or later. Use iCloud services for free (5 gigabytes of file storage included) and buy more storage if you wish.

Setting up iCloud

1 From the Apple menu, choose "System Preferences...." Click the "iCloud" icon.

2 The first time you open the settings, you'll need to sign in with your Apple ID and password (see below).

3 You're given a couple of options to choose from (see below). The first checkbox sets up iCloud for you in your most common applications without any further work on your part. The second sets up the "Find My Mac" feature, which lets you locate your Mac from a web browser or an iOS device with the Find My iPhone app, and will even allow you to lock or erase your machine remotely.

Choose this option to turn on iCloud storage for Contacts, Calendar, Reminders, Notes, and Safari all at once. After you click Next, you can turn on or off iCloud for each individual app.

If you check either of these options, you'll see some explanatory or warning alerts confirming your choice of these options.

Your Mac will keep track of and broadcast its location periodically when it's on.

Customizing iCloud

After you activate iCloud as in the steps on the previous page, you'll be able to customize particular apps and how they behave in the cloud. Go back to the iCloud settings by clicking the "iCloud" icon in the "System Preferences."

You should see all the applications that will work with iCloud listed on the right. Click on an individual application's checkbox to turn on or off its iCloud access. Most will open an alert asking for further instructions.

Checking the box next to most apps will require you to answer a further question about the iCloud storage you want to set up. Unchecking boxes will open questions about saving your data locally or warnings that it will all be lost if you carry out the operation.

The amount of green in this bar indicates how much of your free 5 GB of storage you've used up. If you're running out, you can either delete some things or purchase more by clicking the "Manage" button.

Managing iCloud

Is your green bar almost all the way across? You can either buy more storage or delete some of the iCloud data you're storing. Open System Preferences and choose the iCloud preferences. Click the Manage button on the bottom of the iCloud preferences pane (see below).

Clicking on any application on the left opens a list of files saved for that application (see below). Click any file you don't feel needs to be available on other devices. Deleting files frees up more of your free 5 GB. The file is not deleted from your Mac!

If you can't delete enough to stay within your free 5 GB quota, you can buy more storage by clicking here.

Select any of these files and then click Delete (circled) to remove it from the iCloud, but not from your computer. Or (if you're sure you don't need it) you can click Delete All.

Share Files on a Local Network

File sharing on a local network is so great—as Apple says, your Mac just "discovers" other Macs. But it can't discover them unless the computers are connected in some way. So first, a wee bit about networking.

Simple networking

The Macs you want to share files between must be **networked** together—which means you must have some sort of cable connecting them to each other or both to the same printer, or AirPort cards installed so they can connect to each other wirelessly. Networking can get very complex and specialized! We're only going to explain the simplest method to get a couple of Macs talking to each other.

Wireless

If you have working wireless connections on your Macs in your home or office or coffee shop, you're all set. Skip to page 408, "Turn on Personal File Sharing."

Ethernet cables

If you're not wireless, you'll need Ethernet cables, available at office supply stores.

- If the cables are going from the computer into a hub, router, or switcher, or into a cable or DSL modem, you need **straight-through cables**— not *crossover* cables. Straight-through cables are more common.

- If the cables go directly between two computers (or between any two Ethernet devices, like a Mac and a printer), you need **crossover cables** (see below).

To tell if an Ethernet cable is crossover or not, hold both ends up, facing the same direction, with the locking clips facing up. Look at the colored wires.

- A straight-through cable has the colored wires in **exactly the same order.**

- A crossover cable does **not** have the colored wires in the same order.

Just two computers?

Two computers can be connected with one crossover Ethernet cable **or** a FireWire cable for easy and instant file sharing on two working Macs.

If you have one Mac that is having trouble and you want to copy files off of it onto a reliable machine, use a FireWire cable and Target Disk Mode (see Lesson 26).

What else you need

If you have a number of machines in your office (and it's not wireless), you will need something called an **Ethernet switch** that can connect all of your machines, including your modem. The switch will have a number of Ethernet ports; you connect each Mac *to that box* with straight (not crossover) Ethernet cables. (If you want to share printers, see Lesson 19; it's easy once you have your network working.)

If you have several computers in your office, a broadband connection, and all your Macs get on the Internet at the same time, you're probably using a **router**—you're already set up for networking. An AirPort base station can function as a router.

If the router doesn't have enough ports for the items in your office, buy the small **hub** or **switch** mentioned above and connect the router to it with an Ethernet cable.

Peer-to-peer network

This simple network in a small office is called a **peer-to-peer network,** where every computer is considered a "server," which is a computer that can "serve" files to others. This is different from a client-server network in a large corporation, where lots of computers connect to one huge, main server and everyone gets files from that main server, rather than from each other's computers.

Sharing files on one computer

If you have created more than one user on a Mac, as explained in Lesson 20, all users can share files with each other yet still remain perfectly private.

Turn on Personal File Sharing

Now that your computers are connected, you need to set up who is allowed to share and which files they can have access to. The default File Sharing settings might work perfectly fine for you, where any user on the network can log in with her own password, then see files in your Public folder and drop files into your Drop Box; any user with *your* user name and password can access all the files on your computer and drop files anywhere on your Mac. If the defaults sound fine, follow Steps 1–3, then skip to the next page. If you want to control who has access and to what, see below.

To turn on File Sharing:

1 On each Mac, go to the Apple menu and choose "System Preferences…." Click the "Sharing" icon.

2 Your computer has a name, shown in the "Computer Name" field. Give it a new name that clearly identifies which Mac it is (Kitchen Mac, Teenagers' iMac, Dad's Laptop, Mom's Office Computer, etc.).

3 Put a checkmark in "File Sharing."

4 In the bottom-right of the pane, you see that your Public folder is now shared, and to its right you see who is allowed in.

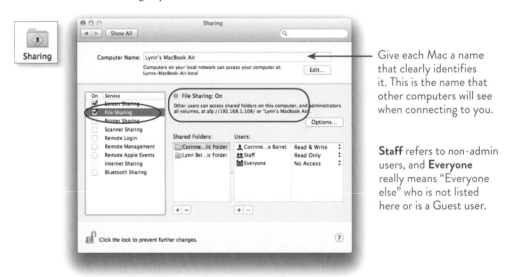

Give each Mac a name that clearly identifies it. This is the name that other computers will see when connecting to you.

Staff refers to *non*-admin users, and **Everyone** really means "Everyone else" who is not listed here or is a Guest user.

5 This might be all you need, if the conditions mentioned above (in the first paragraph) apply to you. Skip to page 410.

Any user you've set up on a Mac can access their own Home folders (and your Public folder) from anywhere on the local network. They can also access the Shared folder and any folders for which you have provided permission.

6 If you want to be more specific about which folders others can share with you, add a folder to the "Shared Folders" pane, select its name, and then add or delete the users who are allowed to use it. Also determine what kind of privileges they can have.

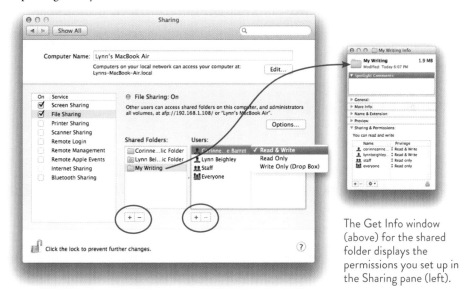

The Get Info window (above) for the shared folder displays the permissions you set up in the Sharing pane (left).

Share files with Windows users

You can share files with Windows users: Click the "Options…" button on the Sharing pane and check the box for **SMB** (Server Message Block) users (Apple uses AFP, Apple Filing Protocol). You will need to enter the Windows user's password.

Connect to Another Mac

Once the Macs are connected in some way and they all have File Sharing turned on in the Sharing preferences (as explained on the previous pages), you're ready to connect.

Make sure you are in the Finder (single-click any blank space on the Desktop). Then follow *either* Process **A** or **B**. Process A is simpler, faster, and more dependable.

Process A, directly through the Finder window:

1 Open any Finder window. Click the Column View icon (circled below).

2 In the Sidebar, if your "SHARED" group is not visible, hover over the word "SHARED" to display the word "Show." Click "Show" to display the other computers on the network.

3 Single-click the name of the computer to which you want to connect.

   You are automatically connected as a *Guest*. What you see in the window below is the Public folder of a shared computer on the local network. As a Guest, you can take a copy of any folder in the Public folder, and you can select the "Public Folder" and put files into the shared computer's Drop Box.

   Now, all of this depends on what the administrator of the other computer has set up as privileges or permissions, but the features above are the defaults.

Your connection status is shown here.

A Guest can drop files in the Drop Box. What else a Guest can do depends on the settings in the Sharing pane, shown on the previous page.

> **TIP** —— To keep track of which computer you're working on and which computer you are viewing in a window, use Column View (as above) so you can see where a folder originates.

4 **To access your own user account on this other computer,** click the "Connect As…" button (circled on the opposite page). You need to know your name and password to log in as a "Registered User" (see below).

If you have the correct information, click the "Connect" button and log in. You will have access to all the files *in your user account* on that Mac.

To access ALL files on this other computer *and* to be able to copy files to it, you need to know the name and password of the Admin user to whom this computer belongs (that might be you, if you're trying to get access to your own computer from somewhere else). Click the "Connect As…" button, and choose to log on as a "Registered User." If you have the correct information, you will have full access to everything on that Mac, plus you will be able to transfer files onto it.

On your computer, this box shows up with *your* name in the "Name" field, deluding you into thinking it wants *your* name and password. No! If you're trying to connect to another computer, it wants the name and password of the Admin (or a user) on *that* computer!

Guess how long it took me to figure *that* out.

TIP —— If you need to share files on a local network regularly, you can drag a folder from another computer and put it on your computer and even in your Sidebar. Then you can move and save files directly into that folder on the other computer. You don't even have to go through the connection process—as soon as you put something in that folder, it acts as an alias and makes the connection.

Process B, through the Go menu:

1   From the Finder's Go menu, choose "Connect to Server...." The window below appears.

If you know the name of the Mac you want to connect to (as shown in the Sharing pane of the *other* Mac; see page 408), type it in the "Server Address" field, with ".local" after its name.

Or enter the **afp://** number that you see circled in the Sharing preferences pane on page 408.

If you connect to the same computer regularly, click this button to put the address in the "Favorite Servers" list.

2   Click the "Connect" button. You'll see this window:

To connect as a **Guest,** you won't need a name and password; see the previous page.

To connect as a **Registered User,** you need to enter a name and password of someone who has a user account on the other computer. **Important!** Even though this window shows up with *your* name in the field, it doesn't want *your* name and password (unless you have a user account on that machine)— it's asking for the name and password *of an account owner on the computer you're trying to connect to!*

To access all files as if you are the Admin of that computer, enter the Admin name and password as a Registered User.

3   Enter the name and password for the account on the other computer, then click "Connect."

4   The next window that appears lists the available disks for that registered user. If you entered the Admin name and password, you will see the hard disk, the Home folder, any partitions or other hard disks attached to the other Mac, and any other volumes that are currently shared (you won't have access to the files belonging to any other user account). Double-click the disk to which you want to connect.

To have access to more than one of the available volumes, Command-click the others. You can also repeat this entire process if you decide later you need to connect to another volume.

This is the Home folder of the shared computer.

5   In the Sidebar of any Finder window on the computer you're working from, you'll see a shared volume icon, shown below. Single-click that icon to open its window, as shown below.

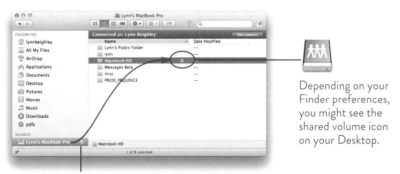

Depending on your Finder preferences, you might see the shared volume icon on your Desktop.

This icon means the disk is connected.
Click this *eject* button to disconnect.

It's not easy to keep track of which windows are on which machine since the default folders all have the same names! Don't *open* any applications or documents from the window of the other Mac because you will actually be working on the other machine at that point, which might affect the person using it. It's best to drag the necessary documents to your own computer before you open them.

Disconnect from a Shared Server

Disconnect from any connected servers in the same way you disconnect from any other hard disk.

- Click the *Eject* symbol next to the server name in the Sidebar:

- *Or* if the server is visible on the Desktop, drag its icon to the Trash.

- *Or* select the server icon; go to the File menu and choose "Eject."

- *Or* select the server icon and press Command E for Eject.

- *Or* Control-click a server icon to get the contextual menu; choose "Eject *'disk'*."

This is a server icon. Whether or not a server icon appears on your screen when you're connected is determined by the Finder preferences, as explained below.

To hide or show the servers on the Desktop or in the Sidebar:

1 In the Finder, go to the Finder menu and choose "Preferences…."

2 Click the "General" tab, if it isn't already selected.

3 Check or uncheck the box to show "Connected servers."

   When the box is unchecked, you won't see the server icons on the Desktop, but they will all be accessible in the Sidebar.

4 You can go to the Sidebar pane in that same Finder preferences (click the "Sidebar" icon in the toolbar) and choose to take connected server icons *out* of the Sidebar and leave them on the Desktop.

   Don't take the server icons out of both the Sidebar *and* the Desktop or you won't be able to find them!

AirDrop

If you have a new Mac running Mountain Lion, you'll see "AirDrop" in your Finder window Sidebar. This makes it extremely easy to send files back and forth over any local wireless connection, as in a coffee shop, tea house, office building, or anywhere.

Just click "AirDrop" in your Sidebar (which you've probably done by now). When anyone else on the same network opens their AirDrop window while you're looking at your AirDrop window, you will all appear in the window together. Just drop a file on someone else's icon. He will be asked if he is willing to receive it, and then to "Save" or "Save and Open" the file. If you save the file, it immediately downloads into your Downloads folder.

You and another Mac user must click on "AirDrop" in the Sidebars on your laptops.

On your laptop, drag and drop a file on the other Mac user's icon.

The other user has to approve the file transmission.

Screen Sharing

Screen Sharing enables someone else on your local network to see your screen, or you can see his. This is especially great for anyone who has experienced the frustration of trying to give Mac support and instruction over the phone or through email. Now you can activate Screen Sharing and watch someone's cursor as you give instructions, or take control of the buddy's cursor while she watches and listens. When Screen Sharing is activated through Messages or Bonjour (page 419), it also starts an audio chat so you can discuss whatever matter is at hand.

Set up screen sharing on both Macs

Before you start Screen Sharing, both computers need to turn on "Screen Sharing" in the Sharing pane of System Preferences:

1 From the Apple menu, choose "Preferences...." Click the "Sharing" icon.

2 Put a checkmark in the option called "Screen Sharing," shown below.

3 If you have other users on the computer, you can choose to allow only certain ones to share that computer from somewhere else: Check the button "Only these users," then click the **+** button to add the ones you want. Close the preferences and carry on.

Your computer's vnc number (circled) can be useful; see page 418.

Choose who you want to have access to your computer through screen sharing.

Screen Share on your local network via your Sidebar

Below is a fast and simple way to connect to another computer on your home/office network to screen the share and access the computer. Your computers must be connected, of course, as explained on the previous pages, and both computers must have Screen Sharing turned on in the Sharing preferences (see the opposite page).

You must know a user name and password. The other user will *not* be asked permission—her screen will immediately appear on your monitor as a separate and moveable window, and you will have control of her mouse (she can also control it on her end). You will not be able to hear each other. This is kind of creepy because it means someone could watch what you're doing on your Mac and you wouldn't even know it (unless you notice a tiny new icon in the menu bar, toward the right, that looks like overlapping rectangles).

To open a screen sharing session:

1   Make sure your Finder window is using Column View, as shown below.

2   In the list of "SHARED" files in your Finder window Sidebar, select another Mac.

3   You will see a "Share Screen…" button, shown below (if you don't see it, the other user has not turned on Screen Sharing, as explained on the opposite page). Click it, and a Finder window opens the other computer in a window on your Mac. Ta-da. You can go back and forth between the other screen and yours simply by clicking on your Desktop or on the screen-sharing window.

To end a screen sharing session on the computer that started it, close the window as if it's a Finder window, *or* go to the "Screen Sharing" menu in that window and choose "Close," *or* go to the Dock icon, right-click on it, and choose "Quit."

On the other computer, the user can end the session by going to the little overlapping monitor icon in the menu bar and choosing to disconnect.

While screen sharing, you'll see this icon in your Dock.

Screen Share on your local network through the Go menu

This is another method to screen share with a user who is on the same local network, *or* with someone on the Internet if you know their *static* IP address (if neither you nor he knows if he has a static IP address, he doesn't have one, but you can still use Messages; see the following page).

1   First make sure you get the vnc address from the computer you want to connect to. This address appears in the Sharing preferences pane when you turn on Screen Sharing—you can see it circled on page 416.

2   In the Finder, go to the Go menu and choose "Connect to Server…." You'll get the window shown below.

3   Type in the vnc address as shown below. Click the "Connect" button.

If you need to share this screen often, click the + button to make the address a favorite. It will appear in this pane under "Favorite Servers" whenever you open this window.

4   The other person's entire computer appears in a moveable window on your screen. You can open his Mail and have it read aloud to him, or open Sticky notes and leave a message. Or just spy on what he's doing. It's creepy.

5   **To end a screen sharing session** on the computer that started it, close the window as if it's a Finder window, *or* go to the "Screen Sharing" menu in that window and choose "Close," *or* go to the Screen Sharing icon in the Dock, right-click on it, and choose "Quit."

    On the other computer, the user can end the session by going to the little overlapping monitors icon in the menu bar and choosing to disconnect.

You can also use Bonjour to screen share on a local network, as explained on the following page. Using Bonjour, you'll be able to talk to each other as well, plus you can send files back and forth.

Screen Share Globally Through Messages

Of course, the buddy whose screen you want to share (anywhere in the world) must be using a Mac running OS X 10.5 or later, have iChat or Messages turned on, and have turned on Screen Sharing, as explained on page 417.

1   **To screen share globally through Messages or locally through Bonjour,** open your Messages Buddies list.

2   You can tell which buddies are capable of and have turned on Screen Sharing: When you select a name in the list, the *Screen Sharing* button at the bottom of the Messages Buddies list is black (instead of gray).

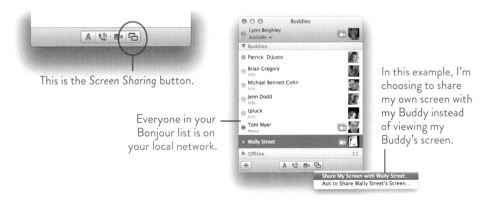

This is the *Screen Sharing* button.

Everyone in your Bonjour list is on your local network.

In this example, I'm choosing to share my own screen with my Buddy instead of viewing my Buddy's screen.

3   Click a buddy's name. Click that Screen Sharing button and choose "Share My Screen..." or "Share (Buddy Name's) Screen...."

4   When you receive and accept the invitation to share someone's screen, the other (remote) screen appears full-size on your screen, while your own Desktop appears as a miniature screen (as shown on page 417). When you mouse over the miniature screen, a "Switch to My Computer" message appears.

   To enlarge your own Desktop to full-size and miniaturize the *remote* screen, click anywhere on the miniature screen. Meanwhile, the buddy who initiated Screen Sharing doesn't see miniature versions on his own screen, even though you can now control his computer, grab files, open applications, or do anything he can do.

   To end a screen sharing session, click the circle-**X** in the top-left corner of the miniaturized screen. *Or* go to the Messages icon in the menu bar and choose "End Screen Sharing."

24

GOALS

Basic Troubleshooting

All computers, even Macs, act funny at times. Fortunately, it's often something that you can fix yourself. These are the steps I follow to fix troubles on Macs, before calling tech support. I go down the list until the problem is fixed (but also check this chapter for other problem-solving tips):

Make sure you've got plenty of free space on the hard disk, at least a gigabyte. If not, clear up space and restart.

Quit and then restart the application that's causing trouble. If it's really having trouble, you might have to force quit the app (see the next page) and then relaunch it.

Relaunch the Finder (see page 423) if it's a problem on the Desktop.

Restart the computer (or Shut Down for a more serious but still quick test, then reboot). See page 423.

Do a Safe Boot (see page 426), then restart to see if that fixed it.

Repair permissions (see page 424) and see if that fixed things.

Then you might throw away the preferences file for the application that's giving you trouble (see page 427) and restart the computer.

If you *transferred* the application to your Mac instead of *reinstalling* it from the original disk, reinstall the application from the disk.

And restart yet again.

I've rarely had an issue that could not be resolved with the above steps.

Hard Disk Is Making Noise?

If your hard disk makes noise, stop everything. Don't create new files, copy, or paste. Call your tech support person right away, or shut down the Mac and take it to the repair shop. The hard disk should never make any sound other than an occasional soft whir. If it's making noise, there is something seriously wrong that could damage your data. Don't risk your data!

Force Quit an Application

Sometimes just one application has trouble and you need to force it to quit. There are two ways to **force quit** any application. This doesn't affect any other application or the system. If an application isn't responding to anything you ask it to do, if it's hung up and the wheel keeps spinning, or it won't let you quit, then force quit the app. After you've force quit an application, try restarting it. It should be fine.

- Hold down the Option key and **press** *(don't click)* on the application's icon in the Dock. A menu pops up with a choice to "Force Quit." Choose it.

- **Or** press Command Option Esc. The window called "Force Quit Applications" appears. From this window, select the application you want to force quit (if it isn't already selected), then click the "Force Quit" button.

Relaunch the Finder

You can't force quit the Finder, but you can **relaunch** it, which only takes a minute. If things are acting a little squirrely, try this. It doesn't hurt anything.

■ Hold down the Option key and **press** *(don't click)* on the Finder icon in the Dock. A menu pops up with a choice to "Relaunch."

■ *Or* press Command Option Esc (as explained on the opposite page) to open the "Force Quit Applications" window. Select the Finder in the list, and the "Force Quit" button changes to "Relaunch." Click it.

Quit All Apps Before Restart

Mountain Lion has a "resume" feature in that when you restart, it automatically reopens every application that was opened when you chose to restart or shut down. If you're troubleshooting, you usually don't want that to happen. So quit all open apps before trying other troubleshooting techniques.

Restart

It's amazing what a simple **restart** will fix. If you rarely turn off your Mac (like me), sometimes little things may start acting a bit quirky. Perhaps your Mac can't find the printer you've been using for months, or icons for new files don't appear. For little unexplainable things, restart. Because the Mac will *resume* all of your applications that you have open, it's a good idea to first **quit** every application before you restart.

■ **To Restart,** go to the Apple menu and choose "Restart…."

■ On most laptops, **press the Power button for one second** and you'll get a little message with a button to restart.

If you **can't restart,** then Shut Down; see below.

Shut Down

Sometimes shutting down fixes small problems that a restart doesn't fix. This is especially useful when you're having connection problems. For a clean shut down and reboot, first **quit** all of your open applications.

■ **To Shut Down,** go to the Apple menu and choose "Shut Down…."

■ Sometimes things are so bad you can't even get to the Apple menu. In that case, **hold down the Power button** (the one you push to turn on your Mac) for at least five seconds. This forces it to shut down.

Repair Permissions

Due to occasional file corruption issues, something called "permissions" can go bad and cause trouble. Repairing the permissions can solve many mysterious things.

1   Open Disk Utility: Open Launchpad and look in Other *or* go to the Applications folder, then open the Utilities folder.

In the Utilities folder, find the Disk Utility and open it. You'll see this:

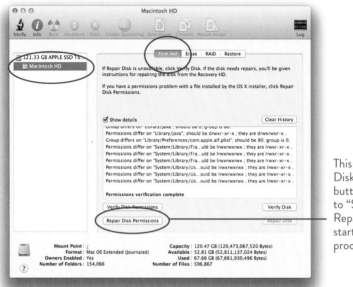

This is the "Repair Disk Permissions" button. It changes to "Stop Permission Repair" when you start the repair process.

2   Make sure the "First Aid" tab is selected.

3   Select the hard disk in the left pane.

4   Click the button "Repair Disk Permissions."

Depending on how much stuff you have on your hard disk, the process can take up to 20 minutes or so. If the Mac finds any permissions that need to be repaired, it will repair them.

If it finds things it can't repair, then you need to go to the next step and verify and repair the *disk*. See the following page.

5   Quit the Disk Utility.

Verify and Repair Disk

First, go through the steps on the previous page to repair permissions, just to clear up any little issues. Don't quit the Disk Utility yet.

If you think the disk might need to be repaired, or if you just want to check to see if the disk has a problem, click the button in Disk Utility (shown on the previous page) to "Verify Disk." This will check the disk to see if it really does have a problem that needs to be (and can be) repaired.

If the disk needs to be repaired, restart your computer using the original OS X install disk or Flash drive, because *Disk Utility can't repair the same disk it's running on.* If you have an external drive that has been set up as a "boot" drive (with an operating system on it), you can use that to start up your computer.

So get the original install disk/Flash drive that came with your Mac, or attach your boot drive. Then:

1 Insert the original install disk. Double-click the "Install" icon as if you were going to install the system again.

2 At the Welcome window, DO NOT INSTALL! Go to the Utilities menu at the top of the screen. Choose "Disk Utility...."

3 You get the window shown on the previous page. *Now* you can click the button to "Repair Disk." Let it run through its process. It might take up to a half hour or more. Be patient.

4 When it's done, it will probably tell you it has repaired the disk. If it can't, it must be a serious problem and you need to take it to a repair shop.

5 Quit Disk Utility and quit the installer.

6 It might ask you to choose a startup disk because if you don't, when you restart your Mac, it will boot up from the disk again. If it asks, you will see the disk options; single-click your internal hard disk, then click the "Restart..." button.

Or restart without choosing a disk and hold the mouse button down until it has restarted. Holding the mouse button down forces the disk to eject so it can't be used to boot the machine. If you're using a trackpad, press on the lowest area of the trackpad, the part closest to you.

Safe Boot

This is one of my favorite troubleshooting techniques. During a *safe boot,* the Mac actually goes in and fixes little things, such as minor file corruptions that build up over time, eventually causing problems. If you've ever used the terminal commands to do the fsck (file system check) technique, you'll be pleased to know the safe boot does the same thing but without having to use the terminal. This is safe, easy, and comfortable, and fixes lots of mysterious problems.

1 Go to the Apple menu and choose "Restart…." If you're having such problems that you can't even get to the Apple menu, hold down the Power button for five seconds to shut down the machine. Then push the Power button again to restart.

2 Immediately upon hearing the startup sound, hold down the Shift key and keep it held down. This might take a while, five minutes or even more. Be patient. Keep that Shift key down. You'll eventually get to a log-in screen that says, in red, "Safe Boot." If not, start over—perhaps you didn't get the Shift key down in time.

3 When you get to the Desktop or to the log-in screen, restart again (either click the restart button if you see one, or go to the Apple menu and choose "Restart"). Because a safe boot turns off everything that's not essential to run the operating system, the Mac needs to restart to put everything back and turn everything on. See if things work a little better now.

Delete the Application Preference File

Another tip to troubleshoot an application that isn't acting right is to delete that application's **preference file.** This is perfectly safe—when the application opens up again, it will re-create a new preference file from scratch. You will lose any preferences you had personally changed in the application, but it can be worth it because this works pretty well to solve inexplicable annoyances in applications.

1   Quit the application.

2   Open a Finder window and view it by columns, as shown below.

3   This step is tricky! Open the Go menu; hold down the Option key and you'll see a new item appear called "Library"—choose "Library."

4   The Library folder appears in the Home column of the Finder window, and it is selected, displaying its contents in a column to the right.

5   In that Library contents column, single-click the "Preferences" folder.

6   In the next column to the right, find the ".plist" file for an application that's giving you trouble. That is the preference file.

7   Drag the application's preference file to the Trash. Empty the Trash.

8   Restart the application and hope it works better. The Library folder will disappear all by itself.

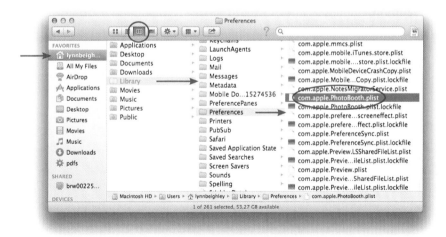

The preferences for non-Apple applications may have their own method to delete preferences—check the support pages for your app.

Check for Software Updates

Make sure you are using the latest versions of all your software. For your Mac OS software, use the Software Update preferences to see if everything is up to date (open it in the System Preferences from the Apple menu). It's especially important to check for updated *application* software when you update your *operating system,* just as you would do when moving from any other OS to Mountain Lion.

TIP ———— If your connection to the Internet is a dial-up through a telephone modem or some other really slow connection, do *not* check the boxes "Check for updates: Daily/Weekly/Monthly" and "Download updates automatically" because it will tie up your connection for hours. Instead, check for updates manually: Click the "Check Now" button.

Keep in mind that if you installed your software through the App Store (very likely) you should open it and check for updates there as well.

Create Another User and Test

If you install new software and it just won't work right, or perhaps it won't even open, one good troubleshooting technique is to create another user (see Lesson 20) and install the software in that user's Home folder. Open the application and see if it works properly. If it *doesn't* work for the new user, the software itself has a problem (I have to assume you checked to make sure it works with your operating system *before* you installed it).

If the software *does* work for the other user, that indicates there is something in your system that is conflicting. Try throwing away the preferences, as explained on the previous page. If it still doesn't work, you may need to contact the vendor to find out what may be conflicting with that particular software.

If You Forgot Your Password

If you forgot the password you chose when you first set up your new Mac or installed your new system (called the Admin password), you can change it *if* you also set up your Apple ID *or* if you have the original install disk or thumb drive.

With your Apple ID

When you log in, you've probably noticed a question mark in the password field. Click that question mark to get the hint for your password, as well as an option to use your Apple ID and password to change your user password. **This only works,** however, if you previously "set" your Apple ID in the Users & Groups system preferences *and* checked the box to "Allow user to reset password using Apple ID," as shown in Lesson 20. If you didn't, an Admin user can log in and do that for your account so next time you forget your user password, you'll be able to change it.

With the original disk or drive

You can use these steps to change the password of any user.

1   Get the original disk or thumb drive. Put it in and double-click the "Install" button. Follow the directions to restart. No, you are not really going to reinstall the entire system.

2   Wait until the Welcome screen appears. Then go to the Utilities menu at the top of the screen and choose "Reset Password...."

3   Enter your new password—twice. And add a hint.
    And write that password down where you can find it again. Click OK.

4   Quit the installer from the Installer menu. Your Mac will restart: If you have a DVD in the Mac, hold down the mouse button during the restart to force the disk to pop out so it won't restart from the DVD again. If you accidentally restart from the DVD, go to the Utility menu and choose "Startup Disk" to tell the Mac to start up from its internal drive.

If you did not enter a password when you first set up your Mac, then you can leave the password field empty; just hit the "OK" or "Continue" button and it will work just fine (although it's not secure at all). The problem with not having a password is that you will probably forget there is no password and so when it asks you for one, you'll spend hours trying all sorts of possibilities that don't work before you remember that there is no password. Guess how I know this.

Use Target Disk Mode

It's not unusual to need to move lots of files from one computer to another. If both computers are working fine and you just need to share files, there are lots of ways to do it. See Lesson 23, and check the index for "sharing files."

But sometimes one computer is just about defunct or maybe won't wake from sleep and you've got to get the files off quickly. Use **FireWire Target Disk Mode.** This makes the other computer act as a hard disk that you're connected to. You'll need a FireWire cable that can connect to both Macs—check your ports carefully before you buy!

- Unplug all FireWire devices from both computers that you are going to connect to each other.

- If FileVault is enabled on the computer you want to take files from, turn it off.

- If either machine is a laptop, plug in its power source.

- The machine you are going to transfer files **to** is the **host** computer. The machine you are going to take files **from** is the **target** computer.

In this process, the *target* computer will appear as a hard disk icon on the Desktop of the *host* computer and you can copy files to and from it.

1 Turn off the *target* computer (the one that's probably going bad). The *host* computer can stay turned on.

2 Connect the two computers with the FireWire cable.

 3 Turn on the *target* computer and immediately hold down the T key and keep it down. Keep it held down until you see a FireWire symbol (shown to the left) moving about its screen.

4 On the *host* computer, you will see a hard disk icon representing the *target* computer. You can copy files from the *target* computer and put files onto it.

   If you don't see the *target* computer's hard disk on the host screen, make sure all the cables are securely attached and reboot the *host* computer.

5 When you're done, eject the *target* hard disk icon from the *host* computer— drag it to the Trash, or select it and choose "Eject" from the File menu.

6 Press and hold the *target* computer's power button until it turns itself off.

7 Unplug the FireWire cable.

Force a CD or DVD to Eject

If a disk is stuck in the drive and won't come out, this trick almost always works:

1   First make sure you've unmounted the disk: Click the eject icon next to its name in the Sidebar of the Finder window,
    or drag the disk icon to the Trash,
    or Control-click (or right-click) the disk icon and choose "Eject disk."

    But you're probably reading this page because you already did that and there *is* no icon on the screen and you can't get it out. So . . .

2   Restart your Mac. Immediately hold the mouse button down. Hold it down until the disk pops out.

    On a laptop, press the area at the bottom of the trackpad instead of the mouse (unless you have a mouse attached to your laptop).

If that doesn't work, see if there is a tiny hole next to the CD/DVD drive slot. Not all Macs have a tiny hole here. But if you see one, that hole is specially made for a paper clip (not the kind with the plastic coating). Unfold a metal paper clip and gently but firmly press it into the hole to snap open the mechanism.

One thing that can cause a huge problem in a CD/DVD player is a disk with a paper label glued to the top. If the tiniest little edge peels up, it can get stuck in the drive and ruin not only the disk but the drive itself. So don't buy those CD labels that you can print yourself, and don't put any disk with a paper label into your Mac!

One last warning: Never put one of the mini-disks into a slot-loading optical drive! If your computer has a tray-loading optical drive, you should be able to put a mini-disk in it and eject without a problem. However, the safest thing to do is just use standard disks.

Report Crashes

Often when an application crashes, an alert box appears and asks if you want to send a report to Apple. Now, Apple is not going to write you back—this is just an anonymous report you send in so Apple can figure out if there are common issues among many users, enough to warrant looking into. It's good to go ahead and send in the report.

25

GOALS

Learn your
security options

Protect yourself from
malware with Gatekeeper

Use passwords
to log on to your Mac

Require a password
to wake computer
and unlock preferences

Securely empty the Trash

Protect information
using Keychain Access

Use FileVault
to secure data

Secure Your Mac and Its Files

In these days with so much of our personal and financial data being stored on our computers and rampant identity theft, it's important to take some precautions to make it more difficult for troublemakers to gain access to our Macs.

The tips in this lesson will make your files more secure, plus you'll discover some useful features and tricks that help ensure your privacy, such as password information, Gatekeeper, Keychain Access, and securely emptying your Trash.

Know Your Security Options

There are a number of **security features** on your Mac. Apple has installed lots of security stuff like Kerberos, Secure Shell, Wired Equivalent Privacy (WEP) data encryption, Virtual Private Network (VPN), firewalls, and other features. It doesn't matter to most of us what those are—they work behind the scenes. Your Software Update software (found in System Preferences) can automatically update security features through the Internet as Apple releases them.

The above features work without you having to do anything. The features that require your participation are explained on the following pages:

- You might need security from humans who walk past your desk when you're not there. Your Mac has a number of **low-level security features** to protect your information from the curious. These are good for laptops as well.

- There are a number of **password-protect** options on your Mac that make it difficult for others to gain casual access.

- **Gatekeeper** can keep you more aware of the risks you may face when installing third-party software.

- **Keychain Access** stores many of your passwords in locked "keychains." This includes passwords to your servers, eBay account, PayPal, and more. Keychain Access also lets you store passwords and codes for other things, such as credit card numbers you might like to use while shopping online. Keychain Access does double-duty—it makes things easier for you and harder for thieves. See pages 444–445 for details.

- If you have highly personal or valuable files on your Mac, you can use **FileVault** for maximum security. If you have a laptop, this is especially important to prevent thieves from accessing your data. See pages 446–447.

- And don't forget about the **Secure Empty Trash** feature. This deletes files from your Trash in such a way that no one can retrieve them again. See page 443.

Passwords on Your Mac

You have several different passwords on your Macintosh.

- **Administrator password:** When you first turn on your Mac, you are asked to create a password. Write this down in a safe place! You will need this password whenever you install new software or when you make certain system-wide changes.

Many operations, such as changing settings in various System Preferences, require an Admin name and password to allow changes.

You can choose *not* to have a password. Your Mac will still *ask* you to enter a password, however—if you never created one, just leave the password field blank, and click OK or the "Continue" button. But keep in mind that it's not very safe (from a security perspective) to neglect this password.

- **Apple ID:** An Admin user can change her own password or allow another user to change her own password using their own Apple IDs; if the user doesn't have an Apple ID, she can get one on the spot. Go to the Users & Groups preferences to set this option (see Lesson 20).

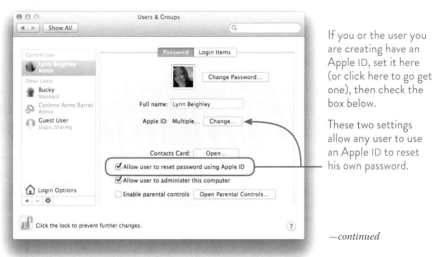

If you or the user you are creating have an Apple ID, set it here (or click here to go get one), then check the box below.

These two settings allow any user to use an Apple ID to reset his own password.

—*continued*

If you don't know (or forgot) your Admin password *and* you did not set up the use of your Apple ID, use the original install disc or USB Flash drive installer **to reset the Admin password:**

1   Insert the original OS X installer disc or USB Flash drive.

2   Double-click the "Installer" icon to start the process of reinstalling. You are not really going to reinstall!

3   When you get to the Install screen, go to the Utilities menu. Choose "Reset Password...."

4   Enter your new password. Write it down in a safe place!

5   Quit the Installer from the Installer menu.

■ **Login passwords:** If you have set up multiple user accounts on one Mac, each user has his own password to log in. *An Admin password is also the login password for that Admin user.* By default, your Mac is set to auto-login the Admin so you don't need your password at startup, but you can turn this off to make the computer less accessible.

If a standard user forgets his password, the Administrator (or anyone who knows the Admin password) can reset the user password in the Users & Groups preferences. If you gave that user the ability to reset his own password using his Apple ID, then he can reset it himself.

■ **Keychain Access password:** This is the same as the login password, whether you are a standard user or the Admin. Keychain Access is the application on your Mac that keeps track of a variety of passwords for you (and other info, if you choose). See pages 444–445.

Password tips

■ A password should be difficult for others to guess, but easy for you to remember.

■ Don't use a word that can be found in a dictionary. Some hackers use software that tries every word in the dictionary in a matter of minutes.

■ Combine caps and lowercase and numbers.

■ Most passwords are case-specific, meaning a lowercase "r" is completely different from an uppercase "R." Take advantage of this and use capital letters where someone wouldn't expect them.

Security System Preferences

Apple makes it easy for you to turn on a number of the low-level security features in one place, the Security system preferences.

1   Go to the Apple menu and choose "System Preferences...."

2   Click the "Security & Privacy" icon.

3   Click the "General" tab, as shown below.

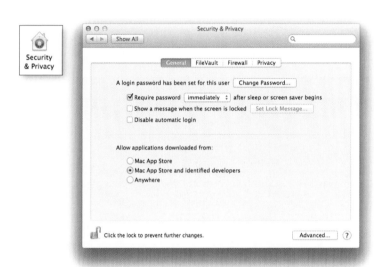

Require password __ after sleep or screen saver begins: See page 442.

Disable automatic login: See page 441 for an explanation of auto login.

Show a message when the screen is locked: To lock your screen, see page 442.

Allow applications downloaded from: This controls what happens when you try to download from the App store, or elsewhere. See the next page for more details.

Gatekeeper security

Mountain Lion can monitor the origins of applications you add to your machine and warn you if they might not be what you prefer. This feature is known as Gatekeeper.

With Gatekeeper, you can choose to only run apps from the App store written by developers registered by Apple. Or you can allow App store apps by unregistered developers, or you can allow any apps from any source to run. Depending on how Gatekeeper is configured, you will see various alerts about the security of apps you add to your machine.

1 Go to the Apple menu and choose "System Preferences...."

2 Click the "Security & Privacy" icon.

3 Click the "General" tab, as shown below.

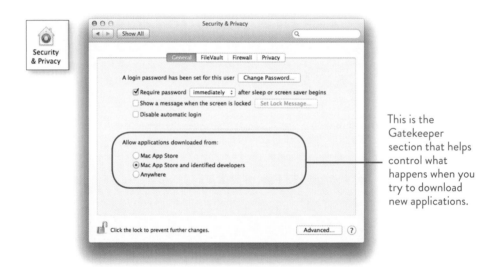

This is the Gatekeeper section that helps control what happens when you try to download new applications.

These options control warning messages that you'll see when you try to install something that this choice doesn't allow.

■ If you choose the first option, "Mac App Store," apps that you didn't download from the App Store will not be allowed to run when you try to launch them.

■ The riskiest option is the third one, "Anywhere." Choose this option and you'll instantly see the warning message shown below. And it's no wonder; this option lets you install anything you want that isn't yet known to be malicious software.

■ The safest option is the second one. Choose "Mac App Store and identified developers" to limit your new programs to only App Store apps created by Apple identified developers.

This means that it's been submitted by a developer who registered with Apple and received a personalized digital certificate they can use to cryptographically sign their apps. Signed apps can be checked to see who developed them and if any modification has occurred since the developer submitted it to the App Store.

Firewall

The **Firewall** pane of the Security & Privacy preferences is not something you will mess with very often, if at all. The most important thing to understand is that as you use Sharing features (in the Sharing preferences), the Mac lets down the firewall (a protective barrier) for the features you have turned on so others can access your machine to share. This means you are at a little more risk than if that feature was not turned on. So if you're not using a sharing feature, turn it off so the firewall goes back up.

To disable various sharing features (Screen Sharing, File Sharing, Bluetooth Sharing, etc.), go to the Sharing preferences pane and uncheck them.

Click the "Turn Off Firewall" button (shown above) to toggle between off and on. When the Firewall is on, your Mac determines which programs are allowed incoming connections based on your "Sharing" preferences. If you want to override any of those settings and allow or block specific applications or services, click the "Advanced..." button in the lower-right corner. A dialog sheet drops down, as shown below. To add items to the list, click the **+** button; to block a service or application, select it, then click the **–** button.

After you customize your settings, click "OK."

This option permits "trusted" sites to make an incoming connection and provide services accessed from the Internet. "Trusted" sites have been verified as authentic and secure.

This option provides an extra level of security and privacy.

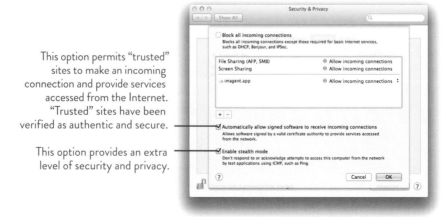

Low-Level Security Features

Here are some simple and quick features to use if you have any worry at all about casual access to your computer.

Automatic login

■ **Turn off automatic login:** Automatic login lets your Mac start up without a password—it automatically logs in to the account of the person who has chosen "automatic login." This means *anybody* can log in to that computer!

Turn off automatic login and then be sure to **log out** before you leave your computer for a while. This ensures that people walking by will need a password to log in to your account, even if they restart your Mac. Laptops should always require a login password (because they're easy to steal or lose).

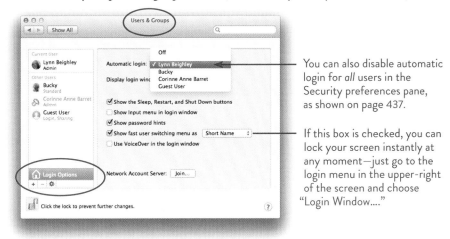

You can also disable automatic login for *all* users in the Security preferences pane, as shown on page 437.

If this box is checked, you can lock your screen instantly at any moment—just go to the login menu in the upper-right of the screen and choose "Login Window...."

■ **If you don't want to turn off auto-login,** you might want to at least take the extra step to *un*check the box to "Show the Sleep, Restart, and Shut Down buttons." If auto-login is on and you log out and leave your Mac, the login screen appears and you think you're safe. But someone can just click the Shut Down button. When the computer starts back up again, it automatically logs in to your account (if automatic login is enabled). By unchecking this box, no one can restart your computer so easily.

However, this precaution isn't going to help much if your laptop is stolen because someone can just reboot the computer and it will automatically log in.

■ OS X lets you have multiple users on one computer, and each user has a separate, private Home area (see Lesson 20 for details). Even if you are the only one using this Mac, you can **create another user,** a standard user who has no administrative privileges, and regularly log in as the standard user. This is a simple step that just makes it one level more difficult for someone to get into your main account and make system-wide changes. It won't protect any data that you create as that user, but it will make it more difficult to get into your Mac as an Administrator with privileges.

Require a password to wake your Mac

To prevent access to anyone walking by your computer, you can use these simple, yet effective, features. Open the System Preferences from the Apple menu, and then:

1 Use the "Security & Privacy" preferences to **require a password to wake up the Mac** from sleep or from the screen saver (see page 437). You can add a delay of five seconds to four hours before the password is required.

2 Go to the "Desktop & Screen Saver" preferences to choose a screen saver and tell it when to start.

3 Then go to the "Energy Saver" preferences to tell your Mac to put either the computer and/or the display (the screen) to sleep after a certain amount of time. Now when the screen saver comes on or your Mac goes to sleep, you'll have to enter your password to get back in to it.

An alternative technique is to set up your Mac so you can **lock it with a mouse click,** not just when the screen saver comes on or when it goes to sleep.

1 To open Keychain Access, open Launchpad, click the "Utilities" (or maybe the "Other") icon, then click the "Keychain Access" icon.

2 From the Keychain Access menu, choose "Preferences…."

3 Check the box to "Show keychain status in menu bar." A padlock icon appears on the right side of your menu bar, as shown here:

4 Quit Keychain Access.

5 Click the padlock icon that now appears in your menu bar to get the menu shown to the right.

6 Choose "Lock Screen." The screen saver will start and no one can access your Mac unless they know your login password.

Higher-Level Security Features

- **Secure Empty Trash:** You might think that after you empty the Trash, it's gone. But it's possible to recover many deleted files using special data-recovery software. To completely overwrite deleted files (several times) that are in the Trash so no one can ever get to them, go to the Finder menu and choose **Secure Empty Trash....** This might take several minutes.

- **Encrypt a disk image:** Using Disk Utility, you can make a password-protected "disk image" of a hard disk, a folder, a CD or a DVD (not an individual file, unless it's in a folder). The disk image can then be stored or transferred via email or any other method without any security concerns. A disk image acts just like any other hard disk—you can move files into it, copy files to it, and delete files from it.

To create a disk image:

1 Open Disk Utility: Open Launchpad, click the "Utilities" icon, then click the "Disk Utility" icon.

2 From the File menu, choose "New," then select one of these options: "Blank Disk Image..." (if you don't know what files you'll be adding) or "Disk Image from Folder..." (if you already have a folder of files you want to make a disk image with).

   With either of these methods you can enable adding or removing files at any time: Choose "read/write" from the "Image Format" pop-up menu.

3 **If you choose "Blank Disk Image,"** set your options, including a name and location for the disk image. Choose settings for the other options: Use the "Encryption" pop-up menu to choose an encryption method, or choose "none." If you choose an encryption option, a password dialog opens after you click "Create."

4 **If you choose "Disk Image from Folder,"** select a folder that you want to make a disk image of, then click "Image." A dialog lets you set a name, location, and other options for image format (read/write) and encryption. If you choose encryption, a password dialog opens after you click "Save."

5 Click Save.

Double-click this icon to open the *volume* that you can move files in and out of. **Lynn Disk Image.dmg**

Lynn Disk Image This is the actual *volume* that stores the files.

443

Use Keychain Access for Protection

Keychain Access provides a secure place to store information that can only be accessed with a user name and password. Keychain automatically and safely stores the passwords you create on your Mac, like those for web sites you go to, servers you connect to, email accounts, etc. Every time you see one of those messages that asks if you want your Mac to remember this password in your keychain, it gets stored here in Keychain Access.

You can also add your own secure collections of Keychains to store your credit card numbers, PINs, bank card information, private notes, passwords, and other things that you want easy access to but you want them to be secure. They won't be entered automatically anywhere—it's just a safer place to store them than on a sticky note.

Keychain Access sets up your initial Keychain file, the one based on your user name and password, as the default Keychain. This default Keychain automatically opens when you log in. To make other Keychains more secure, such as your list of credit card numbers or banking passwords, be sure to make *new* Keychain files for them instead of *adding* them to your default file.

To open Keychain Access, click Launchpad in the Dock, click the "Utilities" icon, and then click the "Keychain Access" icon.

Click this button to show or hide the list of Keychains, now showing at the top of the Sidebar. Any new Keychain you create will appear in that list.

To access any password Keychain has been storing for you:

1   Find the item in the list of "Passwords," shown on the opposite page.

2   Double-click that item in the list (the list displayed in the large pane on the right side of the window). You will be asked for your Keychain password, which is the same as your login password. If you are the only user of the Mac, it's the password you assigned yourself when you first set up your Mac, the Admin password. A window like the one below appears.

3   Check the box to "Show password." Your password appears.

To create a new Keychain: Go to the File menu and choose "New Keychain…." Give it a descriptive name, such as Credit Card Info, then click the "Create…" button. In the dialog that opens, create *a password you will remember* (because tough luck for you if you forget it!), then click OK. This Keychain will appear in the top portion of the Sidebar, shown on the opposite page. You will need to know that Keychain's password if you want to access things in it.

With that Keychain selected, go back to the File menu and choose to create a "New Password Item" or a "New Secure Note Item" to store in it.

Keychain is a very powerful and complex application. To use it wisely and well, please study the Keychain Help files.

Consider FileVault for Heavy-Duty Protection

FileVault encrypts, or scrambles, the data on your Mac so unauthorized people
or software cannot read it. While you are working on your Mac with FileVault
turned on, you won't notice a difference, but everything on the startup disk will be
encrypted, safely protected from prying eyes. When you access any of those files,
they are automatically decrypted.

Remember, this is an *optional* security measure. If you don't have extremely
sensitive data on your Mac, you probably don't need this level of protection.

To turn on FileVault:

1   Before you begin, make sure you are the Admin of this Mac and that you know
    your Admin name and password, as well as the passwords for any additional
    user accounts for which you want to activate FileVault.

2   From the Apple menu, choose "System Preferences...."

3   Click the "Security & Privacy" icon, then click the "FileVault" tab.

    Read the warning! If you forget your password or lose the recovery key that
    Apple gives you, your data (every tiny bit of it) **is lost.**

    If you're sure you want to use FileVault, click the lock icon in the bottom-left
    corner and enter an Admin name and password.

4   Now click the "Turn On FileVault..." button.

5   A sheet slides down to show a list of users. A green checkmark appears to the
    right of users who have passwords set.

If a user doesn't have a password, you must assign one in order for that user to use FileVault. Click the "Set Password…" button. After you set a password, click the "Enable User" button, enter the user's password, then click OK.

6 Back in the sheet that shows a list of users, click the "Continue" button.

7 Another sheet slides down with a 24-character recovery key. This key can be used to unlock the disk if you forget your password. Write down this recovery key *and don't lose it.* Click "Continue."

8 The next dialog lets you choose to "Store the recovery key with Apple." If you forget your password *and* lose the recovery key, you can contact Apple to retrieve it. Apple encrypts the key using the answers to three questions you choose from pop-up menus. If you forget the answers to those three questions, you've got a serious problem.

9 Click "Restart" to begin the encryption process. You can continue to use your Mac while the FileVault encryption takes place. To check on the encryption progress, return to the "Security & Privacy" preferences.

Laptop Precautions

Every year, millions of laptops get stolen or lost. They get stolen not only for the hardware, but more and more often for the valuable personal data that is stored on them. So it is imperative if your laptop does happen to get lost or stolen that the data inside is as safe as possible. Here are a few features (most from this lesson) to seriously consider.

- Do not set automatic login for your laptop—use a password to log in.

- Set a firmware password; see Lesson 26. It prevents someone from booting your computer with another disk.

- Password-protect the screen saver and sleep so if the screen saver turns on or the Mac goes to sleep, you need a password to get back in.

- Turn on FileVault (but never forget the users' passwords). FileVault automatically encrypts everything on your startup disk and decrypts it when you want to access it. (If FileVault is enabled, you can't use your Apple ID to change the password.)

- You can subscribe to services that can track a stolen laptop as soon as a person logs on to the Internet with it. Search the web for laptop security devices and services.

26

GOALS

Understand whether
to upgrade
or clean install

Become familiar with the
utilities available from
the installation media

Use Migration Assistant to
move user accounts and
files to a new Mac

Other ways to transfer files
from Mac to Mac

Remote install

Upgrade Your Mac and Migrate Your Files

You may have just gotten a brand-new Mac with Mountain Lion already installed, in which case you can skip this lesson altogether (unless you want more information about transferring your files from an old machine to your new one).

If you upgrade using a Mountain Lion installation DVD or USB Flash drive, the installer presents you with a few options from which to choose before you upgrade. This lesson explains the choices you will need to make along the way and provides some tips for migrating user accounts and files from one Mac to another.

Remember, before you do anything serious like upgrade your operating system, first back up your important files. The easiest thing to do is drag your important folders and files onto an external hard disk. Always create at least two backups *and store them in different places*—it won't do any good if all your important backups are in the same office that gets burglarized or flooded!

> *Remember, ALWAYS before upgrading or installing, make BACKUPS of your important files. If you don't have the install DVDs for certain applications or fonts, back them up to DVDs before you upgrade or install!*

Upgrade to Mountain Lion

To install Mountain Lion, your Mac must have at least an Intel Core 2 duo processor.

To see what kind of processor your Mac has, go to the Apple menu and choose "About This Mac." If your Mac is using something like an i3 or i5, that's even better than a Core 2 duo.

If your Mac is running Lion OS X 10.7, you're in luck! You can upgrade through the App Store (if the App Store icon is not in your Dock, check your Applications folder, or go to apple.com/mac/app-store). *Or* you can order an install DVD or Flash drive from Apple.

If you download Mountain Lion from the App Store, follow the on-screen instructions. If you install from a DVD or USB Flash drive, insert the disk or Flash drive, double-click the "Install OS X Mountain Lion.app" icon, and follow the directions.

Install as an upgrade

A regular install of Mountain Lion upgrades your existing operating system, but leaves all of your files untouched, and most, if not all, of your custom settings for system preferences and applications. Upgrading is faster and more convenient than a clean install, described on the following page. But you still should make a backup of important files because strange things have been known to happen while upgrading an operating system.

Optional clean install

To ensure a pristine computer environment, some people like to completely erase the hard disk before installing a new operating system. This is called a **clean install.** It ensures that you don't inherit any little corruptions or problems or puzzling behavior that might have been occurring in your previous operating system.

Of course, in the case of a clean install, first make sure all important information, applications, and files are backed up to another disk because this process erases *everything* on the computer. The easiest thing to do is go to the office supply store and buy an external hard disk, then transfer your files to it. If you want the fonts you may have bought, make sure you copy those as well (where they are stored depends on how you installed them; see the Help files for your font application). Later you can transfer these to your new machine. You will need to reinstall most of your third-party applications from the original disks or download them again.

Once everything is backed up, follow these steps:

1   Click the "Install OS X Mountain Lion.app" icon that you see on the disk.

2   In the next window, click "Restart."

3   After restarting, from the Utilities menu choose "Disk Utility."

4   Select your hard disk, listed in the left sidebar of the Disk Utility window, then click the "Erase" tab to show the Erase options.

5   Click the "Erase…" button. After the disk has been erased, the installation process continues.

Take Advantage of the Utilities in the Installer

When you run the upgrade or installer and get to the first screen, you'll see a menu item called "Utilities." This menu gives you access to a number of troubleshooting features on your Mac. If you like, you can stop here before installing Mountain Lion and use the Disk Utility to partition your Mac (divide it into several drives; only do this if you know why you are doing it).

All of the utilities mentioned below, except "Reset Password," are in your Utilities folder, which is in your Applications folder. You don't need to use an install DVD or Flash drive to access them. **But if your Mac has totally crashed** and you can't get anywhere at all, insert the original Mountain Lion install DVD or USB Flash drive, then restart your Mac. Immediately hold down the letter C key to make sure it boots from the install DVD or device. *Do not click any of the installation buttons,* but use the tools that are available here.

From the Utilities menu, choose the appropriate tool:

- **Startup Disk:** Choose which disk you want your Mac to check first when starting up. Only disks that contain operating systems can be used as startup disks.

- **Reset Password:** Here you can reset not only the Administrator password, but the passwords for every user on the Mac. You do not need to know the original passwords to set new ones.

- **Firmware Password Utility:** This option prevents others from starting your computer with a different disk. If someone stole your laptop, this won't get it back for you, but setting this password does make it much more difficult for anyone to log in and get your data. Write down the password!

- **Disk Utility:** Select your hard disk and use the "First Aid" pane to see if anything's wrong with the hard disk. The "Repair Disk Permissions" feature has solved some odd problems for our Macs (see Lesson 24). This is also where you can partition the hard disk before (or after) you install.

- **Terminal:** The Terminal lets you use UNIX commands to do all sorts of things. If you don't know anything about UNIX or how to use the Terminal, skip this altogether.

- **System Profiler:** The System Profiler tells you all the gory details about your Mac, the CPU type, the audio, what kinds of devices are attached to your Mac, the speed of everything you can think of, and oh so much more. It will even tell you the serial number of the computer. Much of this information is also available at your Desktop: Go to the Apple menu, choose "About This Mac," and click the button labeled "More Info...."

■ **Network Utility:** This utility has a number of great tools. If you know what it means to finger someone, ping your modem, run a lookup or a port scan, or when to use whois, then you'll have fun with this utility. It's also in your Utilities folder (which is in the Applications folder) in case you need it.

■ **Restore System From Backup:** This utility uses Time Machine. It can't restore the system from a backup unless you've first put it all on Time Machine (see Lesson 22). But once you've done that, you can use this option to restore your system back to a certain date.

Do You Own Two Macs? Migrate!

If you have important information on another Mac (a different computer from the one you're installing Mountain Lion onto) or a partition or volume on the new Mac, you can transfer the information from the older machine, partition, or volume to this new Mac. You'll use a feature called **Migration.** You can either use the Setup Assistant during the Mountain Lion installation (it walks you through it easily) or at any time in the future.

The migration process can automatically transfer:

■ Network and computer settings.

■ User accounts, preferences, and email.

■ Documents and other files.

■ Applications.

   Some applications, however, will need to be reinstalled from their original disks because they install necessary files in different system folders. All you can do is transfer them, then open them and see if they work. The more expensive and complex an application, the less likely it will transfer perfectly.

Requirements for the Migration Assistant

The old Mac must:

■ Be running OS X version 10.1 or above.

■ Have a built-in FireWire port *or* be on a local network with the new computer.

■ Support "Target Disk Mode" if you plan to connect the two computers with a FireWire cable.

—continued

You'll also need:

- A FireWire cable (if you're using "Target Disk Mode") that is long enough to reach between the two computers, *or* temporarily move the computers closer so they can connect via the cable. Be sure to check the ports (where you plug the cable in to the computer) to make sure you get a FireWire cable that can connect the two computers. Not all FireWire ports are shaped the same!

- An Administrator name and password (unless you're doing this during the Mountain Lion installation).

Be aware that:

- This process will tie up both your Macs for hours!

- This process will *not* automatically migrate songs that you bought from the **iTunes Store.** If you want to migrate *all* of your songs, including those you bought at the iTunes Store, you must first **deauthorize the old Mac** before you migrate files:

  1   Open iTunes on your old Mac.

  2   From the Store menu, choose "Deauthorize Computer...."

  3   Enter your account and password. Click the button to "Deauthorize," then click ок.

  4   To deauthorize any Audible content (audiobooks) so you can migrate them over to the new machine, go to the "Advanced" menu and choose "Deauthorize Audible Account...." You'll need your Audible.com name and password.

Migrate now

 Use the **Migration Assistant:** Single-click the Launchpad in the Dock, single-click the "Utilities" icon then single-click the "Migration Assistant" icon.

The instructions on screen are easy to follow and self-explanatory. You can migrate the files from the Administrator (main user), from any individual user, or from both. The information on the old Mac or the partition is not affected at all.

Migrate additional users

At any time you can migrate additional users and their files from other computers. Just follow the directions on the previous pages.

You can also use **Target Disk Mode** at any time to transfer files from one Mac to another; see Lesson 24. This technique is especially useful if one Mac is dying because in Target Disk Mode, the target computer does not use its operating system—it acts like a plain ol' hard disk that shows up as a disk icon on the Desktop of your healthy computer.

What to do after migrating

It's a good idea to do a quick check of the files on your new Mac after migrating. Open every application to make sure it works okay—make a quick file and try to save it. If an application doesn't work, you will just have to reinstall it from the original disks.

Open sample files by double-clicking them to make sure they can open in the correct application and that their fonts appear correctly.

Connect to the Internet, check your mail, and take a peek at your System Preferences to make sure things are really how you like them.

Disconnect after migrating

Do not unplug the FireWire cable before you unmount the icon of your old Mac from your new Mac running Mountain Lion! Even though it's "hot swappable" (which means you don't have to shut down before you unplug), it's still possible to lose data if you unplug the other computer while the FireWire icon is still visible on the screen.

To disconnect: Find the hard disk icon of your old Mac on the Desktop of the Mountain Lion computer. Drag the computer disk icon to the Trash, or click the *Eject* button next to that computer's name in the Finder window Sidebar.

Other Ways to Transfer Files from Mac to Mac

The migration process can take quite a long time because it gathers up thousands of files. If you want to transfer just selected files, you might want to consider these other options. Some you can do before you install Mountain Lion; others are new techniques that can only be accomplished in Mountain Lion (or Lion or Snow Leopard).

Use an external disk

On many older Macs, the best option can be to attach an external hard disk with a USB or FireWire connection. It can be worth it to buy a new drive just for this process. Copy files onto the external disk as you usually would from your old machine (drag them from the hard disk of your old Mac onto the external disk's icon). Then connect the external drive to the new machine and drag the files from the external disk to the newer Mac.

Burn a CD or DVD

If your old machine can burn a CD or a DVD, you can transfer quite a few files by burning discs and moving them to the new machine. Plus you'll have ready-made backups (always the smart thing to do).

Send attachments in email

If you don't have huge files, send them as attachments through email. It's kind of funny to send your files around the world to get to the machine sitting two feet away.

Use your iCloud account

You can set up your iCloud account on both machines. See Lesson 23 to learn about it.

Send files through the network

If both machines are on the same network, connect the two computers and copy files directly from one to the other through a variety of methods, including the Bonjour list in Messages. See Lesson 20 for all the details. It's really easy and you'll love knowing how to do it.

Use a FireWire cable

Connect a FireWire cable between two Macs. The other Mac will appear in the "Shared" group in the Sidebar of a Finder window. You will probably be able to screen share (see Lesson 23). Or at least you can connect to each other and easily move files back and forth (also in Lesson 23). Or consider the FireWire Target Disk Mode option; see Lesson 24.

Remote Install

A MacBook Air has no DVD drive in which to insert a Mountain Lion install DVD, but you can use a USB Flash drive with the Mountain Lion installation software on it. *Or* you can buy an external USB optical drive (a CD/DVD drive) from Apple and connect it to your MacBook Air. This is an easy solution, and the drive is barely larger than a CD or DVD. There's also the option to install through the App Store.

Another solution is to use the optical drive on another computer and install Mountain Lion over a local network, explained below. Or install directly from the App Store, as I did with the Air I'm using right now.

To install Mountain Lion on a Mac that doesn't have an optical drive, such as a MacBook Air, find a nearby Mac that has an optical drive and insert a Mountain Lion install DVD. Both computers (the one with the drive and the MacBook Air) must be on the same local network, either an AirPort (Wi-Fi wireless) or an Ethernet network. (If you need to use an Ethernet connection, you'll need to get a USB Ethernet adapter to connect to the MacBook Air.)

Open the Utilities folder (inside the Applications folder or Launchpad), double-click "Remote Install OS X Mountain Lion.app," then follow the on-screen directions.

After you choose a network type, you'll be prompted to hold down the Option key while you restart the computer (the one with an install DVD inserted). When you see a list of available startup disks on the network, choose your computer's startup disk, then continue to follow the on-screen instructions.

You can also use the "Remote Install OS X Mountain Lion" app to access the "Disk Utility" from the external drive for computer repairs and troubleshooting when certain tasks have to be done with tools that are on a separate disk from the one being repaired.

Index

THREE WAYS TO QUICKSTART

The ever popular Visual QuickStart Guide series is now available in three formats to help you "Get Up and Running in No Time!"

Visual **QuickStart Guide Books**

The best-selling Visual QuickStart Guide series is available in book and ebook (ePub and PDF) formats for people who prefer the classic learning experience.

Video **QuickStart**

Video QuickStarts offer the immediacy of streaming video so you can quickly master a new application, task, or technology. Each Video QuickStart offers more than an hour of instruction and rich graphics to demonstrate key concepts.

Enhanced **Visual QuickStart Guide**

Available on your computer and tablet, Enhanced Visual QuickStart Guides combine the ebook with Video QuickStart instruction to bring you the best of both formats and the ultimate multimedia learning experience.

Visit us at: Peachpit.com/VQS

VISUAL QUICKSTART GUIDE

WATCH READ CREATE

Unlimited online access to all Peachpit, Adobe Press, Apple Training and New Riders videos and books, as well as content from other leading publishers including: O'Reilly Media, Focal Press, Sams, Que, Total Training, John Wiley & Sons, Course Technology PTR, Class on Demand, VTC and more.

No time commitment or contract required! Sign up for one month or a year. All for $19.99 a month

SIGN UP TODAY
peachpit.com/creativeedge